YOUNG STUDENTS ENCYCLOPEDIA

Specially prepared with the Staff of
MY WEEKLY READER

9
Literature
Missouri

American Education Publications/A Xerox Company

Middletown, Connecticut

Acknowledgements

All photographs supplied by Armando Curcio Editore, SpA, except the following:

Aluminum Company of America—page 1536 top.

American Forest Products Industries—pages 1404 top, 1448 bottom.

American Girl Magazine, published by Girl Scouts of the U.S.A.—page 1412 left.

Australian News and Information Bureau—page 1494 bottom.

Bell Telephone Laboratories—pages 1464 bottom, 1465 top, 1465 center.

Jean F. Blashfield—page 1402 bottom.

Canadian Consulate General—page 1420 bottom.

Canadian Embassy—page 1408 top.

Canadian Government Travel Bureau Photo—page 1410 top.

Canadian Pacific Railway—pages 1466 top right, 1514 top right.

Phyllis Cerf—page 1381 bottom.

Colonial Williamsburg, Williamsburg, Virginia—page 1481 bottom.

Crown Zellerbach Corporation—page 1403 top right.

Diamond International Corporation—page 1471.

DICTIONARY OF AMERICAN PORTRAITS BY CIRKER AND CIRKER, Dover Publications, Inc., New York, Reprinted through permission of the publisher—pages 1393 center (Library of Congress), 1443 bottom, 1478 bottom (Engraving by George E. Perine), 1497 bottom right (Painting by Joseph Oriel Eaton, Courtesy Houghton Library, Harvard University).

Dow Chemical Company—page 1403 top left.

Eloise Engle—page 1484 bottom.

Ford Foundation—page 1489 bottom.

General Electric—page 1453 bottom.

General Motors Corporation—page 1446 top.

Philip Grushkin—pages 1392 bottom, 1516 top.

Linda Hirschmann—page 1481 top right.

Russell F. Hogeland—pages 1429 top, 1454 bottom left, 1458 bottom, 1466 bottom, 1473 top, 1487 top, 1489 top, 1508 top.

Richard Hoover—page 1454 bottom right.

Illinois Department of Business and Economic Development—pages 1502 bottom, 1504 top.

Iowa Development Commission—page 1548 bottom.

Kansas Industrial Development Commission—page 1439 bottom.

Charles R. Knight/The Chicago Field Museum of Natural History—pages 1433 bottom, 1434, 1435.

Library of Congress—pages 1384, 1411 top, 1411 bottom, 1452 top, 1458 top left.

Little League Baseball—page 1387.

Louisiana Department of Commerce and Industry—page 1401 top.

Louisiana Tourist Development Commission—page 1399 bottom.

Maine Department of Economic Development—pages 1417 bottom, 1418 bottom, 1420 top, 1445 top.

Marineland of Florida—page 1431 (whale).

Maryland Department of Economic Development—pages 1462 bottom, 1463 top, 1463 bottom.

Massachusetts Department of Commerce and Development—pages 1467 bottom, 1468 bottom, 1469 bottom, 1470 top.

Mexican National Tourist Council—page 1514 top.

Michigan Tourist Council—pages 1518 center, 1518 bottom.

Minnesota Department of Economic Development—pages 1538 bottom, 1540 bottom, 1541 top.

Mississippi Agricultural and Industrial Board—pages 1545 top, 1545 bottom, 1547 top.

Missouri Tourism Commission—pages 1550 bottom, 1552 top, 1552 bottom.

Mary E. A. Mitchell—pages 1398 bottom, 1425 top, 1444 bottom right.

NAACP—page 1460 top.

National Gallery of Art, Washington, D.C.—page 1441.

National Institutes of Health—page 1501 bottom.

Ohio Development and Publicity Commission—page 1537 top right.

Public Archives of Canada—page 1409 bottom.

Rand McNally & Company—page 1448 (road map).

J-L. Ray-C.E.P.A.—pages 1389 bottom left, 1428, 1429 bottom, 1430 (anteater), 1432.

Southern California Visitors Council Photo—page 1394 top.

State of Ohio Department of Development—page 1502 bottom.

Swedish Information Service—page 1385.

Trans World Airlines Photo—page 1394 bottom.

United Nations—pages 1423 top, 1424, 1473 bottom, 1476 bottom, 1519 top, 1519 bottom, 1520 bottom left, 1520 bottom right.

United Press International Photo—pages 1437 top, 1542 top.

United States Air Force Official Photograph—page 1530 top left.

United States Army Official Photograph—pages 1407 bottom, 1498 bottom, 1530 top right.

United States Department of Agriculture Photo—pages 1391, 1450 bottom right, 1484 top left, 1484 top right, 1487 bottom, 1488 top, 1488 bottom left, 1488 bottom right, 1528 top, 1536.

United States Marines Official Photograph—pages 1453 top, 1453 center, 1530 bottom left, 1530 bottom center.

United States Merchant Marine Academy Official Photograph—page 1503 top.

United States Naval Observatory—1531 top right.

United States Navy Official Photograph—page 1531 top right.

WHO/Photo by Homer Page—page 1502 top.

Larry Workman—pages 1421 top, 1444 bottom left, 1500 top.

State seals courtesy of the Council of State Governments

Canadian armorial bearings of provinces and territories from the Dominion Bureau of Statistics, courtesy of Information Canada

Maps from the Pictograph Corporation

▲ *Beneath the surface of the ocean lies a fascinating world of plant and animal life.* (See MARINE LIFE.)

LITERATURE If you have ever cried at a movie or a play or laughed at a story, you already know some of the ways literature can make you feel. Literature is basically a communication in words of human thoughts and emotions. Before most people could read and write, literature consisted of stories and poems that people made up and taught to their children and grandchildren. (In this way, stories and poems were remembered for many years, passing from generation to generation.) Troubadours (singers who traveled from town to town)

made these stories and poems more widely known. Stories and poems that were written down could be copied and distributed to other towns and other countries. Because of this, writing came to be adopted as the best way for literature to reach a large number of people.

Some kinds of writing are not really literature, although they can be very important to people. *Expository* writing is a very common and useful kind of non-literary composition. Its main purpose is to give information to the reader. Your schoolbooks are good examples of

▼*William Faulkner, American novelist and one of the great figures of literature in the 1900s. He wrote about modern life in the South.*

▲ *An illustrated page from* The Chronicles of France, England, and Spain, *written in the 1300s by the French historian Jean Froissart. Some of his chronicles (stories) were made into plays by William Shakespeare.*

▼ *Charles Dickens's novels are full of the joys and sorrows of children who lived in the England of the 1800s.*

▶ *Women have made important contributions to literature. George Eliot (right) was an English novelist of the 1800s. Her real name was Mary Ann Evans. Edna St. Vincent Millay (far right) was one of the best-loved American poets of the 1900s. Her verse is lyrical and easy to read.*

expository writing. Another kind of non-literary composition is *persuasive* writing. Its purpose is to make the reader believe one particular opinion or point of view. Television commercials and newspaper ads are examples of persuasive writing.

Purposes of Literature

Literature can be both informative and persuasive, but it has other goals. For example, the novel *Oliver Twist,* by the British writer Charles Dickens, gives the reader a great deal of *information* about social conditions in nineteenth-century England and tries to *persuade* him that society's treatment of the poor should be changed. However, one of the main purposes of literature is to help people understand human nature and experience. Another important goal of literature is to entertain people. You enjoy reading about other people and their experiences, and this reading often helps you understand more about people in general or yourself in particular. Throughout the ages, people have shared certain characteristics. They love, hate, admire, pity. They are amused, sad, afraid, cruel, and kind. Literature helps people to understand these emotions and their reasons for feeling them.

Literature appeals to the reader's emotions and imagination. Therefore, the writer chooses the words, phrases, and approach (to his subject) that will excite his reader's imagination. A writer chooses words for their sound and the thoughts people associate with them as well as for their specific meaning. For example, snow that is "white as white cow's milk" sounds somehow whiter and snowier than just "white snow." A writer's method of handling words, images (mental pictures), and sentences is called his *style.* Every work of literature is a unique combination of content (subject matter), theme (the author's statement about human experience), and style.

Types of Literature

Literature that deals with imaginary people and situations is called *fiction.* Works of fiction are often realistic—that is, they seem as though they did or could happen. For example, Jane Austen's *Pride and Prejudice* takes place in an ordinary town. The parents, sisters, and friends of the main character are much like people everyone has met.

Many other fictional works are not realistic. They are based on imagination or fantasy. For example, the reader knows that the events in Edgar Allan Poe's horror story, "The Tell-Tale Heart," could not take place, but they fascinate him anyhow. Such unrealistic stories are often given very realistic details to make the plot more believable. Fantasy fascinates you

Ralph Waldo Emerson (far left) was an American essayist and poet of the 1800s. Sir Walter Scott (left) was a Scottish novelist and poet of the late 1700s and early 1800s. He was the first to make the historical novel popular.

An old illustration shows the shipwrecked sailor, Robinson Crusoe. Daniel Defoe, an English novelist, wrote about Crusoe's adventures in 1719.

William Makepeace Thackeray was an English novelist of the 1800s who wrote about the social life of that era. This bust of him stands in "Poet's Corner" of Westminster Abbey in London.

more if you are made to wonder if it actually *could* happen.

Essays (short compositions presenting the writer's personal views), biographies, and histories are non-fiction literature. James Boswell's biography of Samuel Johnson is non-fiction literature. Gibbon's history, *Decline and Fall of the Roman Empire*, is also considered literature.

The various forms of fictional literature differ in the kinds of plots and the number of characters on which they focus. A *short story* is a fictional work that (because of its shortness) usually has only one or two main characters and usually concentrates on one event in the main character's life. Short stories may also cover longer periods of time. A *novel* is a longer work of fiction that may have many characters besides the protagonist (main character) and may cover several incidents over a long period of time in the characters' lives. A *narrative poem*, which tells a story in verse, also has a plot and characters. A *lyric poem* simply expresses in verse the poet's thoughts or emotions about a particular subject. A *dramatic poem* tells a story in verse through the dialogue (conversation) of the characters, just as a prose (not written in verse) drama does. A drama, or play, is written to be acted on the stage. It usually has several main characters and focuses on one or two inci-

dents in their lives. Everything that the audience knows about these characters depends on what they say and do. The playwright cannot tell you directly what a character thinks or feels.

Interpretation

Not every reader will see the same theme, or meaning, in a work of literature. Everyone brings his own emotions and experiences to his reading. Therefore, readers interpret works of literature in different ways. In fact, one of the things that makes good literature meaningful to people is that it can be interpreted and understood in several ways. For example, many people have enjoyed *Moby Dick,* by Herman Melville, as an adventure story about Captain Ahab's search for the mighty white whale, Moby Dick. Many others see this novel as an essay about religion and man's soul. Both of these interpretations are true. Each results from a different view of the plot (series of events), characters (people), and theme of the novel. Sometimes a reader will interpret a book differently at different ages. For example, if you read *The Old Man and the Sea*, by Ernest Hemingway when you are 12 and again when you are 20, you will "see" different meanings. The book is both an adventure story (which might appeal at 12) and a description of man's struggle within himself, which might be important at age 20.

Themes in Literature

The plot and characters in a piece of fiction work together to present the

►*Sinclair Lewis at work. The themes of his books often dealt with the wrongs he saw in American life during the first half of this century.*

author's *theme*. Every writer has his own themes, and interpretations of them always differ. But the ideas that writers—and readers—are concerned with can be grouped into several *kinds* of themes. (Everyone in your class may write a different composition about what's wrong with your school, but all the compositions will be about the same subject.) For example, people have been writing for centuries about such topics as love, death, religion, disappointment, hope—and writers today still have more to say about these subjects.

Writers and readers are always interested in what people learn about life as they grow up, since everyone has to go through this process. Mark Twain wrote *Huckleberry Finn*, about a boy who ran away from home and traveled down the Mississippi River on a raft with a runaway slave named Jim. Huck learned a great deal from Jim and from the trip about independence and true friendship and about what he wanted out of life. Nearly a hundred years later, J. D. Salinger wrote

a novel, *The Catcher in the Rye*, about another boy who was growing up. Holden, like Huck, was basically a good person but also had trouble adjusting to the adult world. Holden, however, who had been put out of several schools, seemed to learn more about what he did *not* want in adult life than about what he wanted. In other novels, such as *A Separate Peace* (by John Knowles) and *The Heart Is a Lonely Hunter* (by Carson McCullers), the main characters are introduced to the sadness—even tragedy—that people learn about when they grow up.

Men and women have written on many other subjects, and there are many ways to interpret their writings. But as long as people share the same emotions and experiences, they will be interested in writing and reading literature.

Literary Awards

A literary award is a prize given for an outstanding work, or group of works, of writing. Many literary awards are presented each year in many places for novels, biographies, histories, drama, poetry, and other kinds of writing.

Perhaps the most treasured and respected literary award is the *Nobel Prize for Literature*. Writers from anywhere in the world may be chosen for this award. The prize, approximately 70,000 dollars, is presented at a ceremony in Stockholm, Sweden, each year. Six U.S. writers have won Nobel Prizes—Sinclair Lewis (1930), Eugene O'Neill (1936), Pearl Buck (1938), William Faulkner (1949), Ernest Hemingway (1954), and John Steinbeck (1962).

Among nearly 100 literary awards presented each year in the United States are the *Pulitzer Prizes*, established in 1917 by the newspaper publisher Joseph Pulitzer. These are given for journalistic achievements and to the writers of works chosen as the best American novel, play, history, biography, and poetry.

Robert Frost won the prize four times for his poetry. John F. Kennedy won in 1957 for his biographical work, *Profiles in Courage.*

Another important group of U.S. literary awards are the *National Book Awards,* given each year by a committee representing the book publishing industry. These awards are presented in important fields of literature.

Many awards are given in the United States for outstanding children's books. Among these are the *Jane Addams Children's Book Award* and the *Newbery Award* medal. The *Caldecott Award* is given for the best-illustrated children's book. Winners of the Newbery and Caldecott awards are chosen by the American Library Association. Other awards for children's literature in the United States include the *Child Study Association Awards,* the *Regina Award* (sponsored by the Catholic Library Association), and the *Laura Ingalls Wilder Award.* In some states, such as Oklahoma and Vermont, awards are given for books judged by children themselves.

Many literary awards are given by organizations for books written about the topic in which the organization is interested. These include books about certain regions of the United States, certain historical periods, and religions. For example, the *B'nai B'rith Award* is presented for the best book on Jewish life or Judaism, and the *National Catholic Book Awards* are given for special achievements in Catholic book publishing. The *Bancroft Prizes* are presented by Columbia University for books on American history, diplomacy, and international relations.

Literary awards take many different forms. The simplest is an official document which states that the writer has been chosen as a winner. Other awards are silver cups, silver and gold medals, and money in varying amounts. Organizations often give their awards in the form

of fellowships and grants to help writers further their studies and careers. One of the most unusual awards is presented each year by the Western Writers of America to the author of the best piece of writing

◄*Nobel Prize winner Pearl Buck receives her award for literature from King Gustav V of Sweden on December 10, 1938.*

about the West. It is a spur, a metal device with a sharp point used by cowboys to prod their horses. Another unusual award is the "Edgar Award," given by the Mystery Writers of America for the best mystery novel. It is a small statue of Edgar Allan Poe, the great American writer of mystery stories.

For further information on:

Kinds of Literature, *see* BIOGRAPHY, NOVEL, POETRY, SCIENCE FICTION, SHORT STORY.

Literary Awards, *see* CALDECOTT AWARD, NEWBERY MEDAL, NOBEL PRIZE.

Works of Literature, *see* BEOWULF, BIBLE, CID.

Related Topics, *see* AMERICAN HISTORY; ART; BOOK; CHILDREN'S LITERATURE; DECLARATION OF INDEPENDENCE; ENGLISH HISTORY; FRENCH HISTORY; FRENCH REVOLUTION; GERMAN HISTORY; GREECE, ANCIENT; GREEK LITERATURE; INDUSTRIAL REVOLUTION; MIDDLE AGES; PHILOSOPHY; PRINTING; RENAISSANCE; ROMAN EMPIRE.

For individual authors, poets, and playwrights, see Index at name.

LITHUANIA

Capital City: Vilna (372,000 people).
Area: 25,200 square miles.
Population: 2,296,000 people.
Languages: Lithuanian and Russian.
Export Products: Food items.
Unit of Money: Ruble.

LITHUANIA The country of Lithuania is a flat land covered with forests, streams, meadows, marshes, and hundreds of small lakes. Lithuania is bordered by Latvia on the north, Russia and Poland on the east and south, and the Baltic Sea on the west. The country has long, cold winters and short, warm summers. The capital is Vilna. (See the map with the article on EUROPE.)

Approximately half the land in Lithuania is suitable for farming. Many of the people earn their living in agriculture. They grow flax, wheat, oats, rye, potatoes, and sugar beets. They also raise many pigs, dairy cattle, poultry, and sheep. Much of the agricultural work is done on collective farms, where each family works its own land, but the products are sold together, and the profits are divided. Other Lithuanians work in manufacturing. The processing of agricultural and dairy products is the most important industry. Lithuanians also manufacture furniture, paper, textiles, clothing, electrical goods, and farm machinery, and build ships. Many people who live along the Baltic Sea coast earn their living by fishing.

The language of the Lithuanian people is one of the oldest in the world. By the 1300s, Lithuanian rulers had built an empire that stretched from the Baltic Sea to the Black Sea. In 1386, Lithuania and Poland were united under a Lithua-

nian Grand Duke. Later, Poland and Russia ruled the land. In 1918, Lithuania regained its independence, and the people elected a democratic government. Lithuania was free only until 1939, when Russian soldiers crossed the border after Poland was divided between Germany and Russia. A Communist government came to power in 1940, and the country became part of the U.S.S.R. During World War II, the Germans occupied Lithuania, and the country suffered much hardship.

Lithuania, along with Estonia and Latvia, became part of the Soviet Union again after the war. Its name officially became the Lithuanian Soviet Socialist Republic. Many Lithuanians who disliked the Soviet occupation of their country fought a guerrilla war for many years. Some fled to other countries. Thousands of people who resisted were sent to labor camps in Siberia. Many Russians then came to live in Lithuania. As a result, about half of the people now living in Lithuania do not speak Lithuanian. The U.S. does not recognize the incorporation of Lithuania into the Soviet Union.
ALSO READ: BALTIC SEA; SOVIET UNION, WORLD WAR I, WORLD WAR II.

LITTLE LEAGUE BASEBALL

The main difference between regular baseball and Little League baseball is size. The players in Little League ball are smaller, the playing

▼*A view of Kaunas, a city in central Lithuania located on the Neman River.*

area is smaller, and so are the ball and bat. Instead of the regulation nine innings of a baseball game, a Little League game has only six.

The game is designed to teach young boys the basic rules of baseball, and to give them a chance to play the game. The first Little League was formed in Williamsport, Pennsylvania, in 1939. Since then, the game has spread throughout the United States, and to 31 other countries. Two million boys play in 8,000 Little Leagues around the world. The best teams attend the world series play-offs in Williamsport each year. The winning team at the series becomes the Little League champion of the world for that year.

Little League baseball is for boys between the ages of 9 through 12. Each team consists of about 15 boys, all of whom get a chance to play. Many teams are named for big league baseball teams, such as the Orioles, Yankees, and Dodgers.

The nine positions on a Little League team are the same as those on big league teams. There are the *infielders—first baseman, second baseman, third baseman,* and *shortstop—*the *outfielders—right fielder, center fielder,* and *left fielder—*and the *catcher* and *pitcher.*

Almost every community in the country has at least one Little League team. If you don't know how you can join a team, ask your physical education teacher or the athletic department of your school.
ALSO READ: BASEBALL.

LIVER   The liver is the largest gland and one of the largest organs in the human body. It is soft and flat in shape, a dark reddish or chocolate brown in color, and weighs 2½ to 3½ pounds. The liver is located in the right side of the abdomen, just below the stomach. It is divided into four *lobes,* or sections.

The liver is one of the most important organs in the body. If the liver is damaged so that it cannot

▲*The batter gets ready to hit the ball in a game of Little League baseball.*

perform its work, the body cannot continue to function, and death will occur. The liver produces *bile,* a liquid substance needed for digesting fats. The bile is stored in a small sac called the *gall bladder.* Bile empties into the small intestine from the gall bladder by means of a bile duct.

Glycogen is stored by the liver. Blood travels from the small intestine to the liver, carrying a sugar, called *glucose.* The liver changes glucose into glycogen and stores it. When the body needs extra energy, the liver rapidly changes the glycogen back into glucose sugar. The glucose then travels through the bloodstream, providing energy for the body cells.

Certain poisonous waste products are cleansed by body cells as they do their work. The liver combines these substances with other chemicals to make non-poisonous ones. The wastes are then processed by the kidneys and excreted.

The liver also stores vitamins. Vitamins A and D and the various B vitamins are held in the liver for the body to use when necessary. Copper and iron are also stored.

The liver also can make various substances. Two of these are *fibrinogen* and *prothrombin.* They help the blood to clot to stop bleeding. Another product of the liver is *albumin.* This substance helps the

The 1971 Little League champions of the world are from Tainan, Taiwan. The team beat their opponents from Gary, Indiana, with a score of 12–3. Another team from Taipei, Taiwan, won the league championship in 1969.

blood pass through the capillary walls while it is circulating.

The liver may be badly damaged by diseases such as malaria, hepatitis, and dysentery. If these diseases are cured, the liver can go on with its work. If they are not, the liver cannot get rid of the bile that it makes. Bile then goes into the blood, causing the skin to turn yellow—the color of the bile. This condition is called *jaundice*.

ALSO READ: BLOOD, CIRCULATORY SYSTEM, DIGESTION, DISEASE, GLAND, HUMAN BODY, VITAMINS AND MINERALS.

LIVINGSTONE, DAVID (1813–1873) Many people remember the name of the British missionary and explorer, David Livingstone, from the words, "Dr. Livingstone, I presume?" This formal greeting was spoken in 1872 by the British-born explorer, Henry Morton Stanley. For eight months, Stanley had been searching for Livingstone in the jungles of central Africa. When he entered the camp of Dr. Livingstone, he spoke those well-remembered words.

David Livingstone was born in Blantyre, Scotland. He first traveled to Africa in 1841, hoping to convert the African people to Christianity. On his travels to distant villages, he began to explore unknown sections of Africa. He was the first European

▼*The meeting between David Livingstone and H. M. Stanley in the wilds of Africa.*

to see the mighty Victoria Falls, located on the border of Rhodesia and Zambia. *Missionary Travels and Researches in South Africa*, published in 1857, made him famous. In 1866, Livingstone set out to discover the source of the great Nile River. He journeyed deep into central Africa, but he was too far south to find the Nile. He *did* succeed in finding a source of the Congo River.

During his explorations, Livingstone was horrified to see the terrible effects the slave trade was having on the people of Africa. His reports of what he saw, published in 1865, helped to bring about an end to slave-buying and selling. During his long, hard travels, he became dangerously ill. For more than two years, nothing was heard about him. The *New York Herald* newspaper sent Henry Morton Stanley to Africa to find Livingstone. After their famous meeting, the two men explored the region around Lake Tanganyika, located in what is now the Congo. Livingstone remained in central Africa until his death.

ALSO READ: BOTSWANA; EXPLORATION; SLAVERY; STANLEY, HENRY MORTON; ZAIRE.

LIZARD Have you ever seen an animal drop its tail off? Or squirt blood out of its eyelids? Some kinds of lizards can do such things in order to defend themselves.

Lizards are a group (over 3,000 species) of reptiles closely related to snakes. Lizards have dry, scaly skin, which they shed periodically. Most species have four legs, although some have no legs and are often confused with snakes. (The glass snake is actually a legless lizard.) Nearly all lizards have tails that are much longer than their bodies, although the horned toad (actually a lizard) has a rather short tail. Lizards may vary in length from a few inches (geckos and chameleons) to several feet (Komodo dragons). Most lizards are less than two feet long.

▲*Meller's chameleon is an African species that feeds on birds. It maintains a strong grip with its hand-like feet. It can also grip things with its tail.*

Lizards can be almost any color or combination of colors. The male often has brightly colored patches. Some types of lizards, such as chameleons, can change color to match their backgrounds so they are hard to see. Light and temperature influence a lizard's color. The male lizard's color also changes during a fight with another lizard.

These creatures live in nearly all parts of the world, but they are found mainly in tropical and

▼*Geckos are small lizards that are well known for making a variety of interesting sounds—anything from a chirp to a bark. Their suction grip is so good that they can easily walk upside down.*

temperate zones. They can live on deserts, since they can get the water they need from the food they eat.

Like all reptiles, lizards are cold-blooded, which means that their body temperature varies with the temperature of their surroundings. Because of this, desert lizards often must hide in the shade or burrow into the sand when the sun becomes too hot or the night too cold.

Lizards have adapted their methods of movement to their environments. Desert lizards have sharp claws on their feet that enable them to dig into sand rapidly. One type of lizard, the gecko, can walk on walls and ceilings because it has pads on its toes that are made of small, hooked growths. These pads enable the gecko to cling to surfaces that look smooth. One variety of agamid lizard can "fly" (glide, really) from tree to tree. Its ribs grow out of its body and are connected by a *membrane* (a flap of skin). When the lizard spreads its "wings," it can glide for short distances. Legless lizards move by wriggling, as snakes do.

Since most species of lizards are harmless, they have developed ways of scaring off attackers. When a certain type of lizard disconnects its tail from its body, the tail continues to twitch. As the attacker watches—or eats—the tail, the lizard escapes. The lizard then grows a new tail. The horned toad squirts a little blood out of its eyelids to drive away its attacker. The frilled lizard has a wide membrane around its neck that it can spread out like a ruffle to frighten away an enemy.

Many species are carnivorous (meat-eating), while others are herbivorous (plant-eating). Some types eat both plants and animals. In some areas, lizards are valuable to farmers because they eat troublesome pests, such as insects.

Some types of female lizards are *oviparous*, which means that they lay eggs. Other species are *ovoviviparous*, which means that the

▲*A green lizard feasting on a butterfly. Green lizards are European lacertids, small to medium-sized lizards.*

Pet chameleons often like to be stroked lightly on the stomach or under the chin by someone they know. In fact, it almost hypnotizes them.

▲*An iguana has five claw-like toes on each foot which make it easy for this lizard to climb almost anything.*

eggs are warmed inside the mother's body and the young are born alive.

Geckos and the smooth, shiny skinks live in North America and other parts of the world. Iguanas are also found in the Western Hemisphere. The American chameleon is actually one kind of iguana. The only poisonous lizards in North America are gila monsters and beaded lizards, found in the southwestern United States and in Mexico.
ALSO READ: ALLIGATORS AND CROCODILES, REPTILE, SNAKE.

LLAMA see CAMEL.

LOCAL GOVERNMENT Have you ever looked at the words printed on the truck collecting garbage near your home? Do they say something like "City of Chicago," "Arlington County," or "Town of Stuntz"? Who is in charge of sanitation where you live? Your local government. Who is in charge of the water supply, the police and fire departments, or the traffic signs and signals where you live? These activities and responsibilities are also handled by local governments.

The United States Constitution states exactly what the Federal Government (which governs the entire nation) may or may not do. Any power not given to the Federal Government or that is denied to the Federal Government is handled by the state governments. State governments have their own state constitutions, which describe the state's powers and tell what powers local governments may have. Each state constitution is different, so the local governments in each state vary.

Forms of Local Government
The area under the control of a local government may be established in several ways. It may be based on population, land area, or simply on the nature of a region. A region where a large mass of people and industry are situated might have its own government, for example. There are three main forms of local government in the United States—town, county, and municipal.

TOWN GOVERNMENT. In the New England states, the *town* is the main unit of local government. Voters gather in town meetings, where everyone elects officers, sets up taxes, decides how to spend tax money, and passes local laws.

COUNTY GOVERNMENT. The *county* is the main unit of local government in most of the United States. The people elect representatives, usually called the County Board, to impose taxes, supervise county officials, and perform certain administrative functions. These functions may include the management of the school system, fire department, water system, and other local departments. The County Board may also have the power to make local laws and set up local courts.

MUNICIPAL GOVERNMENT. In areas of the United States such as the Northeast, there are a great many people living in cities. Most cities operate under a *municipal* form of government. The governing body of a municipality is usually an elected council, which is sometimes composed of two chambers, or houses, an upper and a lower. The chief officer is an elected mayor. Some municipalities have a city manager. A city manager is a non-elective official hired by the council to manage the affairs of city and to appoint and supervise the heads of the various departments. Under the city manager form of government, the job of mayor usually becomes less important.

State and Federal Supervision
Many of the duties and much of the power of local governments are connected in some way with the state and Federal governments. State authorities supervise many activities of local governments, especially those affecting public in-

stitutions, such as public schools, hospitals, prisons, and boards of health. The local courts are administered by the local, state, or Federal government, depending on the kinds of legal cases they handle. Decisions of judges in local courts may be overruled by judges in state and federal courts. State and Federal government authorities may also help supervise the many local institutions and projects to which they have given financial aid.

AUTHORITY OF LOCAL GOVERNMENTS. The local government usually has total or nearly total authority over the police department, fire department, sanitation department, water and air pollution control, and the transportation system. The local government also provides housing and food for the poor. It keeps records of births, marriages, deaths, house and land sales; collects taxes; and runs elections.

Local Governments in Other Countries

In many countries, the national government appoints somebody to supervise local governments. This person can direct or overrule any action taken by the local government. France, Italy, Portugal, Spain, and many Latin American countries have this kind of system. In most Communist countries, the local governments are strictly controlled by the national government. Local officials simply carry out the orders of the national government.

ALSO READ: CITY, COUNTY, COURT SYSTEM, GOVERNMENT, STATES' RIGHTS, SUBURB.

LOCKS AND KEYS A lock is a mechanical device used to fasten doors, chests, and lids. Most locks consist of a bolt with a guard that can be released by a key.

The earliest lock in existence is an Egyptian lock from about 2000 B.C. It is made of wood and was found with its key in the ruins of an an-

cient city. The Greeks and Romans used locks of simple design and made large keys of iron or bronze. Skilled craftsmen in the 1500s designed beautifully carved locks and keys that were works of art.

The simplest form of lock is a *ward lock*, or a *fixed lock*. It has a bolt that is moved backward or forward by a key. The *tumbler* or *lever lock* contains metal pieces of various heights known as tumblers, or levers. These keep the bolt from being moved until the tumblers are released by a key of the correct shape.

The *pin-tumbler cylinder lock* or *Yale lock* was invented and patented by Linus Yale, Jr., about 1860. It was the first lock to use a small, flat key in place of a large one. It is made up of a revolving cylinder or plug. Five small pin tumblers fall down into the cylinder when it is locked. The key must raise all five

pins, which have different lengths, before the lock will open. The most common form of cylinder lock used in the home is the *night latch*, operated by a key from the outside and a knob from the inside. When the pin tumblers are inside the lock itself, as

▲ *Local governments are responsible for many important services. One of them is to provide an efficient and effective fire department for the community.*

▼ *A long strip of metal is fed from a roll into a key-making machine (left). Roughly shaped keys fall out of the back of the machine (below). Later, the keys will be smoothed into their final shape.*

PIN-TUMBLER CYLINDER LOCK

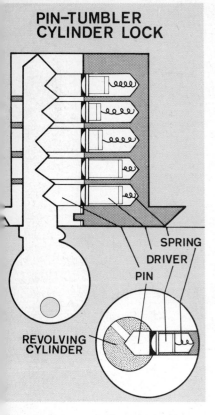

SPRING
DRIVER
PIN

REVOLVING
CYLINDER

in a *padlock*, it is called a *pin tumbler lock*.

The *dial* or *combination lock*, designed for safes and bank vaults, is not operated by a key. Turning a dial in the right sequence of numbers arranges a set of tumblers or wheels so that a bolt is released. Combination locks can have more than one hundred million changes of combination. A *time lock* can be opened only at a certain hour, when a clock releases the bolt or obstacle.

A series of locks can be made so that a *master key* or *skeleton key* will open any of the locks. Each of these locks still has its own key that can open only that lock.

LOCOMOTIVE see RAILROAD.

LOGIC see REASONING.

LONDON London is the capital of Great Britain. It is the fifth largest city in the world, with a population of about 7,764,000.

London is a bustling seaport and world trade and financial center full of warehouses, offices, homes, and markets. But in this modern city are historic buildings and beautiful old cathedrals. The ancient ceremony of the changing of the guard can be seen at Buckingham Palace, the official home of the ruler of Great Britain. The guards wear colorful uniforms and tall black bearskin hats, called busbies. The city is governed by the Greater London Coun-

cil. The person called "lord mayor" is an honorary official.

London is built near the mouth of the River Thames. Shortly after the Romans arrived in Britain in 43 A.D., they built a bridge over the Thames. This was guarded by a walled town called Londinium.

When the Roman Empire collapsed, the barbaric tribes who invaded England had little use for cities. London lay deserted for about 300 years. Alfred the Great, king of the West Saxons, occupied the town in the late 800s. He rebuilt the Roman walls and made London a center for business and trade.

When the Normans from France conquered England in 1066 A.D., London was a busy city. The Norman leader, William the Conqueror, had a fortress built to guard London Bridge. This became the Tower of London, used for centuries as a royal palace and prison.

Most of the buildings in Old London were made of wood, with thatch (straw) roofs. In 1666, the Great Fire of London burned for five days and destroyed most of the city. A brilliant English architect, Sir Christopher Wren, helped plan the rebuilding of the city. Stone and brick were then used for the houses. Many beautiful new churches, including Saint Paul's Cathedral, were built. Over the centuries, London spread far beyond the old city walls. Tree-lined avenues, squares, and spacious parks were built.

London was badly bombed during World War II, but most of the historic buildings were saved. The Tower of London is now a barracks and a museum where the Crown Jewels are kept. The Houses of Parliament are easily recognized by the tower of the huge clock, Big Ben. Nearby is Westminster Abbey, where the kings and queens of England have been crowned since the days of William the Conqueror. The prime minister of Britain lives in a small house at 10 Downing Street.

▼*Soldiers of the Household Brigade marching down a London street. They guard Queen Elizabeth's official home, Buckingham Palace.*

Londoners have parks and gardens to enjoy. Some of the largest are Hyde Park, Kensington Gardens, and Regent's Park, which has a zoo. London is a center for opera houses, concert halls, theaters, art galleries and museums, including the British Museum.

ALSO READ: ALFRED THE GREAT, BIG BEN, CROWN JEWELS, ENGLISH HISTORY, THAMES RIVER, TOWER OF LONDON, WESTMINSTER ABBEY.

LONDON, JACK (1876-1916) Some of the most popular adventure stories in the literature of America were written by Jack London. He was born in San Francisco, California. Many of his stories were based on his own adventures and travels.

London went to sea at 15 and saw much of the world. He was a newspaper reporter in Mexico and Asia, and he searched for gold in the Klondike (a part of Canada's Yukon Territory). He wrote over 40 books and many magazine stories. London's first published book was *The Son of the Wolf*, a collection of short stories about his gold rush days.

One of the best known and most widely read of London's works is *The Call of the Wild*. It tells about a dog named Buck, who is stolen from his California home and taken to the Yukon. Buck is sold to one man after another—some cruel, some kind. He must learn to be tough in order to live. In the end, Buck becomes leader of a wolf pack. He has returned to the life of his untamed ancestors.

In *Martin Eden*, London tells the story of a poor, young man who works hard to become a writer. In this book London is really writing about his own life.

ALSO READ: LITERATURE.

LONGFELLOW, HENRY WADS-WORTH (1807-1882)   Henry Wadsworth Longfellow is one of America's best-loved poets. He is remembered for having written "Paul Revere's Ride" and "The Village Blacksmith." He also composed the beautifully flowing story-poem *Song of Hiawatha*, based on authentic legends of American Indians. One of the most famous passages from this poem describes the home of Nokomis and her son, Hiawatha:

By the shores of Gitche Gumee,
By the shining Big-Sea-Water,
Stood the wigwam of Nokomis,
Daughter of the Moon,
    Nokomis.

The Courtship of Miles Standish, the *Wreck of the Hesperus*, and *Evangeline*, which are all based on American legends, are other well-known poems by Longfellow.

Longfellow was born in Portland, Maine. He attended Bowdoin College in Maine, and studied at several universities in Europe. Before becoming a writer, he taught modern languages at Bowdoin and later at Harvard University.

One of Longfellow's most interesting collections of poems is *Tales of a Wayside Inn*, stories in verse told by travelers staying at a real inn located in Sudbury, Massachusetts. The Wayside Inn, the oldest operating inn in the United States, is now visited by thousands of people every year. Longfellow's house in Cambridge, Massachusetts, is also a popular attraction for tourists. When Longfellow died, a statue of him was placed in Westminster Abbey in London, in the Poet's Corner. He was the first American poet to be honored in this manner.

ALSO READ: LITERATURE, POETRY.
LONG ISLAND see NEW YORK, NEW YORK CITY.

▲*Tower Bridge is a well-known London landmark. It crosses the Thames River.*

▲*Jack London, American writer.*

▼*Henry Wadsworth Longfellow, American poet.*

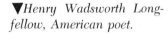

▲*Visitors to Griffith Park in Los Angeles enjoy a ride on an old train.*

LOS ANGELES The city of Los Angeles, California, is one of the fastest-growing localities in the United States. Los Angeles has a population of nearly 3 million people and ranks as the third largest city in the nation. The city covers about 460 square miles, sprawling in all directions. The number of people in the metropolitan area makes it the second largest city. Only the Jacksonville, Florida, metropolitan area is larger. Los Angeles completely surrounds several independent communities, such as Santa Monica and Beverly Hills, which are not part of the city at all. A long, narrow strip of land to the south connects the downtown area with San Pedro Bay. Much of the city's coast is beach.

Besides being the seat of Los Angeles County, the city is one of the major commercial and industrial centers in the United States. Los Angeles ranks first in the production of aircraft and aircraft parts, and second only to Detroit in assembling automobiles. Other leading industries include petroleum refining, printing and publishing, ordnance (military equipment), fishing and fish-canning, and the manufacture of electrical machinery and instruments. Hollywood, a part of Los Angeles, has been famous as a movie-making center since the early twentieth century and has been important to the television industry since the 1950s.

The region surrounding Los Angeles is one of the richest farming areas of California. Among the chief crops are citrus fruits, peaches, apricots, avocados, and figs. The area is dry, having no natural supply of water, and homes and crops have sometimes been destroyed by dry brush fires. Water has been piped to the city from the Colorado River, which is about 300 miles away. This water supply is now threatened by the vital need for water in the desert state, Arizona. A new California State Water Project is under construction to bring water from reservoirs and dams in northern California to where it is needed by homes, farms, and factories in southern California.

In 1781, a Spanish missionary, Father Junipero Serra, and the governor of the Mexican province of Alta California, Don Felipe de Neve, founded a town called "El Pueblo de Nuestra Señora la Reina de Los Angeles de Porciuncula" —The Town of Our Lady, the Queen of the Angels, of Porciuncula. Forty-four settlers lived around a *plaza* (town square) by the Porciuncula River. The old plaza is now a park, located in downtown Los Angeles. One section of the city has been closed to traffic and is preserved as a replica (copy) of a Mexican street of a century ago.

In 1846, Los Angeles was captured by the United States in the Mexican War. It rapidly became a thriving frontier town. After the discovery of gold in California in 1849, Los Angeles served as a source of food, chiefly cattle, for the boom-

▼*An interesting sculpture stands in front of one of the buildings of the cultural center in Los Angeles.*

ing mining towns in the North. The name was shortened to Los Angeles as the region grew, and in 1850 the area was incorporated as the City of Los Angeles.

A transcontinental railroad, completed in 1876, connected Los Angeles with the East and brought in many new settlers. Many immigrants came across the Pacific from China and Japan.

Oil was discovered in the city of Los Angeles and under the waters of San Pedro Bay. Oil wells began pumping inside the city limits in the 1920s. The first motion picture made entirely in the city was produced in 1908. From 1900 to 1920, the vast growth of all the industries in Los Angeles caused the population to triple—from 100,000 to more than 300,000 people! During World War II, the aircraft and other war industries expanded greatly, bringing hundreds of thousands of people to Los Angeles.

Many people come to Los Angeles because of its beautiful climate and scenery. It has a dry, subtropical climate with mild, sunny days and cool nights. The rapid growth of the city has, unfortunately, brought many problems. There are too few buses in this sprawling city, and no subway. Most of the people must depend on automobiles for all their transportation. The many expressways through and around the city have created a traffic problem and increased air pollution. The pollution problem becomes worse when a mass of warm air settles over Los Angeles, which lies in a kind of bowl, or valley, surrounded by ocean and mountains. The resulting smog is trapped over the city in this bowl. The smog of Los Angeles has become a dangerous health hazard, and no solution to the problem has yet been found.

Los Angeles lives under the constant threat of earthquakes. Major earthquakes are rare, but slight tremors, landslides, and mudflows cause thousands of dollars worth of damage each year.

ALSO READ: AIR POLLUTION, AMERICAN HISTORY, CALIFORNIA, EARTHQUAKE, FOG, HARBORS AND PORTS, MEXICAN WAR, MEXICO, MISSIONARY, WESTWARD MOVEMENT.

LOUIS, JOE (born 1914) One of the world's greatest prize fighters was born on a poor farm in Lexington, Alabama. His real name was Joseph Louis Barrow, but in the boxing ring he was known as Joe Louis, or the "Brown Bomber." As a small boy, young Joe moved with his family to Detroit, Michigan. He began boxing as a teenager, and won 50 out of 59 bouts as an amateur fighter. He turned professional in 1934.

Louis defeated James J. Braddock in a Chicago fight in 1937, and became heavyweight champion of the world. He held the championship for almost 12 years. During that time, he defended his title 25 times, winning by knockouts in 20 of those fights. Louis was still the champ when he retired in 1949.

One of Louis's most dramatic bouts was his second match with Max Schmeling, of Germany. Louis had been knocked out by Schmeling in their first fight. When the two met again, Louis knocked out the German in the first round.

Louis's modesty combined with his fantastic skill made him a national hero during the time he held the heavyweight title. He became a symbol of success to many black Americans.

ALSO READ: BOXING.

▲Joe Louis, the great heavyweight boxing champion.

LOUIS, KINGS OF FRANCE France has been ruled by 18 kings with the name of Louis. Their reigns cover a long period of French history—from the days when the monarchy was first being formed to the time when it was replaced by other forms of government.

Louis I (778–840) succeeded his

▲*Louis IX (Saint Louis), king of France from 1226 to 1270.*

father Charlemagne as king of the Franks and emperor of the Romans, in 814. Louis divided his lands among his four sons, who fought each other bitterly and rebelled against their father. Louis I supported the Catholic Church in France, and was called "The Pious."

Louis II (846–879) was called "The Stammerer." He succeeded his father Charles II as king of France in 877, and had a short reign.

Louis III (about 863–882) was the son of Louis II. He became joint ruler of France with his brother Carloman in 879. The brothers won a major battle against the Vikings, who had occupied Normandy in northern France.

Louis IV (921–954) was the son of King Charles III and grandson of Louis II. France was by this time split up into many regions, each ruled by a nobleman. This political and economic arrangement was called the feudal system. No king since the days of Charlemagne had been strong enough to control all of France, and the nobles were often more powerful than the king. Louis's father was overthrown by the nobles and Louis spent much of his childhood in England. In 936, several of the nobles asked Louis to return, and he was crowned king of France.

Louis V (about 967–987) was known as "The Sluggard" (lazy person). He succeeded his father King Lothair as king in 986. Louis V was the last king of the Carolingian dynasty (ruling family), founded by Charlemagne. When Louis died, the French people rejected his son, and chose Hugh Capet of a popular noble family as king of France.

Louis VI (1081–1137) succeeded his father King Philip I in 1108. Louis was a gluttonous eater who became known as "The Fat." But he was a brave soldier and spent most of his reign fighting French nobles.

Louis VII (about 1121–1180) succeeded his father Louis VI in 1137. In 1147 he led the second of the

▼*Louis XI, king of France from 1461 to 1483.*

great Crusades, or Christian military campaigns, against the Muslims in the Holy Land. Louis divorced his wife Queen Eleanor of Aquitaine in 1152. Eleanor then married King Henry II of England, and brought him the large French region of Aquitaine. The English possession of Aquitaine led to quarrels between the two countries, and was one of the main causes of the Hundred Years' War (1337–1453).

Louis VIII (1187–1226) was the son of King Philip Augustus of France and grandson of Louis VII. Before Louis became king, several rebellious English nobles asked him for help against their unpopular king, John. Louis invaded England with an army but he was defeated by the English king. Louis became king of France in 1223, but he died after ruling for only three years.

Louis IX (1214–1270), or Saint Louis, succeeded his father Louis VII in 1226, when he was 12 years old. His mother, Queen Blanche, acted as regent until Louis was old enough to rule. The young king was just and fair to nobles and peasants alike, and greatly loved by the people. Louis tried to end the long struggle between France and England by granting King Henry III of England several provinces in southern France. In return, Henry gave up his claim to land in northern France. Louis also led two crusades to the Holy Land. He died of plague in northern Africa while on the Second Crusade. After his death, Louis was declared a saint by the Roman Catholic Church.

Louis X (1289–1316) was known as "The Quarreller." He succeeded his father King Philip IV of France in 1314. During his reign, the nobles began to regain power.

Louis XI (1423–1483) was a suspicious and ruthless man, who became known as "The Spider." His father was King Charles VII. When Louis became king of France in 1461, he forced the French people to pay huge taxes. But he defeated the most powerful of the nobles, built a strong army, and encouraged the work of the townspeople.

Louis XII (1462–1515) was the son of Charles, Duke of Orleans. Louis became king of France in 1498, after the death of his cousin Charles VIII, who left no heirs. Louis worked to improve the living conditions of the French, especially the peasants. He became known as the "Father of the People."

Louis XIII (1601–1643) was only nine years old when he became king. His father, King Henry IV, was assassinated in 1610. Louis had poor health and never had the strength to rule alone. His mother, Marie de Medicis, first acted as regent. Later, Louis's brilliant chief minister, Cardinal Richelieu, governed France. The cardinal destroyed the castles of the nobles and also fought against the Huguenots (French Protestants). But in the Thirty Years' War (1618–1648), between the Protestants in Germany and the Roman Catholics in Austria, France fought on the side of the Protestants.

Louis XIV (1638–1715) succeeded his father Louis XIII as king of France in 1643. He was only five years old, and his mother, Queen Anne, became regent. During Louis's childhood, France was governed by the chief minister, Cardinal Mazarin. After Mazarin died in 1661, the king took control of the government and eventually became known as the "Grand Monarch." The sun became the symbol of his power, and he is often known as the "Sun King." He built a magnificent palace at Versailles, outside Paris. During Louis's reign the arts flourished.

Louis led France into four wars with other European countries. But he was defeated, and by the end of the wars, much of France's wealth had been used up.

Louis XV (1710–1774) was the great-grandson of Louis XIV. He succeeded Louis XIV as king of

France in 1715, when he was five years old. France was ruled by a regent, the Duke of Orleans, until 1723. Louis was then guided by his capable chief minister, Cardinal Fleury. After Fleury's death, Louis devoted most of his time to the pleasures of court life. He waged two expensive and unsuccessful wars, which the French peasants were forced to pay for with huge taxes. But Louis showed very little concern for their unhappiness.

Louis XVI (1754–1793) succeeded his grandfather Louis XV in 1774. His great passion was hunting, and he left governing to his ministers. The French people were now demanding a change in the system that made them pay enormous taxes while the nobles paid almost nothing. They criticized the king's gay and beautiful wife, Marie Antoinette, whom they accused of spending vast sums of money. The people believed the only answer was violent rebellion, and the French Revolution began. Louis and his family were forced to leave Versailles and live in Paris. In 1793, Louis and Marie Antoinette were condemned for treason by the people, and executed—Louis in January and Marie nine months later.

Louis XVII (1785–1795) was the son of Louis XVI. After his father was executed in 1793, Louis was named king of France by the supporters of the monarchy. But the young prince was imprisoned by the leaders of the French Revolution,

▲*Louis XIV, great king of France from 1643 to 1715.*

▲*Louis XV, king of France from 1715 to 1774.*

▼*Louis XVI, king of France from 1774 to 1793, was beheaded by the people.*

▲*Louis XVIII (seated), king of France from 1814 to 1824, with members of his family.*

and was never crowned. He died in prison at the age of ten.

Louis XVIII (1755–1824) was declared king of France by his supporters after the death of his nephew Louis XVII. As a prince, he had escaped from France before his brother, Louis XVI, was executed. After Napoleon Bonaparte was defeated in 1814, the elderly king returned to Paris. He ruled there for the next ten years except for a time in 1815, when Napoleon returned to France and regained control for the period known as "The Hundred Days." The French people were still divided by the extreme forces of the Revolution, and Louis spent his last years trying to bring peace and unity to France.

ALSO READ: CHARLEMAGNE, CRUSADES, ENGLISH HISTORY, FEUDALISM, FRENCH HISTORY, FRENCH REVOLUTION, HUNDRED YEARS' WAR, ITALIAN HISTORY, VERSAILLES, VIKINGS.

LOUISIANA The colorful traditions of the early French and Spanish settlers in Louisiana are still a part of life in the state today. The descendants of these settlers are called *creoles.* The Spanish style of decorating buildings with lacy iron-work can be seen in the old part of New Orleans. Some people in Louisiana still speak a form of French, called Creole. Louisiana has a state legal system that is based on the French Napoleonic Code.

The Land and Climate
Louisiana is a gulf state. It is not only on the Gulf of Mexico, but it is partly in it. The coast is lined with islands and *peninsulas* (land with water on three sides). The largest peninsual is the Mississippi Delta. It has been built up over the years by the great Mississippi River. The water carries soil downstream and deposits it at the river's mouth. The soil deposits grow, forming a new land area. The delta grows more than a mile every 17 years.

Most of the land in Louisiana is a low-lying plain. The highest point is Driskill Mountain, 535 feet high. It is in the northern section of the state. From here the land slopes southward toward the Gulf. The southern third of the state is only 50 feet above sea level. The lowest point, which is the site of the city of New Orleans, is five feet below sea level. Thick walls of earth and stone keep the lowlands from being flooded.

Louisiana has more than 7,000 miles of waterways deep enough for boats. The Mississippi and Red rivers are the two main rivers. Many *bayous* are located in southern Louisiana. These are slow-moving

▼*Tourists ride through the old French quarter of New Orleans in a traditional open horse-drawn carriage. Wrought-iron balconies are an outstanding feature of the architecture in this section of the city.*

streams that flow through swamps. The bayou country was the setting for part of Longfellow's famous poem, *Evangeline.* This poem tells the story of the French people who came from Acadia (now Nova Scotia) in Canada to settle in the bayous in the 1700s. Some of their descendants still live in the bayous, and are called *cajuns,* which comes from the word "Acadian." The state also has many lakes. The most unusual are ones called oxbows. These semicircular water bodies are the former channels of rivers that have changed their courses.

Louisiana has a semi-tropical climate. Summers are hot and humid and winters are short and mild. The state has plenty of rain throughout the year. Its climate is just right for numerous southern crops.

History

Many different Indian tribes once lived in the area of present-day Louisiana. The Caddoan group lived in the northwestern corner of the state. The Tunicans lived in the eastern and southern part of Louisiana. The Muskogean group lived in the eastern and central areas.

A small fleet of canoes started down the Mississippi in 1682. It carried a group of Frenchmen and Indians led by Robert Cavalier, Sieur de La Salle. The men were searching for the mouth of the Mississippi

River, which they found on April 9. La Salle then claimed all the land drained by the Mississippi for France. His claim included the basins of the rivers that flowed into the great river, too. He named the vast territory Louisiana in honor of his king, Louis XIV.

The French used only a small portion of the land they claimed. They founded the city of New Orleans in 1718. Its location on the Mississippi River and near the Gulf of Mexico made it an important port for ocean and river trade. It guarded one of the main water routes into North America. France lost Louisiana at the end of the French and Indian War. The part east of the Mississippi went to Britain. The part west of it went to Spain.

France had taken the Spanish part back again by 1800. The United States bought the area extending from the Mississippi River to the Rocky Mountains from France in 1803. This land was called the Louisiana Purchase, and included the area of present-day Louisiana. Louisiana became the first state to be carved from this huge piece of land, and the eighteenth state in the Union, in 1812.

The War of 1812 put Louisiana in danger of attack. The British tried to capture New Orleans, but were defeated by General Andrew Jackson and his men in the famous Battle

LOUISIANA

State flower
Magnolia

State bird
Eastern brown pelican

State tree
Magnolia (unofficial)

Capital
Baton Rouge (165,963 people)

Area
48,523 square miles (ranks 31st)

Population
3,643,180 people (ranks 20th)

Statehood
April 30, 1812 (18th state admitted)

Principal Rivers
Mississippi River
Red River

Highest Point
Driskill Mountain, 535 feet

Largest city
New Orleans (593,471 people)

◄*A watermelon eating contest in Kaplan, a town in southern Louisiana, held as part of the Bastille Day (July 14) celebration. Louisiana still has close cultural ties with France.*

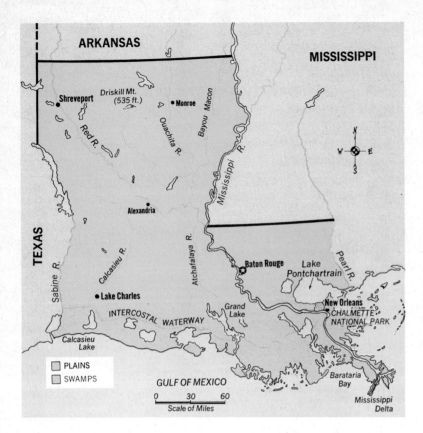

ARKANSAS

MISSISSIPPI

TEXAS

Shreveport
Driskill Mt.
(535 ft.)
Monroe
Red R.
Ouachita R.
Bayou Macon
Mississippi R.
Alexandria
Atchafalaya R.
Calcasieu R.
Sabine R.
Baton Rouge
Lake Pontchartrain
Pearl R.
Lake Charles
INTERCOSTAL WATERWAY
Grand Lake
New Orleans
CHALMETTE NATIONAL PARK
Calcasieu Lake

PLAINS
SWAMPS

GULF OF MEXICO

Barataria Bay

0   30   60
Scale of Miles

Mississippi Delta

Washington. Long ruled like a dictator, but he did some things to help the people of Louisiana. He was assassinated in 1935.

Louisianians at Work

History was made in Louisiana in 1901. Oil was discovered in that year. The discovery was made at just the right time—automobiles were soon to become popular. Today, Louisiana produces more oil than any state except Texas. It leads the country in producing natural gas. (Like oil, natural gas comes from wells.) These two underground resources have given the state its biggest industry.

Manufacturing is second. Its two principal products are chemicals and food products. Oil refining is the third most important kind of manufacturing. Refineries produce gasoline and other things from oil.

Tourism is far below manufacturing in terms of the dollars it earns, but it is the third most important industry in Louisiana. Visitors come from all over the United States to the annual Mardi Gras festival in New Orleans. The celebration includes colorful parades and gay costume balls. In French, "Mardi Gras" means "Fat Tuesday"—so called because it is followed by the very lean 40 days of Lent. The celebration is an old French custom and takes place on the Tuesday before Ash Wednesday—the day Lent begins. Many tourists also take boats through the winding river harbor of New Orleans and the bayous beyond it. Others drive through rolling green country and stop at old French-style villages. Here and there they see beautiful houses built before the Civil War. Visitors are allowed to go into some of them.

Agriculture is also important. The principal crops, in order of value, are cotton, soybeans, rice, and sugar cane. Livestock and animal products bring the state about two-thirds as much money as crops. Louisiana,

of New Orleans in January, 1815. This battle occurred two weeks after a peace treaty between the U.S. and Great Britain had been signed. But communication was so slow the soldiers had not received the news.

Two things brought wealth to Louisiana in the years that followed. One was the river-and-ocean trade of New Orleans. The other was agriculture. Thousands of Negro slaves raised cotton and sugar cane on large plantations in the state. Louisiana voted to join the Confederacy and entered the Civil War in 1861. Union forces took over the state in 1862. The state was bankrupt after the war, and many different groups began to struggle for power. On one side were the freed Negroes and some whites. On the other were the whites who wanted to regain their power over the blacks. This group won. The result was much bitterness. It is still felt in Louisiana—as in some other states.

Huey Long became the most powerful politician in Louisiana in the early 1930s. He served as governor of the state and as a senator in being a coastal state, has a large fishing industry. A major part of the nation's shrimp catch comes from the gulf waters of Louisiana.

The old trapping trade of Indians and frontiersmen is still carried on in the woods and swamps of Louisiana. These areas are the homes of many fur-bearing animals, especially muskrats. No state except Alaska earns as much money from the sale of fur as Louisiana. The woods also provide much timber.

ALSO READ: CIVIL WAR; CONFEDERATE STATES OF AMERICA; FRENCH AND INDIAN WAR; GULF OF MEXICO; HURRICANE; JAZZ; LA SALLE, SIEUR DE; LAW; LONGFELLOW, HENRY WADSWORTH; MISSISSIPPI RIVER; RECONSTRUCTION; WAR OF 1812.

LOUISIANA PURCHASE   The Louisiana Purchase has been called the most important event that occurred in American history during the first half of the 1800s. President Thomas Jefferson bought the entire Louisiana territory from the French in 1803. This territory extended from the Mississippi River to the Rocky Mountains, and from the Gulf of Mexico to the Canadian border. It added almost a million square miles of land to the south and west of the United States. America could then expand westward.

The Louisiana territory had been owned by European countries for many years before its purchase by the United States. First France and then Spain controlled it. Napoleon, the French leader, regained Louisiana from Spain in 1800. The Spanish governor in New Orleans, however, did not know this, and closed the port to American shipping. Americans needed the seaport to ship goods up and down the Mississippi River and to other countries. President Jefferson knew that France really controlled New Orleans. He sent James Monroe to Paris with an offer to buy the port from France for 2 million dollars.

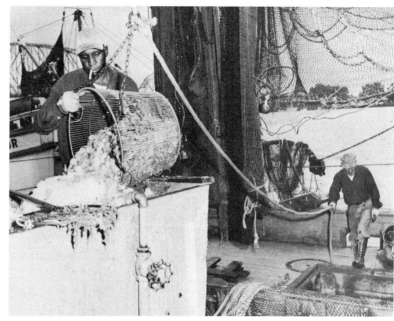

Napoleon surprised Jefferson by offering to sell not only New Orleans but the whole Louisiana territory. Napoleon asked for 20 million dollars for all the land. But he later agreed to take 15 million dollars. The United States paid France 11,250,000 dollars, and agreed to pay French debts to U.S. citizens.

The purchase treaty was signed by France and the U.S. on April 30, 1803. Then all of the Louisiana territory belonged to the United States. The territory made up all or part of what became 15 new states. The United States had bought enough land to double the country's size.

ALSO READ: JEFFERSON, THOMAS; LEWIS AND CLARK EXPEDITION; LOUISIANA; MONROE, JAMES.

LOUSE   A louse is a tiny, wingless insect that can cause a lot of trouble. Lice are dangerous *parasites*—living things that live on or in other animals. These insects, which look like tiny crabs, cause great discomfort and spread serious diseases.

There are two main types of lice—biting lice and sucking lice. Biting lice have mouth parts that are made for chewing and biting. They usually live on birds, and eat flakes of dried skin and feathers. Sucking lice have mouth parts that

▲*Great numbers of fish are to be found in the waters along Louisiana's coastline. Shrimp, being unloaded here, are an important part of the great amount of seafood caught by fishermen in Louisiana.*

▼*French soldiers fire a salute as the French flag is lowered and the American flag is raised as the U.S. takes possession of Louisiana on December 20, 1803.*

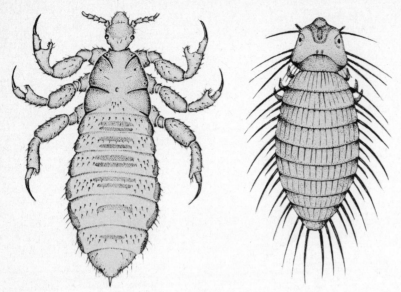

▲*A head louse (above) is a sucking louse that can be found on man. The chicken louse (right) is a type of biting louse.*

older buildings. The leaders of the French Revolution decreed that all works of art seized from royal palaces, the homes of nobles, and from convents and churches should be brought to the Louvre.

The Louvre is now one of the world's largest art museums. It covers almost 50 acres on the north bank of the Seine River. The museum's 140 exhibition rooms house 275,000 works of art, including 5,000 paintings. Among the Louvre's greatest treasures are the ancient Greek statues, *Venus de Milo* and *Winged Victory*, and Leonardo da Vinci's painting, *Mona Lisa*. The only American artists represented are Mary Cassatt and James Whistler. One of Miss Cassatt's mother-and-child paintings hangs in the Louvre, and so does Whistler's famous painting of his mother.

All the works of art in the Louvre were removed and hidden in different places throughout France during World War II. After the war, they were returned—not one item was lost.

ALSO READ: ART, ART HISTORY, FRENCH REVOLUTION, MUSEUM.

LOW, JULIETTE GORDON see GIRL SCOUTS.

LSD see MOOD MODIFIER.

LUBRICANT see FRICTION.

are specially made for piercing skin and sucking blood. They live on many mammals, including man. Their bodies are flat, and they have powerful claws which grip an animal's hair and make them hard to pull off. Both biting and sucking lice cause much itching. Biting lice also spread disease. They are the main carriers of typhus fever.

Body and head lice can attack human beings. They live in people's hair, where they attach themselves to the strands. They lay their eggs, called *nits*, in the hair, or in the seams of clothing. Anyone with lice should get medical treatment.

ALSO READ: INSECT, INSECT PEST, PARASITE.

LOUVRE For hundreds of years, the Louvre was a great royal palace in the city of Paris. Various kings had added new buildings to the huge estate and had artists redecorate the

▼*The Louvre, the great art museum in Paris, was originally a palace of the French kings. Only one wing of the huge building is shown here.*

LUMBER AND LUMBERING The chair you are sitting on was very likely made from lumber. Lumber is also used in making, among other things, houses, telephone poles, railroad ties, and plastic. Look around you now and notice all the things that are made of wood.

Lumbering (the business of preparing timber for use in building and manufacturing) is one of the oldest and biggest industries in the United States. Lumber was important in the early development of the colonies, when settlers lived in log cabins and had only wood for fuel. Many settlers were able to earn a living from logging, since lumber

▲*The top branches of a big tree are trimmed off before the tree is cut down to allow the tree to fall clear of other trees nearby.*

was needed both in the colonies and in Europe. At that time most logging was done in New England.

Today, most of this country's lumbering is done in the pine forests of the South and in the Pacific Northwest. The United States is the world's second largest producer of lumber. The building (construction) industry uses most of the lumber, but the paper industry also uses a great deal of wood.

Lumbering

Logging is the first of the three main branches of the lumber industry. Foresters mark the trees that are to be cut down. Then loggers *fell*, or cut down, the marked trees with a power saw. After they cut the felled trees into smaller sections, these logs are taken to the sawmill.

Logs are sent through the sawmill on a moving belt. After the bark is removed from the logs, they are cut into boards. Then the lumber must be *seasoned*, or dried, since untreated wood contains a great deal of water. If lumber were not seasoned, it would stain, rot, and warp (twist out of shape) quite easily. Sometimes lumber is dried in the open air. But often it is dried artificially in a *dry kiln*. The boards are graded before and after they are

seasoned according to their size, kind, and quality.

Lumber is finished, or given a smooth surface, at the planing mill. Lumber used in construction is also cut into the proper shapes for floors, shingles, and house trim.

Types of Lumber

Hardwood lumber comes from deciduous trees (trees that lose their leaves in autumn), such as maples and oaks. Hardwood is used primarily for floors, furniture, paneling, and tools. Conifers (evergreen trees), such as pines, firs, and spruce, produce *softwood* lumber. Softwood is used in construction and in making pulp, from which paper is made. (Pulp is wood that has been ground up and moistened.) The cellulose in pulp is used in making plastic, linoleum, and rayon. Plywood, used in construction, is made of several thin layers of wood that have been glued together to form large sheets. Tar and turpentine are also obtained from wood. Sawdust, from cutting lumber, is used as industrial fuel.

Conservation

Lumbermen consider the future of our forests when they fell trees. Lumber companies usually either reforest (plant new trees) in an area or leave some "seed" trees so that nature will reforest the region. In some areas, lumbermen cut down all the old trees so that they will not die and create a fire hazard or fall on

▲*Floating the logs down river is a traditional and efficient way of getting them to the sawmill. This logger is forming a raft of the logs.*

▼*Logs with the bark removed are piled outside a sawmill. They will be cut into lumber.*

▲*A power saw is used to remove the bark from a log and to square it off.*

younger trees. Foresters also leave some trees on a hillside (called *selective cutting*) whose roots will grasp the earth and prevent erosion.

Many wood products, such as paper and cardboard, can be recycled (ground up and re-used) so that fewer trees need to be felled. Recycled wood is used to make such products as building boards, shoe boxes, paper towels, and newsprint. Find out if a group in your neighborhood collects paper and cardboard for recycling. If no one does, perhaps your class would like to start a recycling project.

ALSO READ: BARK, BUILDING MATERIAL, CONIFER, CONSERVATION, CONSTRUCTION, ECOLOGY, EROSION, FOREST FIRE, FORESTRY, FURNITURE, HOUSE, NATIONAL FOREST, NATURAL RESOURCES, SHELTER, TREE, WILDERNESS AREA, WOOD.

▼*Martin Luther, leader of the Protestant Reformation.*

LUTHER, MARTIN (1483–1546) One of the greatest upheavals in the history of the Christian religion was started by a German monk named Martin Luther. Luther was born in Eisleben, Germany. He studied at the University of Erfurt, intending to become a lawyer. Toward the end of his course, he changed his mind and entered the Augustinian monastery in Erfurt.

He became a priest in 1507. He was made a professor of religious studies at the University of Wittenberg, where he was very popular with his students.

Luther was not able to accept many of the teachings of the Roman Catholic Church. In 1517, a Dominican monk named Johann Tetzel arrived in Wittenberg to sell *indulgences*, or releases from suffering the Church's punishment for sin. The money was to be used to help rebuild St. Peter's Church in Rome. On October 31, 1517, Luther nailed his Ninety-Five Theses, or statements, on the door of All Saints' Church in Wittenberg. In them, Luther attacked the selling of indulgences. He also said that a person received forgiveness by having faith in God and Christ and by showing that he was sorry for having done wrong. He said that the Church was too interested in money.

This date in 1517 is considered the beginning of the *Protestant Reformation*. The Church, under Pope Leo X, tried many times to make Luther take back what he had said, but he refused. At a meeting in the city of Worms, Germany, Luther said: "Here I stand; I cannot do otherwise." He was excommunicated (put out) from the Roman Catholic Church.

Under Luther's leadership, and with the support of the German princes, a large number of Christians split away from the Roman Catholic Church. Many other groups broke away from the Roman Church soon afterwards. Luther married Katherine von Bora, a former nun, in 1525, and they had six children. He translated the Bible from Latin into German and wrote many hymns, including "A Mighty Fortress Is My God." Luther's religious ideas became the faith called Lutheranism.

ALSO READ: PROTESTANT CHURCHES, PROTESTANT REFORMATION, ROMAN CATHOLIC CHURCH.

LUXEMBOURG Old castles and walled towns give Luxembourg a medieval look. It is a tiny picture-book country surrounded by France, Belgium, and West Germany. Rivers have carved deep valleys into the rocky hills. The narrow valleys sometimes make the hills look taller and more rugged than they really are. Along the rivers are peaceful little villages built during the Middle Ages. The nation's official name is the Grand Duchy of Luxem-

who grow grapes, oats, potatoes, and wheat. They also raise dairy cows, beef cattle, and pigs.

The capital is lovely Luxembourg City, the largest community in the country. The city has many bridges because two winding rivers cut through it. Luxembourg City began to grow when a small castle was built there a thousand years ago. The counts of the House of Luxembourg lived in this castle. It was a small fortress where corridors

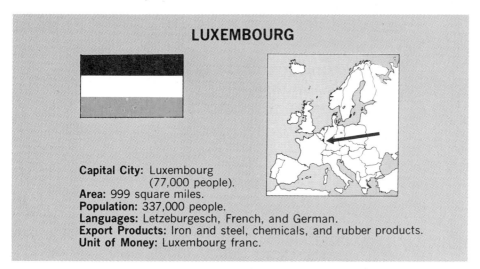

LUXEMBOURG

Capital City: Luxembourg (77,000 people).
Area: 999 square miles.
Population: 337,000 people.
Languages: Letzeburgesch, French, and German.
Export Products: Iron and steel, chemicals, and rubber products.
Unit of Money: Luxembourg franc.

bourg. (See the map with the article on EUROPE.)

Luxembourg, a land with a cool, moist climate, is divided into two regions. The Ardennes forest and high hills cover the northern third of the country. The southern, hilly part of the country is called *Le Bon Pays,* or "Good Land." Once most of Luxembourg was covered with trees, but only one-third of the land is forested now. Vineyards, famous for their wine, are in the east.

Most Luxembourgers are of French, German, or Belgian origin and belong to the Roman Catholic church. They speak French and German. Their own language is a mixture of these two, called *Letzeburgesch.* The Luxembourgers mostly work in banking and industry, especially iron and steel. In the southwest, the country has some of Europe's richest iron mines. About 11 per cent of the people are farmers

gouged through solid rock connected outer forts with the main citadel.

Luxembourg became a constitutional monarchy in 1836 under King William of the Netherlands as Grand Duke. It has been ruled by a grand duke or grand duchess ever since. The country was later invaded and occupied by the Germans during both world wars. Part of the Battle of the Bulge was fought there during World War II. United States troops liberated Luxembourg in both wars. Today, the country belongs to the North Atlantic Treaty Organization, the Benelux economic union with Belgium and the Netherlands, and the Common Market. Luxembourg was one of the original UN members.

ALSO READ: COMMON MARKET, EUROPE, NORTH ATLANTIC TREATY ORGANIZATION, WORLD WAR I, WORLD WAR II.

▼*The city of Luxembourg, capital and largest city of the Grand Duchy of Luxembourg.*

Mm

▼A sedan, a portable chair, is used in funeral ceremonies in Macao.

MACAO Macao, an overseas province of Portugal, is the oldest European settlement in the Far East. Cobblestone streets, brightly colored houses, and medieval Portuguese churches blend with Chinese shops and Buddhist temples. Fishing junks visit the harbor.

Macao is situated on the southern coast of mainland China at the mouth of the Canton River. Part of the colony lies on a peninsula. The islands of Taipa and Coloane to the south contain the rest of the colony. The total area covered is only six square miles and is low and flat. The monsoons bring warm wet summers and cool sunny winters. (See the map with the article on ASIA.)

Hong Kong lies 40 miles east across the Canton River delta. Ferries travel to Macao from Hong Kong and from Canton, China, about 70 miles north of Macao.

About 99 per cent of the people in Macao are Chinese. The others are Portuguese or mixed Portuguese and Chinese. The main religion is Buddhism. There are about 17,000 Roman Catholics. The official language is Portuguese, but Chinese, mainly Cantonese, is spoken.

MACAO

Capital City: Macao City
(161,000 people).
Area: 6 square miles.
Population: 260,000 people.
Languages: Chinese and
Portuguese.
Export Products: Fish, textiles, and handicrafts.
Unit of Money: Pataca.

Fishing is the main industry in Macao and provides the chief local food supply. Most of Macao's food and all of its fresh water are imported from mainland China. Fireworks, matches, and textiles are manufactured in Macao.

Portuguese traders stopped at Macao on their way to Japan during the 1500s and developed the area as a trading post. In 1557, the Chinese agreed to let the Portuguese settle in Macao. The right of perpetual occupation of Macao was granted in 1887. This agreement was called the Protocol of Lisbon. The People's Republic of China does not recognize this agreement, but has generally lived peacefully with Macao.

Macao has a governor appointed by Portugal and sends a member to the Portuguese National Assembly.

ALSO READ: CHINA, PORTUGAL.

MacARTHUR, DOUGLAS (1880–1964) "I shall return," U.S. General Douglas MacArthur promised the people in the Philippines when Japanese troops forced him to leave the islands in February, 1942. He kept his promise, and his forces drove the Japanese out of the Philippines only 2½ years later. MacArthur accepted the Japanese surrender in World War II aboard the U.S.S. *Missouri* in Tokyo Bay on September 3, 1945.

MacArthur was born on an army reservation in Little Rock, Arkansas.

His father, Arthur MacArthur, was a Union colonel in the Civil War, and became a general in the Spanish-American War. Douglas graduated from the U.S. Military Academy at West Point, New York, in 1903, at the head of his class. He served as a colonel and later a brigadier general in Europe during World War I. He returned to the United States after the war, and became superintendent of the U.S. Military Academy. He was appointed chief of staff in 1930, becoming, at 50, the youngest man to hold this position.

President Franklin Roosevelt appointed MacArthur commander in chief of U.S. armed forces in the Far East when World War II broke out in December, 1941. MacArthur was chosen supreme commander of all Allied Forces in the Southwest Pacific in 1942, and led the Allied troops to victory. He was put in charge of setting up a democratic government in Japan after the war. MacArthur became commander of United Nations forces in Korea when the Korean Conflict broke out in June, 1950. He thought he could end this conflict by attacking military bases in Red China, but President Harry Truman disagreed with him and discharged him from his post in 1951. MacArthur was honored by the U.S. Congress in 1962 for his great leadership.

ALSO READ: ARMY, KOREAN CONFLICT, PHILIPPINES, WORLD WAR II.

In Macao, tourists visit the Kwan Yin Temple and its nearby garden. The first treaty between the United States and China was signed on July 3, 1844, on a table in this garden.

▼*General Douglas MacArthur, American military leader in the Pacific.*

In his speech to Congress in 1951, Douglas MacArthur spoke the words from an old military song, "Old soldiers never die, they just fade away."

▲ *John A. Macdonald, first prime minister of the Dominion of Canada.*

▼ *An old archway partially hides from view a modern apartment building in Salonika, the capital and chief city of Greek Macedonia.*

MACDONALD, JOHN A. (1815-1891) Sir John A. Macdonald was a great statesman and the first prime minister of Canada. He was born in Glasgow, Scotland, in 1815. When he was a young boy, his family moved to Canada, and he was brought up in Ontario. Macdonald's parents were able to send him to school only until he was 15 years old. After that, they arranged for him to become a lawyer's assistant. Macdonald soon became a lawyer himself, and a highly respected leader in the town of Kingston.

Macdonald opposed the old-fashioned, conservative views of the political leaders in Canada. He played a leading role in making the Conservative Party more modern and up to date. Macdonald was one of the first to work for a united Canada that would include the seven remaining British colonies in North America and stretch from coast to coast. With the help of a newspaper publisher named George Brown, Macdonald was successful in bringing about the creation of Canada in 1867. He became the country's first prime minister.

Macdonald's government purchased the Northwest Territories from the Hudson's Bay Company and began construction of the Canadian Pacific Railway. His government was defeated in 1873, but he was elected prime minister again from 1878 to 1891.

ALSO READ: CANADA, FATHERS OF CONFEDERATION.

MACEDONIA The region of southeastern Europe known as Macedonia has a very ancient history. Macedonia is in the Balkan Peninsula on the northern coast of the Aegean Sea.

The region was settled around 3000 B.C. by wandering tribes. Historians are not certain where these first settlers came from. Tribes from the neighboring countries of Thrace and Illyria occupied parts of Macedonia around 2000 B.C. After 1000 B.C., the great civilization of ancient Greece was established to the south of Macedonia. The Macedonians admired the Greeks and copied many of their ways.

In 359 B.C., King Philip II became ruler of Macedonia and began a campaign to extend the borders of his country. He invaded Greece and gained control over most of the Greek city-states. Philip was assassinated, and his son Alexander III (Alexander the Great) became king. Alexander, a brilliant military leader, built one of the greatest empires the world has ever known. He united all of Greece, conquered Persia and Egypt, and even went as far as India. After Alexander's death in 323 B.C., the mighty Macedonian Empire fell apart. The Romans conquered much of it, and in 148 B.C. made Macedonia a Roman province. The Roman Empire split in two in 395 A.D., and Macedonia became part of the Eastern Roman, or Byzantine, Empire. Many other conquerors—Bulgarians, Turks, and Serbians—have since invaded the mountainous land of Macedonia.

Today, Macedonia is divided into three parts, belonging to Bulgaria, Yugoslavia, and Greece. Salonika, in the Greek part, is Macedonia's largest city. Farming is the most important occupation in Macedonia. Grain, tobacco, and fruit are grown in the valleys, and sheep and goats graze on the hillsides. The people are descended from many different nationalities. The southern Macedonians mainly speak Greek. The northerners speak Bulgarian or or Macedonian.

ALSO READ: ALEXANDER THE GREAT; BULGARIA; GREECE; GREECE, ANCIENT; YUGOSLAVIA.

MACHIAVELLI, NICCOLO (1469-1527) Many modern-day ideas about politics and government were first written about in the 1400s and 1500s by Niccolo Machiavelli, an

Italian statesman and soldier.

Machiavelli was born in Florence, at a time when Italy was completely divided into independent city-states. When he was a young man, the powerful Medici family, which had ruled Florence for many years, was overthrown. Machiavelli was given an important position in the new government.

It was the general custom of the time to hire soldiers. Machiavelli started a "citizens' army" in Florence, believing that the natives of Florence would be more patriotic and better defenders of the city than hired soldiers. Machiavelli's duties required him to make many trips to the various governments of Italy, France, and Germany. In those countries, he was able to see how the rulers plotted and schemed to stay in power.

Machiavelli was banished from Florence when the Medici came to power again. During his exile, he wrote *The Prince*, stating his ideas about how a country should be governed. Machiavelli wanted Italy to be united into one nation. He believed that this could only be achieved by one strong leader who had unlimited powers. He dedicated *The Prince* to Cesare Borgia, an Italian soldier-statesman who wanted to rule all of Italy and often used treachery to get what he wanted.

The word "machiavellian" is used today to describe someone or something that is shrewd and cunning.

ALSO READ: BORGIA FAMILY, FLORENCE, ITALIAN HISTORY, MEDICI FAMILY.

MACKENZIE, ALEXANDER (about 1764-1820) Sir Alexander Mackenzie was the first white explorer to travel across the continent of North America to the Pacific Ocean. He traveled through the wild regions of northwest Canada.

Mackenzie was born in Scotland but moved to New York as a child. A few years later he went to Mon-

treal, Canada, and joined the fur-trading North West Company in 1778. Mackenzie was stationed at a trading post on Lake Athabasca in northern Alberta. His outpost, Fort Chipewyan, was at the edge of the wilderness. No Europeans knew what lay beyond to the north or west. Mackenzie was determined to find out. In 1789, he traveled north on the huge river that was later named after him, to where it reaches the Arctic Ocean. Mackenzie was a strong man and a tireless paddler. He led his exploring party in three large canoes more than 1,000 miles to the Arctic Ocean, traveling at the almost unbelievable average rate of 99 miles a day.

Mackenzie returned to Fort Chipewyan, but set out again in May, 1793, this time to the west. His route lay through the Rocky Mountains. He followed dangerous, twisting rivers never before explored, narrowly missing death many times. He reached the Pacific coast of what is now British Columbia after two months. Mackenzie then traveled back to eastern Canada, where he became a successful fur trader. He later returned to Britain, where he was knighted. He died in Scotland.

ALSO READ: CANADA, FUR TRADER, MACKENZIE RIVER.

MACKENZIE RIVER Take a look at the map of Canada. Put your finger on Great Slave Lake in Canada's Northwest Territories. Now trace the path of the Mackenzie River as it flows out of Great Slave Lake northwestward to the Arctic Ocean. Another large river—the Slave River—flows into Great Slave Lake from the south. Before it reaches Slave Lake, it is joined by the Peace River, which starts high in the Rocky Mountains. If you paddled a canoe from the beginning of the Peace River, across Great Slave Lake, then through the length of the Mackenzie, you would have traveled about 2,635 miles!

▲ *Niccolo Machiavelli, Italian statesman and political philosopher.*

▲ *Alexander Mackenzie (right) reaches the Pacific Ocean after his long journey across the northern part of North America.*

▲*An aerial view of the Mackenzie River delta in Canada's Northwest Territories.*

The Mackenzie-Peace River System is the second longest waterway in North America. The Mississippi-Missouri River System in the United States is the longest. Small ships can sail about 1,700 miles of the Mackenzie-Peace System.

The Mackenzie River was discovered by the Canadian explorer, Sir Alexander Mackenzie, in 1789. Mackenzie traveled down the river hoping to reach the Pacific Ocean. He arrived at the Arctic Ocean instead, so he named this river the "River of Disappointment." The name was later changed to Mackenzie, in honor of this brave explorer.

ALSO READ: CANADA; MACKENZIE, ALEXANDER.

MADAGASCAR see MALAGASY.

MADISON, JAMES (1751–1836) "The great little Madison," as James Madison was called, was a small man with a brilliant mind. He began his political career early, and helped draw up the United States Constitution more than 20 years before he became the fourth President of the United States. He was responsible for some of the basic ideas used in this American plan of Federal Government. For that reason, he is gratefully remembered as the "Father of the Constitution."

James Madison grew up at Montpelier, a handsome plantation house that his father had built in Orange County, Virginia. He suffered from poor health, but studied hard, and enrolled at the College of New Jersey (now Princeton University) at the age of 18. He became interested in problems of government, and he was elected a delegate to the Virginia Convention in 1776. This Convention declared Virginia to be independent of Great Britain several weeks before the Declaration of Independence was adopted. Young Madison was appointed to the committee that wrote the new state constitution. Later he was a delegate to the Continental Congress (1780–1783).

Madison was chosen as delegate from Virginia to the Constitutional Convention of 1787. His "Virginia Plan" of government became a kind of basis for the Constitution which was written at this convention. He also helped to write *The Federalist Papers* with two other members of the convention, John Jay and Alexander Hamilton. This series of essays explained the new plan of government to the people. A new Congress took the place of the old Continental Congress after the Constitution became the law of the land. James Madison was elected to the House of Representatives, and one of his first acts was to urge that some amendments be added to the Constitution. The first ten amendments that were adopted and *ratified*, or approved,

The President's house was not always called the White House. Madison had the mansion painted white after it was burned by the British in the War of 1812. People then began to call it the White House.

JAMES MADISON

FOURTH PRESIDENT   MARCH 4, 1809—MARCH 3, 1817

Born: March 16, 1751, Port Conway, Virginia
Parents: James and Eleanor (Nellie) Conway Madison
Education: College of New Jersey (now Princeton University), Princeton, New Jersey
Religion: Episcopalian
Occupation: Lawyer
Political Party: Democratic-Republican
State Represented: Virginia
Married: 1794 to Dolley Payne Todd Madison (1768–1849)
Children: 1 stepson
Died: June 28, 1836, Montpelier, Virginia
Buried: Montpelier, Virginia

by the states, are called the Bill of Rights. This bill guarantees the basic rights, such as freedom of speech and of religion, of all American people.

Madison served as Secretary of State under President Thomas Jefferson. During this time, American seamen and ships were being taken over by both the British and French, who were at war. Madison succeeded Jefferson as President in 1809. He tried to make the French and British respect American shipping without going to war, but was unsuccessful. The War of 1812 broke out between the United States and Great Britain over this issue.

Madison was re-elected President. The British invaded the country, and were approaching Washington in August, 1814. The President left the capital hurriedly to hold a council with one of his generals. His wife, the popular Dolley Madison, was left alone with the servants in the Executive Mansion (now the White House). She had Gilbert Stuart's portrait of George Washington cut from its frame, and gave it to two gentlemen from New York, who promised to take it to a safe place. Her quick action saved this famous portrait, which now hangs again in the White House. Dolley then packed some of the President's important papers in a trunk, and took them away with her in a carriage sent by friends.

British troops soon entered the city and set fire to the Capitol, the White House, and other public buildings. Then they retreated, fearing that U.S. troops were coming. The Executive Mansion was still standing when the Madisons returned, but it was blackened by fire. The inside of the building had been almost destroyed. The President and First Lady lived in several different houses until the Madison administration left office.

The war ended in December, 1814, and the country entered a pe-

riod of nationalism later called the "era of good feelings." Americans wanted to build up their new country, and stay out of foreign affairs. This era lasted far beyond Madison's administration, which ended in 1817. Madison spent his last years at Montpelier.

ALSO READ: BILL OF RIGHTS; CONSTITUTION, UNITED STATES; CONTINENTAL CONGRESS; VIRGINIA; WAR OF 1812; WHITE HOUSE.

MAGAZINE One of the best ways of reaching a large number of people is to publish a magazine. Magazines are published and read in countries all over the world. They provide entertainment and information on a wide variety of subjects. Many magazines contain a variety of articles, stories, drawings, and photographs. Magazines are produced on many different subjects, for readers with all kinds of interests. Magazines often influence people's political opinions, values (what they consider important), and tastes in hobbies and clothing.

Unlike books, which are published only once, magazines are issued in periodic installments, some weekly, some monthly, some quarterly (four times a year), and some annually (once a year). Therefore, magazines are often called *periodicals*. Unlike newspapers, which are not bound together permanently, magazines are stapled or sewn together and have a cover. They are

▲ *In 1814, during the War of 1812, the British sailed down the Potomac River and burned part of Washington, D.C. This event occurred during Madison's Presidency.*

▲ *Dolley Madison, the wife of James Madison, was a popular First Lady.*

▲ *Like many magazines, American Girl (above) keeps pace with the changing interests of its readers. An art director (right) discusses the design of a layout with his assistant. Each page of a mgazine is planned separately.*

Newsstands in large cities sell foreign magazines as well as a variety of American periodicals. Students of a foreign language—French, for example—can use such magazines as *Paris Match* to improve their reading in the language.

also cheap, so most people can afford to buy the ones that interest them. Readers often *subscribe* to their favorite magazines, which means that each issue is mailed directly to them as soon as it is published. Magazines are also sold at drugstores, markets, and newsstands.

One of the first publications that could be called a magazine was published in London in 1704. It was called the *Review.* Its publisher, and the author of most of its contents, was a young man named Daniel Defoe, the man who wrote *Robinson Crusoe.* In the *Review*, politics, business, religion, and London social life were discussed.

Benjamin Franklin published one of the first magazines in the United States in 1740. His publication, *The General Magazine and Historical Chronicle,* did not last very long, but many popular, successful magazines were started in the 1800s. People then had few sources of entertainment and news, so general magazines such as the *Saturday Evening Post* and *Collier's* were widely read. In recent years, the market for such general interest magazines has been reduced because many people get most of their news and entertainment from television. Today, the most successful magazines serve

special-interest groups. Many mass-circulation magazines have stopped publication because they have so few readers now and costs are very high. For example, the *Saturday Evening Post,* a general-interest magazine, had to stop regular publication. *Collier's* was a popular and influential magazine during the first half of this century, but during the 1950s its circulation fell so low it was forced to close. Most special-interest magazines, such as *Ladies' Home Journal* and *Popular Mechanics,* still have a wide circulation. *Cosmopolitan,* a popular general-interest magazine during the 1930s and 1940s, managed to survive by becoming a special-interest periodical. It is now written for young, unmarried women.

Several new types of magazines have appeared in this century. A digest contains selected articles and stories from other publications, written in condensed (shortened) form. The *Reader's Digest* is the best-known example. It became very successful and widely imitated. Weekly news magazines have also become popular. Such magazines as *Time, Newsweek,* and *U.S. News and World Report* contain news photographs, political cartoons, and articles on the week's news. Other weekly news magazines, such as *Life,* concentrate on picture stories.

Magazines for Young People

Youth's Companion, begun in 1827, was the first magazine written especially for children. It soon became one of the most popular magazines in the country with both adults and children. It was soon followed by *St. Nicholas,* edited by Mary Mapes Dodge, who wrote *Hans Brinker, or the Silver Skates.* These magazines published children's stories written by many well-known writers. *St. Nicholas* also published stories and poems written by children. Robert Benchley, William Faulkner, and Edna St. Vincent Millay were successful authors who wrote for *St. Nicholas* while still children. *American Boy* and *Open Road* were popular with boys. The first comic books were made in the 1930s and are still popular with children today. Other children's magazines today, such as *Boy's Life, American Girl, Wee Wisdom,* and *Jack and Jill,* contain stories, interesting information, and ideas about hobbies and games. *Current Events* and *My Weekly Reader* are very popular with children in the elementary grades. *Scholastic* magazines are published for several grade levels. Your school library can give you a list of children's magazines. Schools often print their own magazines. Most junior high and high schools print magazines or newspapers containing short stories, poems, and essays written by students.

Publishing a Magazine

The price of most magazines is rather low. Therefore, magazine publishers do not make such money from sales to readers. Most magazines make a profit by selling advertising space to manufacturers of products their readers might want to buy. In fact, most magazines could not survive without the money they make from advertising.

The editors of a magazine are the men and women who put together each issue. The editor in chief and his staff decide what kinds of articles an issue should contain. The editor in chief may then ask free-lance (independent) writers for some or all of the articles. (These writers are often called contributing editors.) He may also assign articles to his own editors and writers. In a large magazine, each editor is responsible for a different subject, such as politics, fashion, fiction, or art. After the articles are written, they must be checked by the editors. The editors must arrange with photographers for pictures to illustrate the articles. Many magazines use free-lance photographers. Magazines with a large circulation (many people who buy it) have full-time photographers.

Each issue of the magazine, including the cover, illustrations, and the arrangement of articles, must be designed by the art director and his staff. The magazine is then printed, and copies are sent to subscribers, drugstores, and newsstands.

ALSO READ: ADVERTISING; CARTOONING; CHILDREN'S LITERATURE; COMICS; DODGE, MARY MAPES; FRANKLIN, BENJAMIN; JOURNALISM; PRINTING.

MAGELLAN, FERDINAND (1480-1521)

The first expedition to sail all the way around the world was organized by a Portuguese navigator and explorer named Ferdinand Magellan. Magellan died before the end of the journey. But his courage and leadership inspired his men to complete the dangerous voyage through unknown seas.

◄American Girl *is a magazine of special interest to young girls, especially Girl Scouts. Fiction stories, non-fiction articles, and things to do keep the readers looking forward to each month's issue.*

▲*Ferdinand Magellan, Portuguese explorer and navigator.*

▼*A magical rite in a secret society in Africa. The person drinking the potion is supposed to be protected against evil spirits.*

Ferdinand Magellan was born in Sabrosa, Portugal. As a young man, he served with the Portuguese army in India. A sea route to that land, around the southern tip of Africa, had been discovered in 1497 by the Portuguese explorer Vasco da Gama.

Magellan dreamed, however, of finding a shorter route to Asia by sailing around the Americas. He especially wanted to reach the Molucca (Spice) Islands, where cloves were grown. The Portuguese were not interested, but the Spanish king gave him 5 ships and 240 men. In 1519, Magellan began his voyage across the Atlantic.

After sailing down the east coast of South America, Magellan discovered a narrow passage, or *strait*, running west. To the south was a wild and icy land. As the explorers sailed through the strait, they could see the fires in the Indian villages along the coast, and they named the land *Tierra del Fuego* ("land of fire"). The strait was later named after Magellan. In November, 1520, the expedition sailed out into the Pacific Ocean. Magellan headed west, expecting to reach China in a few days. After several weeks, supplies ran out, and his men began to die of starvation.

At last, after more than three months without sight of inhabited land, the exhausted and battered fleet reached what is now Guam Island in the West Pacific. Refreshed and revived, those who had survived pressed on to the Philippine Islands. There, a tragedy occurred. Magellan tried to make peace between two warring tribes, and was killed.

Heartbroken, his men returned to their two remaining ships. Under a new leader, Juan Sebastian del Cano, they set sail again. Magellan had planned for the expedition to go back to Spain by the way they had come. But the winds were too strong and one ship was wrecked. The last ship continued west, loaded with cloves and nutmeg from the Molucca Islands. In September, 1522, del Cano and 17 survivors finally reached Spain, the first men to sail around the world.

ALSO READ: EXPLORATION; GAMA, VASCO DA; NAVIGATION.

MAGIC You may have been to a party where a clever entertainer called a magician, or conjurer, performs tricks. He holds up his empty top hat, says the magic word—"abracadabra!"—and pulls a rabbit out of the hat. The conjurer calls his trick magic, because few people watching can be certain how he makes the rabbit appear.

In ancient times, when events happened that people could not explain, they called them magic. When the sun suddenly disappeared in the middle of the day, this could only be magic. We now know that this is an eclipse of the sun. Such "magical happenings" were thought to be the work of the gods or spirits, who controlled all things. People called magicians were thought to be able to perform magic to make the gods and spirits do certain things. For example, if many months passed without rain, people asked a magician to perform special rites, or ceremonies, to soothe the angry rain god. If the rain came, people thought the magician had brought it. Modern scientists have been able to explain most of the things that used to be called magic. But primitive tribes in some parts of the world still believe in magic.

The actual methods magicians use to perform their tricks have varied widely at different times and in different regions. But most magicians use special words (charms such as "abracadabra"), songs, sayings, and gestures to cast their spells. They often have a collection of magical objects (such as herbs, eels, and pieces of someone's hair or clothing) that help them cast the spells. Some such objects and techniques are still considered magic by superstitious people. Have you ever heard that having a rabbit's foot is lucky? Have you ever seen people knock on wood when they say something hopeful? These superstitions are left from days when people thought magic warded off evil spirits.

Today, the word "magician" refers to an entertainer who performs tricks that seem to be impossible. He may pull a rabbit out of a hat, saw a woman in half, or read someone's mind. He often uses the charms and gestures of ancient magicians in performing his stunts.

All of his tricks are based on mechanical help or on his own skill at deceiving the audience. A man who seems to have disappeared from a locked box was actually released through a trap door in the floor of the stage. Magicians use *sleight of hand,* or *legerdemain,* to make small objects "disappear." Both of these terms mean quickness of hand. A magician must be able to use his hands skillfully to get rid of the "disappearing" object before anyone notices. He must also be able to distract the audience's attention by talking or by using misleading facial expressions or gestures. A magician

▼*Card tricks are one of the most popular acts performed by magicians. It takes lots of practice and quickness of hand to do such tricks.*

may juggle three balls and suddenly slip one of them up his sleeve while his eyes—and the audience's—follow the movement of the other balls.

The most famous American magician was Harry Houdini. He specialized in escaping from many kinds of locks and chains. He would allow himself to be handcuffed and locked into a heavy metal container (perhaps filled with water), such as a trunk. Houdini could get himself out of the trunk and the handcuffs within a few minutes. At one time, he had himself bound in ropes and locked in a packing case, which was then bound with steel tape. The case was then dropped into the New York City harbor, Houdini reappeared on the surface in 59 seconds.

Mind reading is an easy magic act to perform for a group of people. Arrange 12 different objects, such as playing cards, record album covers, or magazines, in rows on the floor. (When someone picks one of these, you will "read" his mind and tell the group which one he has chosen.) Choose a friend to be your secret assistant. You and your assistant should decide on a secret code or signal to let you know which objects have been chosen. (The signal may be that your assistant will touch his left ear or clench his fist when someone points to the chosen object. Think of a signal that the others won't notice.) Then turn your back and close your eyes while a member of the group points to one of the objects. When you turn around, someone in the group will point to one object after another. Your assistant, using the code, will let you know which was chosen. Amaze people with your "mind-reading" ability.

ALSO READ: FORTUNE-TELLING; HOUDINI, HARRY; WITCHCRAFT.

MAGNA CARTA The contract, or agreement, known as Magna Carta ("The Great Charter") was one of the most important docu-

▲*The people of the Solomon Islands in Melanesia believe this good luck charm (amulet) has magical qualities. They think its owner will be protected against harm.*

▲*King John and the barons at Runnymede, near London, where Magna Carta was signed on June 15, 1215.*

ments of all time. Magna Carta was an agreement between the noblemen, or barons, of England and the English king, John. It was signed in 1215. The charter gave less power to the English kings and gave the English barons certain rights and privileges. This was the first time in English history that such an agreement had been set down in writing.

Most of the later laws that helped England become a democracy were based on Magna Carta. In a democracy, the people or their elected representatives take part in the government of the country. In a democratic system, no ruler can gain absolute power. For example, Magna Carta stated that a council of barons and churchmen should be set up. The king would have to get permission from this council before raising taxes or making any important decisions. This council became the basis of the present English Parliament, which is similar to the U.S. Congress. Magna Carta also stated that a man can be convicted of a crime only if a group of his equals judges him guilty. This became the jury system.

There were no written laws in England before Magna Carta. Instead, people were supposed to follow certain customs. For example, each nobleman owed the king a certain amount of tax money. This king was not supposed to ask for a penny more. Such customs were part of a complicated organization of society known as the feudal system. When John became king of England in 1199, he needed extra tax money to fight a war with France. The barons did not want to pay higher taxes, but King John forced them to pay. The barons finally revolted. They wrote Magna Carta and had King John meet with them at a place called Runnymede. There, on June 15, 1215, the barons forced John to sign Magna Carta.

Magna Carta did not help all the English people. Only the noble-

men were considered important in those days. But in later years, the agreements of the charter were applied to everyone.

ALSO READ: DEMOCRACY; ENGLISH HISTORY; FEUDALISM; GOVERNMENT; JOHN, KING OF ENGLAND; LAW; MIDDLE AGES; PARLIAMENT.

MAGNET You have probably seen toy magnets, but magnets are more than toys. Large magnets are used to lift heavy pieces of iron and steel. Magnets are used in compasses. When you talk on the telephone, your voice travels through wires as electric signals. A magnet on the receiving end picks up these signals and makes them sound like your voice.

More than 2,000 years ago, the ancient Greeks discovered *lodestones*, or *magnetite*, pieces of iron ore that are natural magnets. Lodestone can still be found today, but it is easier to make your own magnet.

You can make a magnet from another magnet with a large blunt needle (such as a tapestry needle) and a bar magnet—like the one shown in the drawing. Slowly rub the needle with the magnet from the middle down to the point 25 or 30 times. You can rub with either end of the magnet, but do not change ends, and only rub in one direction. Try to pick up a pin with the needle. If the needle-magnet does not work, rub it again with the magnet, and test it.

What is magnetism? No one is really sure, but scientists think that a special arrangement of iron molecules causes this force. Each tiny molecule is a magnet. In nonmagnetic iron, the molecule-magnets pull in all possible directions. In magnetic iron, the molecules are arranged so that they all pull in the same direction. The greater the number of molecules pulling in the same direction, the greater the force of the magnet. When you rubbed the needle with a magnet,

▼*An electromagnet used for lifting and raising. When the current is turned off, the object being lifted drops off.*

the magnetic force pulled the molecules in the needle in one direction—making the needle a magnet. If you drop a magnet or hit it with a hammer, the molecules get shaken and pull in different directions. All you have left is a piece of iron.

There are two types of magnets—*permanent magnets* and *electromagnets*. In permanent magnets, the iron molecules stay set in one direction—unless the magnet receives a hard blow. In an electromagnet, the molecules are turned in one direction when a current of electricity is passed through the iron. An electromagnet loses its magnetism when the current stops.

Permanent magnets are used for picking up small objects, holding refrigerator doors closed, holding objects such as ashtrays or pieces of paper onto metal surfaces, and so on. Electromagnets have become far more important than permanent magnets. Big ones are used in industry. Around the home, you can find electromagnets in doorbells, telephones, radios and TV sets, vacuum cleaners, tape recorders, furnaces, and other things run by electric motors.

ALSO READ: ATOM, COMPASS, EARTH, ELECTRICITY, NORTH POLE.

MAGNIFYING GLASS see LENS.

MAINE Maine lies the farthest north of any state in the East. It makes up the northern half of New England. It has almost as much land as the other five New England states put together.

The Land and Climate
Canada curves around northern and eastern Maine. New Hampshire lies to the west of Maine and the Atlantic Ocean is south of Maine. The southern part of Maine is flat land. Towards the north and west, the land changes. It becomes first hilly and then mountainous. The mountains are part of the White Mountain group, extending west-

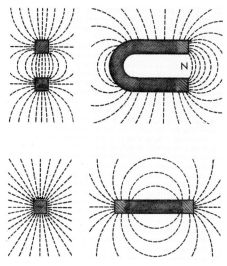

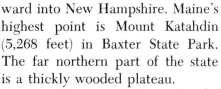

▲*The magnetic field around a horseshoe and a bar magnet as seen from the side and from the bottom* (above). *The magnetism is strongest at a magnet's ends, or poles. Iron filings form along the lines of force of magnets* (right).

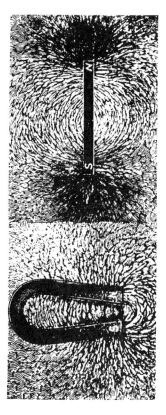

ward into New Hampshire. Maine's highest point is Mount Katahdin (5,268 feet) in Baxter State Park. The far northern part of the state is a thickly wooded plateau.

Maine has an irregular and rocky coastline. Many of the bays make fine harbors. Portland, the largest city in the state, is located on Casco Bay. Islands are sprinkled along the Maine coast. The largest is Mount Desert Island. Its wooded hills and deep blue water make it a beauty spot.

When most people think of Maine and the water, they think of the seacoast. But the state also has many large lakes and rivers. The biggest is Moosehead Lake, about 60 miles northwest of Bangor. Other large lakes are Sebago Lake and those in the Rangeley Lakes chain. The rivers in the state are not used much for transportation. They have too many falls. But the falls are an important source of electric power needed for industry. The most important river is the Penobscot. Other long rivers are the Saco, St. Croix, Kennebec, and St. John.

Winslow Homer, an American artist, painted many pictures of the sea while living in Maine during the late 1800s and early 1900s.

▼*Seashore picnics are a popular pastime on the rocky coast of Maine. This family is enjoying a clambake.*

MAINE

State flower
White pine cone and tassel

State bird
Chickadee

State tree
White pine

Capital
Augusta (21,945 people)

Area
33,215 square miles
(ranks 39th)

Population
993,663 people
(ranks 38th)

Statehood
March 15, 1820
(23rd state admitted)

Principal river
Penobscot River

Highest point
Mount Katahdin (5,268 feet)

Largest city
Portland (65,116 people)

Winters are cold and summers are cool in Maine. Precipitation falls throughout the year. During the winter, greater amounts of snow fall in the western part of the state than in the eastern, seacoast region. The climate makes the state a popular place for sports all year round. Camping and sailing are popular in the summer, and skiing is a favorite winter pastime.

History

No one knows when the first Europeans sighted the coast of Maine. John Cabot explored the shoreline in 1498. He claimed the area for England. In 1524, Europeans arrived on *La Dauphine*, a ship belonging to the French navy. Its commander was the great Italian sea captain, Giovanni da Verrazano. With him was his brother, Girolamo, a skilled map maker. *La Dauphine* sailed north along the coast of North America. In May, it dropped anchor in Casco Bay, off the coast of southern Maine. Here the explorers met the Abnaki Indians. This tribal group spoke an Algonkian language and included the Malecite, Penobscot, and Pennacook tribes. They were hunters and fishermen. Verrazano noted the region's many harbors and its strik-

ing scenery. When he returned to France, he gave a good report of the area.

In 1604, some Frenchmen tried to settle on a small island in the St. Croix River. A hard winter and sickness killed half of the settlers. The rest left. Three years later, a group of Englishmen started a settlement on the banks of the Kennebec River. Their luck was no better than that of the French. Finally in 1622, the English established a permanent settlement in southern Maine at Monhegan. Colonies were soon set up at Saco and York, which have also survived.

By the early 1620s, the name Maine was being used. Some people think that the region was named for a province in western France. But Maine may have received its name in another way. We know that English colonists divided the region into "the islands" and "the main" (mainland). Did main become Maine? It may have.

Maine was made part of the colony of Massachusetts in 1647. It became a battleground during the French and Indian War and during the American Revolution. During the War of 1812, the British took the northern part of Maine. But they gave it back at the end of the

▶*Vacationers find plenty of facilities in Maine to aid their exploration of the state's forests and mountains. Katahdin Stream Campground is located in Baxter State Park.*

fighting. A few years later, Maine was separated from Massachusetts and became a state in 1820.

At Work in Maine

Much of Maine's history is the story of hard work. This northern land of mountains and rocky coast does not give people a living easily.

The first English colonists were fishermen and fur traders. Both fishing and trade turned them toward the ocean. The North Atlantic was dangerous for sailing vessels. It was especially hazardous during a nor'-easter—a fierce storm out of the northeast. In Maine fishermen's family records, the words "lost at sea" appear over and over beside the names of husbands and sons.

Before very long, the Indians, the fur animals, and the fur trade began to disappear. The Maine colonists then found that the beautiful pine forests around them could be cut down for lumber. They shipped some abroad. The colonists also used it to make ships. The tallest trees made strong masts for the sailing ships.

Colonial fishermen and woodcutters were likely to be farmers, too. People raised crops during the summer. The rest of the year they did other work. A change came in the 1800s. The prairies south of the Great Lakes were opened to settlement. The rich soil there drew many New England farmers westward. But not all went. Maine has some of the level, fertile land that farmers like. Most of it is in big Aroostook County.

Since the 1890s, the most valuable crop has been Aroostook potatoes. Maine is second only to Idaho in the number of potatoes grown. Blueberries are the state's most important fruit crop. Today, Maine's livestock products are worth more than all crops put together. Chickens, eggs, and milk are the principal livestock products.

Industries are located in various

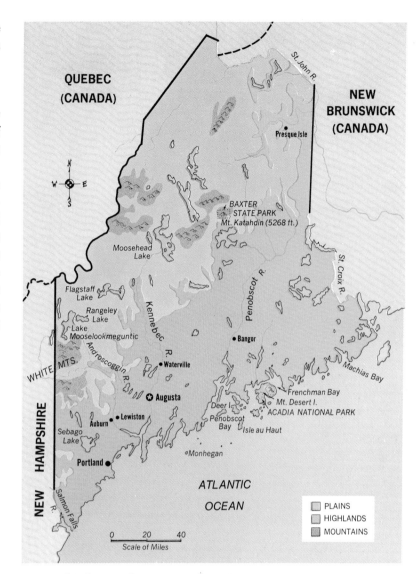

parts of Maine. Cutting timber is still important. This valuable natural resource once used for making lumber is now used for making paper. The state's leading product is paper. Leather goods are second.

Fishing remains an important economic activity. Lobsters, the most important single variety of seafood caught, account for half of the total annual income from fishing. Cod, salmon, bass, flounder, mackerel, and haddock are also caught off the Maine coast.

Recreation and tourism are growing industries in Maine. Many visitors are attracted by the cool climate and beautiful scenery. Many people have built vacation homes there, some on the seacoast, others on lakes or rivers in Maine's pine country. Thousands of city dwellers

A Maine woman, Sarah Orne Jewett, wrote a beautiful book about Maine and the people who lived there in the late 1800s. The book, *The Country of the Pointed Firs,* tells about strong, hardworking, delightful human beings.

from New York, New Jersey, and other mid-Atlantic states go north to enjoy a cool summer in Maine's climate. Hundreds of young people go to summer camps, as well. Tourists visit the state parks, such as Acadia National Park, with their scenic trails and campsites. They also visit the house in Portland where the poet Henry Wadsworth Longfellow once lived. Or they may tour the monument dedicated to John Paul Jones, a Revolutionary War hero.

ALSO READ: DIX, DOROTHEA; FUR TRADER; LONGFELLOW, HENRY WADSWORTH; VERRAZANO, GIOVANNI DA; WAR OF 1812.

MAKE-UP   Many women wear make-up, or cosmetics, on their faces in order to make themselves more attractive. Both actors and actresses use theatrical make-up on their faces and any exposed parts of their bodies in order to change their appearance for the roles they are playing. The usual types of cosmetics ordinarily used by women are also used in stage, screen, and television make-up. But theatrical make-up is more dramatic and much heavier than everyday cosmetics. The shades and amounts of cosmetics used depend largely on the lighting and the effects desired.

Stage make-up stresses highlights

and shadows. In a theater, the audience is seated at a distance and cannot see the actors too closely. The bright stage lights also make any normal coloring or ordinary make-up appear very pale, or washed-out. Dark make-up with heavy lines and shadows is needed simply to make the actors appear "natural."

Make-up used in television and motion pictures is lighter and less exaggerated, since the camera comes quite close to the face. But the bright lights still make the use of make-up necessary. For television, natural bone structure is emphasized. Colors to which the television camera is sensitive, such as green, blue, and violet, are used widely. Make-up is used very sparingly for color motion pictures because the film-developing process tends to exaggerate colors and make them appear unnatural.

Besides the powder, rouge, mascara, lipstick, and other cosmetics in everyday use, theatrical make-up includes wigs, false beards, mustaches, and noses. *Putty* (a kind of wet clay) is used not only to create false noses, but also to change the bone structure of the entire face. Beards and mustaches are stuck on the face with *spirit gum*. Make-up is also used on other parts of the body

to create "wounds" or "scars" or just to cover blemishes.

Many different materials have been used as make-up throughout history. Since the late 1800s, the most popular theatrical make-up has been *grease paint*—a thick greasy solid that is made in the form of a stick. It comes in many colors and is easy to use. One color is usually smoothed over the entire face as a *base*. Then lighter and darker shades are applied to create highlights and shadows. Deep shadows at the inner corners of the eyes make the eyes appear to be closer together and evil. Deep shadows under the eyes and cheekbones make the face appear to be thin, tired, and older. Lines drawn downward at the corners of the eyes and mouth make a sad face.

An actor can look like almost anyone he chooses, with the careful application of make-up. If a young actor is playing the part of an old man, he can make his face appear older by drawing the lines and wrinkles of old age, adding putty to make his skin appear to sag, and wearing a white wig or beard. By using other make-up, an older actor can be made to look younger.

The skillful application of theatrical make-up is a great art. Some performers apply their own make-up, but the "make-up artist" is an extremely important person in any theater, or television or movie studio.

You might like to try applying make-up to see what effects you can create. Ask some adult if she will let you experiment with some old cosmetics she no longer uses. Sit before a mirror in a well-lighted room. Try using light and dark bases to create shadows and hollows. Use an eyebrow pencil to draw lines extending from the corners of your eyes and mouth. Try to follow any natural "lines" or "creases" you already have. You can see creases at the corners of your eyes and mouth when you smile. If you frown, you can see creases across your forehead. What happens when you make upward lines? Or downward lines? Can you make yourself look like a very old man or woman? How about making up like a clown? Be sure to wipe the make-up off carefully when you have finished "creating." Spread cold cream over the make-up and wipe it off with a tissue. Then scrub your face well with soap and water. Be sure to keep the make-up off your clothes.

ALSO READ: ACTORS AND ACTING, COSMETICS, DRAMA, LIGHTING, MASK, THEATER.

MALAGASY Madagascar is the fourth largest island in the world. It is in the Indian Ocean, about 250 miles off the southeast coast of Africa. The island is about 1,000 miles long and 375 miles wide at its broadest point—a little smaller than

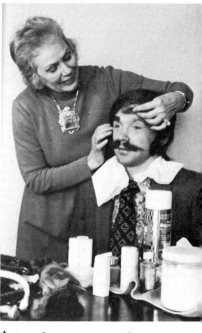

▲ *A make-up artist applying a false eyebrow to a television actor, who is already wearing a big artificial moustache.*

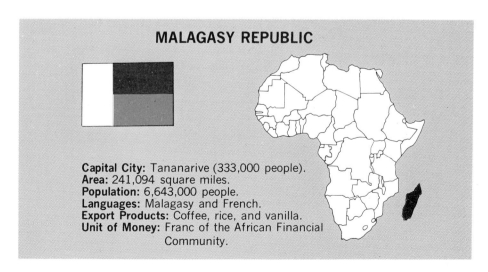

MALAGASY REPUBLIC

Capital City: Tananarive (333,000 people).
Area: 241,094 square miles.
Population: 6,643,000 people.
Languages: Malagasy and French.
Export Products: Coffee, rice, and vanilla.
Unit of Money: Franc of the African Financial Community.

▲*People of Malagasy use long boats to bring their products to market.*

The *valiha* is a musical instrument that is played in the Malagasy Republic. It sounds like a guitar and is played like a harp.

the state of Texas. It and several small neighboring islands make up the Malagasy Republic.

Mount Ankaratra, nearly 9,000 feet high, is one of the many extinct volcanoes on Madagascar. The island is rugged with high plateaus and mountains. Low plains lie between the mountains and the sea. The climate in the highlands is cool and pleasant and in the coastal regions, hot and damp.

In a plateau setting surrounded by hills overlooking the east coast, the capital and largest city, Tananarive, reveals both ancient and modern sides of the country. Modern buildings show the French influence in the city.

Plant and animal life of the Malagasy Republic are different from those found on the African mainland and in other countries. Among the rare animals are the many types of lemur (small, monkey-like animals). Fossil bones of strange prehistoric animals now extinct have been found on Madagascar and have not been found elsewhere.

Although Malagasy lies off the coast of Africa, the country has an Asian appearance because of its people and their customs. The Malagasy people are mostly either of African or Indonesian descent. They speak French and their own language, Malagasy. Farming is the most important occupation in Madagascar. Rice is the basic food crop

and coffee is the chief export crop. More than half of the world's supply of vanilla is grown on the coastal plains of Madagascar. Rich mineral deposits are being mined. Trade with other countries is important, and Malagasy's dependence on passing freight ships to transport food, spices, and minerals has often been a problem.

Several thousand years ago, people crossed the Indian Ocean from the region that is now Indonesia and settled on Madagascar. Later, Arabs and other people from Africa came to the island. Diego Dias discovered Madagascar for Portugal in 1500. Traders from other European countries followed him. In the late 1800s, the French seized the island and set up the colony of Madagascar. In 1958, the colony was given self-rule as the Malagasy Republic, but the French kept some control over the government. In 1960, the country became completely independent of France. The republic is now governed by a president and a parliament consisting of a national assembly and a senate.

ALSO READ: AFRICA, LEMUR.

MALAWI   The Republic of Malawi is a narrow sliver of land that stretches about 500 miles north and south along the western and southern shores of Lake Malawi (Lake Nyasa) in East Africa. The region was formerly known as Nyasaland.

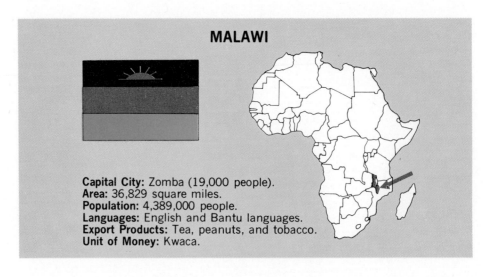

MALAWI

Capital City: Zomba (19,000 people).
Area: 36,829 square miles.
Population: 4,389,000 people.
Languages: English and Bantu languages.
Export Products: Tea, peanuts, and tobacco.
Unit of Money: Kwaca.

(See the map with the article on AFRICA.)

Malawi is about the size of the state of Indiana. It has very beautiful scenery, with high mountains, sparkling lakes, and fertile highlands. Mlanje, the highest mountain in Malawi, towers 9,843 feet in height. The climate in the lowlands along Lake Malawi is hot and damp. But the highland areas are pleasantly cool.

Most of Malawi's people, called Malawians, live in small villages and grow their own food. Tea and tobacco crops are grown for export. Malawi has very few industries, and many of the men work in Zambia, Rhodesia, and South Africa. Some factories are now being built in Malawi to produce cement, bricks, textiles, shoes, and farm tools. In 1970, construction was completed on the country's second railroad, running into the neighboring country of Mozambique. A new capital is being built at Lilongwe to replace the present capital of Zomba. The University of Malawi graduated its first class in 1969.

British explorer David Livingstone was the first European to come to the region of Malawi, in 1859. He found the people almost destroyed by the terrible effects of the slave trade. In 1891, Great Britain took over the territory and set up the Protectorate of Nyasaland. Independence was granted on July 6,

▲Fish merchants on Lake Chilwa in Malawi wait for the fishermen to bring in their catch.

1964. The name was changed from Nyasaland to Malawi, the name of the people who once lived in the region. Malawi is governed by a president and a national assembly elected by the people.

ALSO READ: AFRICA, COMMONWEALTH OF NATIONS.

MALAYSIA Malaysia is a country of Southeast Asia a little larger than New York State. The country is divided into two parts by the South China Sea. The mainland part is West Malaysia, on the Malay Peninsula. Thailand lies north of West Malaysia. The Malacca Straits border Malaysia on the west and the South China Sea and islands of Indonesia are to the south and east. East Malaysia consists of the states of Sarawak and Sabah, which are 400 miles away from the mainland on the island of Borneo. Kuala Lumpur

Mount Kinabalu (13,455 ft.) in the Malaysian state of Sabah is the highest point in Southeast Asia. It is in the Crocker Mountains.

MALAYSIA

CHINA

AUSTRALIA

Capital City: Kuala Lumpur (316,000 people).
Area: 129,374 square miles.
Population: 10,583,000 people.
Languages: Malay, English, Chinese, and Indian dialects.
Export Products: Rubber, tin, and forest products.
Unit of Money: Malay dollar.

▶*Malaysian soldiers in dress uniform in front of the sultan's palace in the state of Kedah.*

▼*The main industry on the island of Ketam in Malaysia is fishing. This fisherman is spreading out shrimp to dry in the sun.*

is the capital of Malaysia. (See the map with the article on ASIA.)

Malaysia is almost entirely mountainous, with narrow plains along the coasts, and a few fertile upland plateaus. Tropical rain forests cover most of the area—a wonderland of rare orchids, evergreens, bamboo, and palms. The climate in all parts of Malaysia is hot and wet, with an average rainfall of 100 inches in most places.

Many fields and hills in Malaysia are lined with rows of leafy rubber trees. Malaysia produces more rubber than any other country in the world. Thousands of people work on the rubber plantations. Others are farmers who raise rice, tea, coconuts, fruits, and other crops. Additional rice must be imported to meet the country's needs. Many Malaysians work in the tin mines. Tin is one of the country's major natural resources.

The people of Malaysia, known as Malaysians, are mostly of Malay, Chinese, and Indian descent. People from Ceylon and Pakistan also live there. The people of Malaysia show their different backgrounds through their languages, dress, religions, and festivals. Traders from the Middle East, India, and Persia visited the area in the 1400s. The first European trading posts were set up in the 1500s. The region was controlled by the British for many

years. In 1963, independence was declared and the new country was established as the Federation of Malaysia. It is now a member of the British Commonwealth of Nations. Malaysia is ruled by a sultan and a prime minister. The parliament, or legislative assembly, is elected by the people.

ALSO READ: BORNEO, COMMONWEALTH OF NATIONS, RUBBER.

MALCOLM X (1925–1965) Malcolm X was born Malcolm Little in Omaha, Nebraska, and grew up in Lansing, Michigan. His father, a Baptist minister, was a follower of Marcus Garvey, a black man who urged American Negroes to return to Africa and establish a black nation. When Malcolm was six years old, his father was killed by unknown men who disagreed with his ideas about a separate black nation. Malcolm spent the next ten years in and out of foster homes and reform schools.

After completing the eighth grade, Malcolm moved to Boston to live with a married sister. His job as a railroad porter enabled him to travel to Harlem in New York City. Malcolm admired the "hip" people he met in Boston and Harlem. Soon he was gambling, stealing, and taking drugs. He was sent to prison for robbery at the age of 20.

Malcolm read many books while in prison. He also heard about the Black Muslims, who followed a religion based on that of Islam and believed in a separate state for black people. Malcolm remembered what his father had told him about Marcus Garvey. When he was paroled from prison, Malcolm became a spokesman for the Black Muslims. He changed his last name to "X" in the style of the Black Muslims.

In 1963, Malcolm X had a disagreement with Elijah Muhammad, the Black Muslim leader. He went on a pilgrimage (holy journey) to the Middle East. There he saw Muslims

Malcolm X began his self-education program at the age of 20 while in prison. By reading and copying an entire dictionary, he greatly improved not only his vocabulary, but also his penmanship.

of all colors and nationalities worshiping together in true brotherhood. Malcolm realized that men could not be judged by the color of their skins. He returned to the United States to tell U.S. Negroes that although black people should be proud of their African heritage, their future was in a united America.

The Black Muslims did not agree with this idea, and black people were soon divided. In 1965, while speaking in Harlem, Malcolm X was shot and killed by an unknown person. Three days before his death, Malcolm X spoke at Columbia University: "It is incorrect to classify the revolt of the Negro as simply a racial conflict of black against white. . . . We are interested in practicing brotherhood with anyone really interested in living according to it."

ALSO READ: ABOLITION, ARABIA, BLACK MUSLIMS, CIVIL RIGHTS MOVEMENT, ISLAM, MUHAMMAD, NEGRO HISTORY, SLAVERY.

MALDIVE ISLANDS An ancient story tells about a prince named Koimala who sailed into a lagoon of the Maldive Islands, where his ship was becalmed. He stayed on to bring the religion of Islam and to rule as the islands' first sultan.

Sultans ruled the Maldives for many years. The islands lie southwest of Ceylon in the Indian Ocean. The Maldives are a group of approx-

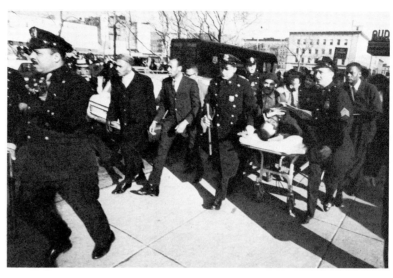

imately 2,000 small coral islands. The total land area is only about 115 square miles. Most of the usable islands are only a few feet above sea level. (See the map with the article on INDIA.)

The climate of the Maldives is damp and hot, with heavy rainfall the year round. The humid weather produces a dense tropical growth of coconut palms, breadfruit, and fig trees on many of the islands. The Maldivians live on about 215 of the islands. Most of them make their living by fishing. Tuna and bonito fish are exported to India and Ceylon. Rice, one of the most important foods, must be imported.

The Maldive Islands were once under British protection. Since 1965, they have been an independent republic, governed by a president and an elected assembly. The

▲ *A police officer clears the way as the body of Malcolm X is taken from the Audubon Ballroom in New York City where he was killed by a gunshot.*

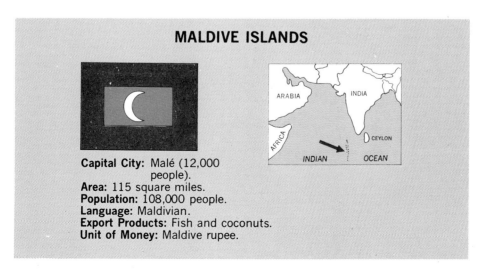

MALDIVE ISLANDS

ARABIA INDIA
AFRICA CEYLON
INDIAN OCEAN

Capital City: Malé (12,000 people).
Area: 115 square miles.
Population: 108,000 people.
Language: Maldivian.
Export Products: Fish and coconuts.
Unit of Money: Maldive rupee.

Maldive Islands are members of the United Nations. The capital island is Malé. It is also the island with the greatest population.

ALSO READ: ASIA, INDIAN OCEAN.

MALI The Republic of Mali is in northwest Africa. It is bigger than the state of Texas and is completely surrounded by land. Mali links the countries of the Sahara Desert with the coastal nations of West Africa. (See the map with the article on AFRICA.)

processing plants. The major exports are cotton, livestock, peanuts, and fish.

The region that is now Mali was once a part of several great West African trading empires. These empires—Ghana, Mali, and Songhai—flourished between the 300s and the 1500s A.D. Timbuktu, one of the cities in Mali along the caravan trade route, became a center of learning for many Arab scholars during the 1500s. The University of Sankore was there. In the 1800s,

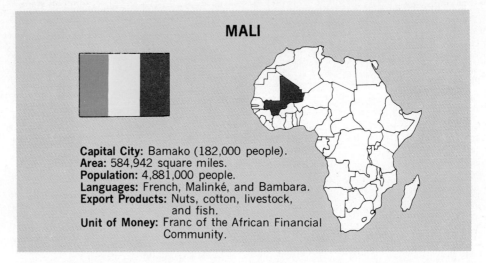

MALI

Capital City: Bamako (182,000 people).
Area: 584,942 square miles.
Population: 4,881,000 people.
Languages: French, Malinké, and Bambara.
Export Products: Nuts, cotton, livestock, and fish.
Unit of Money: Franc of the African Financial Community.

Two major rivers, the Niger and the Senegal, run through southern Mali. The capital city Bamako is on the banks of the Niger. The rainfall in this area is fairly heavy, and farmlands and pastures line the river valleys. In the extreme south of Mali is a flat region of grassy plains. Northern Mali is a hot area on the southern fringes of the Sahara Desert.

The people of Mali are called Malians. Several different groups of people live in this large country. In the fertile river valleys, a people called the Bambara grow crops such as millet, rice, peanuts, and cotton. They also catch fish in the rivers. On the grasslands, the nomadic Fulani herd cattle, goats, and sheep. Another group of nomadic herdsmen, the Tuareg, live in Mali's desert areas. Other people are the Voltaic and the Songhai. Most of the factories in Mali are small food-

the territory was occupied by the French, who set up a colony called the Soudan. The Soudan united with the neighboring country of Senegal in 1959 to form the Federation of Mali. But the federation collapsed the following year. In September, 1960, the Soudan declared itself the independent Republic of Mali. The army threw out the government in 1968 and has ruled the country since then.

ALSO READ: AFRICA.

MALTA The five sunny Maltese Islands, lying in the Mediterranean Sea, form the independent nation of Malta. The nation's capital, Valletta, is located on the largest of the islands, Malta Island. The other islands are Gozo, Comino, and the tiny, uninhabited Cominotto and Fifla. Malta, Gozo, and Comino comprise only 122 square miles—

▼*The railroad station in Bamako, capital of Mali. People can board a train here and travel by rail as far as Dakar in Senegal, about 700 miles to the west.*

about twice the area of Washington, D.C.—but Malta is one of the world's most densely populated countries. An average of 2,700 people live on each square mile of land.

The strategic location of Malta —58 miles from Sicily and 180 miles from Africa—and its many excellent harbors have made it an important place for 35 centuries. (See the map with the article on EUROPE.) Malta became a Phoenician colony around 1000 B.C., but earlier inhabitants of the islands had erected large,

ceived its independence as part of the Commonwealth of Nations in 1964. The nation is ruled by an elected House of Representatives and an elected prime minister. After the elections in 1971, the victorious Labor Party demanded the removal of all British military installations and personnel from the islands—or the payment of a fee in the return for their use. But the income provided by British civil service jobs and the money spent by British military personnel have been the

During World War II, the Maltese Islands were heavily bombarded by Germany. In 1942, King George VI of England awarded the George Cross (a medal) to the entire nation of Malta, to honor the heroism of its people.

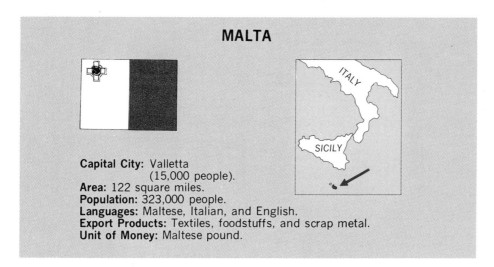

MALTA

Capital City: Valletta
    (15,000 people).
Area: 122 square miles.
Population: 323,000 people.
Languages: Maltese, Italian, and English.
Export Products: Textiles, foodstuffs, and scrap metal.
Unit of Money: Maltese pound.

stone buildings and monuments that are still standing today. Malta was also ruled, at various times, by the Carthaginians, Romans, Arabs, and Normans.

In 1530, Charles V, Holy Roman Emperor, granted the islands to the Catholic Order of St. John of Jerusalem (Knights of Malta). The Knights built the huge stone foundations and walls of the city of Valletta, which Napoleon once called "the greatest stronghold in Europe."

Malta was seized by Napoleon and his army in 1798. Two years later, the Maltese managed to drive out the French, with the aid of the British. Malta became a colony of the British Empire in 1814, and has been a vital British stronghold ever since. But there have been increasing demands by the Maltese people for greater freedom. Malta was granted home rule in 1961, and re-

main source of Malta's wealth, and the controversy remains to be solved.

The next largest source of income in Malta is agriculture. The farms of Malta produce cereals, tomatoes, potatoes, onions, and grapes. Although the Maltese people cultivate every bit of the rocky soil that they can, they must import about 80 per cent of their food. Other important industries are shipbuilding, wine making, and fishing.

In recent years, tourism has become one of Malta's largest industries. Visitors come from all over the world to enjoy the mild, sunny climate and beautiful beaches. Tourists buy Maltese lace and tour the ruins of centuries-old cities and temples.

ALSO READ: COMMONWEALTH OF NATIONS; ENGLISH HISTORY; EUROPE; MEDITERRANEAN SEA; NORTH ATLANTIC TREATY ORGANIZATION; PAUL, SAINT; PHOENICIA.

▼*A narrow street in Valletta, the capital of Malta for over 400 years.*

▲ *A young donkey gets milk from its mother. All female mammals produce milk in the mammary glands to feed their young.*

MAMMAL Mammals are *vertebrates*—they have backbones. They breathe with lungs, they usually have four legs, and they are warm-blooded. Other vertebrates, such as amphibians, birds, and fish, share some of these characteristics. But unlike all other vertebrates, mammals have hair that grows out of their skin at some time in their lives. The female mammals have special glands, called *mammary glands*, that produce milk on which the young feed. True mammals are born alive from the mother's body. They do not hatch from eggs laid outside the mother's body.

The Importance of Skin and Hair
Mammals can live in deep oceans and on blazing deserts, in polar snows and steamy jungles. Mammals can live in all these places because they are *warm-blooded*. Their bodies stay about the same temperature, no matter what the temperature of their surroundings. The body temperature of cold-blooded animals, such as reptiles, changes with the surrounding temperature.

Hair helps keep the mammal's body temperature at an even level. Each hair is controlled by a tiny muscle in the skin. When it turns cold, these muscles raise the hairs so that more air is trapped in the fur for insulation. If the weather turns hot, the muscles stand the fur even

straighter so that air moves around the hairs to cool the body. Human beings and other mammals without much hair have *sweat glands* in the skin. These glands secrete perspiration. Evaporation of perspiration cools the skin and keeps the body temperature in its normal range.

Each hair has at its base a tiny oil, or *sebaceous*, gland. These glands produce a grease-like substance that coats the fur to keep it soft and waterproof. If water soaks through the fur down to the skin, the fur cannot keep the body warm.

From Eggs to Living Young
Mammals and birds developed from egg-laying reptiles. Birds still lay eggs, but most mammals developed another way of producing and feeding their young. When early mammals were evolving, some of the sweat glands in females took on a special job. Instead of producing sweat, these glands, called *mammary glands*, produce a whitish fluid called milk. A female mammal can carry her babies' food supply right in her body. She does not have to leave her babies to find food for them, as birds do. Female mammals can stay with their young and never leave them unprotected.

Along with the milk glands, most mammals evolved a system of caring for the very young *inside* the mother's body. Other animals lay eggs in which the baby develops. When the food supply in the egg is used up, the baby hatches. The spiny anteater and the duck-billed platypus show an early stage in mammal evolution—they still lay eggs. When the eggs hatch, the young feed on milk that oozes from the mother's abdomen. The babies lap it from her hair.

The pouched animals, called *marsupials*, are a type of mammal that developed in the region of Australia. Marsupial eggs grow inside the mother's body. When food in the egg runs out, the young are born. At that stage, they are only tiny masses of living cells. They squirm into the mother's pouch and start feeding on milk from the mother until they have grown enough to live outside.

The true mammals are *placental mammals*. Mammal babies develop inside the mother's body attached to a special organ, called a *placenta*. From the placenta, the growing babies, called *embryos*, receive nourishment from the mother's bloodstream through the *umbilical cord* (the remains of which shows on people as the navel). This food supply does not get used up as the food in an egg does, so the baby stays inside the mother until it is ready to live in the outside world. Being protected inside the mother's body allows a mammal's brain to grow bigger in proportion to its body than that of other animals.

The time it takes for a mammal to grow enough to be born is called the *gestation period*. The smaller mammals have shorter gestation periods, the babies grow into adults very quickly, and they live very short lives. The bigger mammals have

▲ *Several of these tiny baby mice could fit into a teaspoon. They are blind and hairless at birth and need their mother's care to survive and grow.*

longer gestation periods, the babies take longer to grow into adults, and they live a long time.

Babyhood is very important to mammals. During this time, they must learn to hunt and defend themselves. While they are learning, young mammals are under the protection of their parents. For this reason, more mammal babies survive infancy and childhood than any other animal young. Reptiles, amphibians, and fish lay thousands of eggs at one time, but the adults do not stay to take care of the eggs and babies. Many of the eggs are destroyed or the babies killed. Mammals do not give birth to large numbers of young because it would be impossible to feed and protect thousands of babies at one time. Such a great number of babies could not fit inside the mother's body during the gestation period. Once they were born, the mother would not be able to produce enough milk to feed them all. Mammals give birth to fewer babies and each one is well protected and cared for during infancy and childhood. After childhood, the mammal young become adults, ready to breed and teach the skills of hunting and defense to the next generation.

Energy for Living
The heat inside the bodies of warm-blooded animals comes from

▼ *A baby wallaby hitches a ride in its mother's pouch. Pouched mammals take good care of their young. A wallaby may carry its baby in its pouch for six months.*

▲A brown bat. Bats are the only true flying mammals.

▶Hedgehogs are cousins of moles. They eat insects.

▲Wombats, like kangaroos, carry their young in a pouch.

▼Squirrels are rodents, which have teeth for gnawing.

▲Raccoons are carnivores, with sharp teeth for tearing meat.

▶The spiny anteater is one of the few mammals that lay eggs.

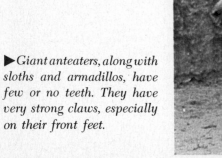

▲Most mammals have hair, but the pangolin has scales on its upper body instead. It has no teeth. Its tongue is almost a foot long.

▶Giant anteaters, along with sloths and armadillos, have few or no teeth. They have very strong claws, especially on their front feet.

major mammal groups

▼*Monkeys, like man, are primates who can walk upright and can grasp things well.*

▲*Rabbits and hares are rodent-like mammals with well-developed hind legs that are used for jumping.*

▲*The elephant's upper lip and nose developed into its trunk. The two tusks are actually teeth.*

▼*Seals have flippers instead of legs. They spend much of their time in water.*

▶*Zebras belong to the group of hoofed mammals with an odd number of toes.*

◀*The hyrax looks like a rodent but is related to the elephant. It lives on rocks or in trees and comes out mostly at night.*

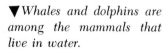

◀*Camels belong to the group of hoofed mammals with even-numbered toes.*

▼*Whales and dolphins are among the mammals that live in water.*

▲ *The Tasmanian devil is a ferocious little pouched animal found only in the Australian state of Tasmania. Its strong jaws can crush the life out of its prey with ease.*

the production of energy from food. Many mammals, such as deer, cattle, and rabbits, are *herbivores*—plant-eaters. There are probably no mammals that eat nothing but meat, but those that eat mostly meat are called *carnivorous*. A mammal's eating habits show in its teeth. Anteaters have no teeth. They catch insects with their tongue and drop them straight into their stomach. Most herbivores have flattish grinding teeth for breaking up tough plant stems and leaves. A carnivorous mammal has long canine teeth, or fangs, with which it can stab and rip its prey. Its big back teeth grind the food. *Omnivores* (mammals that eat both plant and animal matter) have teeth for each purpose. Man's teeth show that he is an omnivore.

Flippers, Hoofs, Wings, and Feet
The legs and feet of mammals have developed in many different ways. The legs of whales and dolphins evolved into flippers and their tails became flattened. This is necessary for a life spent swimming in the water. Walruses and seals are half water-living and half land-living. Their feet are flattened paddles with webbing between the toes.

Mammal ancestors had five toes on each foot. Some mammals lost a few toes during evolution and developed hard coverings called *hoofs*. Hoofs do not sink down into the ground when an animal is running. Running is the hoofed mammals' primary means of defense. Mammals such as flying squirrels have large flaps of skin between the feet and body. The flaps act like a parachute, allowing the animals to glide out of harm's way. These animals do not fly. Bats are the only true flyers among mammals. Their front feet have evolved into long, web-like fingers that support a wing of skin. Mammals such as rodents can hold things by clasping both front feet together. Shrews and moles can dig rapidly into the ground with their

spade-like toes. Bears walk using their whole feet. Cats and dogs are built to move on their toes. The heel bone is located far up on the leg.

Monkeys, apes, and human beings have front feet that evolved into hands. Monkeys use their hands to catch hold of branches. Chimpanzees can grasp and handle small objects with their fingers. Human babies crawl on all fours, but as adults, humans no longer use their front legs for moving around. Humans stand upright. This frees man's hands for making things, using his brain, and exploring and changing the world around him.

For further information on:
Body Functions of Mammals, *see* CIRCULATORY SYSTEM, DIGESTION, GLAND, MUSCLE, NERVOUS SYSTEM, REPRODUCTION, RESPIRATION.
Body Structure of Mammals, *see* ANIMAL TRACKS, BRAIN, CLAWS AND NAILS, FLYING MAMMALS, FUR, HAIR, HANDS AND FEET, HOOFED ANIMALS, HORNS AND ANTLERS, HUMAN BODY, SKIN, TEETH.
Evolution of Mammals, *see* AMPHIBIAN, ANIMAL KINGDOM, ANTHROPOLOGY, ARCHEOLOGY, EVOLUTION, FISH, FOSSIL, MAMMALS OF THE PAST, MAN, PALEONTOLOGY, REPTILE, VERTEBRATE.
How Mammals Live, *see* ANIMAL DEFENSES, ANIMAL HOMES, ANIMAL MOVEMENT, ANIMAL VOICES, DOMESTICATED ANIMALS, INTELLIGENCE, MARINE LIFE, MIGRATION, PETS, PROTECTIVE COLORING, WALKING.
For individual mammals see Index at name.

MAMMALS OF THE PAST
Many strange animals roamed the Earth long before the first ancestors of man appeared. These prehistoric (before written history) animals included fish, insects, and dinosaurs. When dinosaurs ruled the Earth about 180 million years ago, several mammal-like reptiles were already on the scene. Many scientists believe that mammals developed from

a group of mammal-like reptiles. As millions of years passed, the teeth, bones, and feet of these reptiles began to look more and more like those of mammals.

The Earliest Mammals

The *Pantotheria*, a small group of insectivores (insect eaters), were probably the ancestors of present-day mammals.

STORIES TOLD BY FOSSILS. The first "true" mammals to appear were probably no bigger than rats or mice, and ate leaves, fruits, insects, birds, and birds' eggs. When the dinosaurs became extinct about 70 million years ago, the Age of Mammals began. With the decline of the reptiles, the mammals had fewer enemies. The mammals swiftly increased in size, number, and variety of types. The descendants of some are still found today. But other mammals grew to tremendous sizes and simply disappeared from the face of the Earth, leaving no descendants to carry on the species.

What were these strange beasts? No man has ever seen most of them, since they lived long before the first ancestor of man appeared. But scientists have managed to learn a great deal about the appearance of these animals from fossils (animal bones or impressions of bones left in mud that hardened into rock).

How these animals lived and why they died can only be guessed at.

Perhaps the changes in the Earth's climate drove them from their homes to warmer—but barren—places. When the colder climate killed all the trees and plants, forcing the herbivores (plant eaters) away, the carnivores (meat eaters), who preyed on the herbivores, no longer had food either. Perhaps new land bridges between continents brought new enemies.

The Age of Mammals

Scientists divide the Age of Mammals into seven periods of time, or epochs. The Paleocene Epoch began about 70 million years ago. During that time the climate of the Earth was cold. All the mammals of that time appear to have developed in northern Asia and to have migrated to other parts of the world. All were four-footed, having five toes on each foot and walking on the soles of the feet. The Paleocene mammals also had slim heads, with narrow muzzles and small brain cases.

A number of direct ancestors of modern mammals appeared during the Eocene Epoch, which began about 55 million years ago. The Earth was warm and forests were abundant. The continents were still separated by oceans, limiting migration. Among the mammals of that epoch, all of which were small in stature, were four-toed horses no bigger than a collie dog, tiny camels, and tapirs. The first aquatic

▼*The horned Uintatherium* (right) *lived about 50 million years ago. The four-toed horse Orohippus* (left) *is a relative of the modern horse. (Pictures of mammals of the past painted by Charles R. Knight, © Field Museum of Natural History.)*

▲ *The enormous cave bear, the largest of all bears, lived about 800,000 years ago.*

mammals also appeared in Eocene times. The *Zeuglodon,* an ancient whale, was about 70 feet long, but very slender—almost snake-like. The main exception to all the tiny land mammals was the *Uintatherium,* which lived in what is now the Uinta Mountains in Utah. The Uintatherium was a grotesque rhinoceros, having six horn-like knobs sticking out from its skull, and two tusks on its lower jaw. About the size of an African elephant, it ate plants.

GIANT BEASTS OF LONG AGO. The Oligocene Epoch began about 35 million years ago. The Earth's climate had begun to change, but was still rather warm. The first true carnivores, resembling dogs and cats, evolved at this time. Other animals of the period include the ancestors of modern beavers, camels, mice, rabbits, and squirrels.

The Beast of Baluchistan *(Baluchitherium),* a giant hornless rhinoceros, lived in Central Asia about 25 million years ago. The Beast was the largest mammal ever to walk the Earth. It was about 34 feet long from nose to tail and stood 18 feet high at the shoulder. When the Beast stretched out its neck to reach the twigs and leaves that were its diet, its nose was 25 feet above the ground. The formation of the Himalaya Mountains cut off the moisture-filled warm winds from the South. The Beast could not find food or travel far. It became extinct.

The Miocene Epoch began about 25 million years ago. The first grasses appeared, promoting the further growth and development of grazing animals, such as horses, camels, and rhinoceroses. Various carnivores, including cats and wolf-like dogs, ranged much of the world. A gorilla-like ape was common in Europe and Asia.

The *mastodon,* an elephant-like mammal, having tusks on both the upper and lower jaws, ranged in the forests. Mastodons were covered with shaggy hair. *Mastodon ameri-*

canus, about the size of an Indian elephant, was common in America.

Modern-Day Mammals

The Pliocene Epoch, beginning about 14 million years ago, is regarded by many scientists as the high point in the Age of Mammals. Primitive mammals began evolving rapidly into modern species. Herds of grazing animals roamed over all the continents, which were connected by land bridges. Hoofed horses and *glyptodonts,* or giant armadillos, were numerous.

The Pleistocene Epoch began about 3½ million years ago. It was a period of dramatic changes on the Earth. There was an abundance of large mammals, most of which were very modern in type. The *mammoth,* an extinct species of elephant, lived in cold climates, moving northward as the glaciers of the Ice Age receded. Mammoths existed in North America, Europe, and Asia. All mammoths had a shaggy covering of long, thick hair, a large hump on the back, and long, curving tusks that reached a length of 10½ feet. Mammoths were probably hunted for food by early man, who captured them in deep pits. If not killed by hunters, many mammoths probably starved to death or drowned.

The *giant ground sloth (Megatherium)* was an ancestor of the modern tree sloth. It lived in warm climates, from the southern part of North America to the jungles of South America. The giant ground sloth was a huge, slow-moving plant eater, with great claws and a thick, heavy tail. Although it walked in a stooping shuffle, it would have been about 15 feet tall if standing upright. When there were no meat eaters in the South American jungles, the sloth lived in peace. But when the land bridge of Central America developed, enabling tigers, bears, and dogs to migrate to South America, the sloth did not know how to defend itself.

The perfectly preserved skeleton of a mastodon was found on the Brewster farm in Orange County, New York, in 1845. It is now at the American Museum of National History in New York.

The *saber-toothed tiger* (which belonged to the cat family, but was not really a tiger), lived during the Pleistocene Epoch in Europe and North America. It resembled a tiger in its general appearance, but it had a shorter tail and heavier, shorter legs and feet. The most striking feature of this extinct mammal was the development of the upper canine teeth. They reached to about seven inches below the jaw and were shaped like sabers, which could easily slash the skins of the larger mastodons and mammoths. Some scientists believe that the animal

mammals that lived more than a million years ago survived the combination of climate changes and the presence of man. Most of the huge beasts that remained became extinct about 10,000 years ago, at the beginning of the Recent Epoch.

But the dying out of a species is not uncommon to modern times either. The *aurochs*, a long-horned wild ox, roamed the forests of Europe about 400 years ago. The hunting of this ancestor of modern-day cattle provided great sport for Europeans. In the sixteenth century, some scientists realized that the aurochs

became extinct because the over-development of these saber-like teeth became an obstacle in getting food. The animal may not have been able to open its mouth wide enough to use the teeth for biting, and the space between the teeth and the lower jaw would only allow small bits of meat to enter the mouth.

THE AGE OF MAN. Many animals appeared, developed, and died out long before man appeared on Earth. But some extinct mammals were very well known to primitive man, and their extinction can be chiefly attributed to him. Man has hunted and killed animals for food and clothing for many centuries. Man used animal bones for weapons and tools. As man began to kill animals, the rates of reproduction in animals could not make up for the losses in their numbers. Few of the big

was in danger of becoming extinct, and they put the remaining aurochs on a game preserve in Poland. But the game preserve was often raided by hunters. The last aurochs on Earth died in 1627.

The process of extinction has been greatly speeded up since man appeared on Earth. More than 100 major species of mammals have died out since the time of Christ. Scientists estimate that an average of one animal species has died out each year since 1900. You will never see a saber-toothed tiger or a woolly mammoth. Your children may never see a grizzly bear, a graceful Arabian oryx, or many other animals that enrich men's lives today.

ALSO READ: ANIMAL, ANTHROPOLOGY, ARCHEOLOGY, DINOSAUR, EARTH HISTORY, EVOLUTION, FOSSIL, HORSE, MAMMAL, MAN, PALEONTOLOGY.

▲*Mammoths lived close to the edge of the ice sheet about 25,000 years ago. Can you see the resemblance between mammoths and elephants?*

▶*Doctor Louis S.B. Leakey, a noted anthropologist, holding a very old human skull. The study of the bones of early man helps anthropologists discover fascinating things about the way early man lived and how he evolved.*

▼*Man's first tools were stones. He learned the advantage of chipping away at the sides of the stones to make them sharp.*

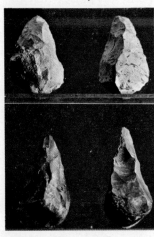

MAN Where did human beings come from? How did man get to be the way he is? Man is probably well over a million years old. Men and women who lived in prehistoric times wrote no history books, but they did leave a record of themselves and their way of life. There are special scientists who study this record of prehistoric man. *Physical anthropologists* study fossil bones and teeth to discover what prehistoric people looked like and how they moved about. *Archeologists* study fossil man to learn what prehistoric men made and did.

The Earliest Beginnings
In the 1930s, an archeologist digging in the hills of India found a jaw bone belonging to a very ancient kind of ape. The bone was 14 million years old, and was shaped like a man's jaw bone! All the teeth in this jaw bone were about the same size. Apes and monkeys have sharp eyeteeth (called *canines* or fangs) for ripping food apart and for defending themselves by biting. Their canines are always larger and longer than the other teeth. Human beings have canine teeth, too, about the same size as the other teeth. Scientists decided that this ancient jaw and teeth that looked so much like a man's must belong to some new kind of ape. The ape was named *Ramapithecus*. Ramapithecus died out about 12 million years ago.

No leg, hip, or spine bones of Ramapithecus have been found. Such bones would show if Ramapithecus could stand up like a man, or only try to, like an ape. Monkeys and apes can move around on their hind legs, but only for short distances and for short lengths of time. Monkeys and apes are not built for living on two feet. They stand in a crouch, walk on the sides of their feet, and they cannot stretch out their legs all the way. Man is the only mammal whose body is built for standing and walking around on two feet all the time.

The Ape that Walked
Archeologists and anthropologists working in Africa about the middle of this century discovered some very ancient bones—about one to three million years old. They seemed to be the bones of a small ape, but this ape was different. This ape's body was built to walk upright on two feet. Also, this ape's teeth were not very different from human teeth. This new type of ape was called *Australopithecus*.

Australopithecus no longer lived in trees like the monkeys, but lived on the ground. The change took a very long time. Millions of years ago, Europe, Asia, and Africa were mostly hot, tropical forests and jungles. In some places, apes could find more food on the ground than in the trees. If the food remained plentiful year after year, the apes best able to stay on the ground would spend more and more time there.

This is probably how Australopithecus changed from a tree-ape to a ground-ape and began to stand upright. Apes have good eyesight for moving from branch to branch, and they use their hands for grasping and picking food from the trees. The apes that searched for food on the ground began to use their hands in new and different ways. With their hands, they began to use tools to help them find food—a stick to dig for insects or a stone to kill a small animal. As the ground apes became able to stand upright and use tools as weapons, they were able to move farther away from the safety of the trees because they could use the weapons to defend themselves.

As Australopithecus practiced using his hands to make and use tools, he gradually became more intelligent. Scientists know this because the size of his brain got larger. To make the tools, Australopithecus had to think about how to do it. This meant he had to experiment with his hands. To use his hands, he had to stand upright so his hands would be free. Since his hands were free, he was able to experiment with more tools. Hands, tools, brains, and standing all worked together.

Archeologists in Africa have discovered very crude tools which Australopithecus made by chipping stones a little bit to make them sharper. As Australopithecus got more intelligent, he also grew larger and more powerful. Finally he became so like a man, that he could properly be called a human type, rather than an ape.

The First True Man

Homo erectus (standing man) lived from 300,000 to 800,000 years ago. His body looked much like modern man's, but his face was made up of very heavy bones. He had no chin. His forehead was quite small and sloped directly back from his eyebrows, which were thick and heavy. His brain was larger than Australopithecus's. Homo erectus used to be called *Pithecanthropus*.

Homo erectus could walk better than Australopithecus. Australopithecus's leg and hip bones show that he could run well, but he walked with his feet turned way out, in a kind of waddle, swaying from side to side. The leg and hip bones of Homo erectus show he was an excellent walker. His leg and hip bones are the same as modern man's.

Homo erectus must have traveled a lot by walking. His skeletal remains have been found in Europe, Asia, and Africa. Homo erectus was a better tool maker than Australopithecus. He made big axes by chipping away a lot of stone to form a sharp edge. He could hunt very large animals with such weapons. Small groups of Homo erectus men also killed herds of wild animals by driving them over steep cliffs or into swamps.

Archeologists have found bits of burned wood and bones in the caves where Homo erectus sometimes lived. These show that Homo erectus knew how to use fire. No one knows how or when he first began to use fire. Perhaps he saw the fires caused by lightning, and started to save burning twigs and branches. His fires probably went out many times before he learned how to keep them going and how to carry them from place to place. Homo erectus used fire for cooking. Man's stomach, like the stomachs of apes, is made to digest vegetables. Cooking helps soften and break down meat so man can more easily digest it.

Scientists have decided that Homo erectus must have had some form of language. Speech was necessary for teaching children how to make more complicated tools and how to make fire. Speech was also needed for planning the large animal hunts. Homo erectus's brain was large enough to do most of what modern man can do. But a brain develops only as it needs to be used. Homo erectus did not have to understand all the things that modern man must think about. His life was very simple. But he *could* think—even though his thoughts may not have been very complicated.

The Beginning of Religion

The first prehistoric skull ever found that was known to belong to a human being was that of *Neanderthal man*, who lived 35,000 to 110,000

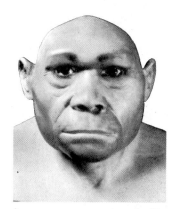

▲ *Homo erectus probably looked something like this. Notice how his small forehead slopes sharply back from his eyebrows.*

▼*Some skulls of Neanderthal man with a fuller forehead than Homo erectus have been found.*

▲ *Later man learned to make arrowheads of chipped stone to provide himself with a more effective and deadly weapon.*

years ago. Neanderthal man was a skillful hunter and ate a great variety of animals—from mice to mammoths (huge, woolly elephants, now extinct). Neanderthal man used fire most of the time and even dug shallow hearths in his caves. Not all Neanderthalers lived in caves. Some preferred tents made of animal skins and branches.

Neanderthal man's face was similar to that of Homo erectus. He had no chin, but in some areas of the world, Neanderthal skulls with more prominent foreheads have been found. The Neanderthalers had a heavy, overhanging brow that connected in a ridge over the nose. Neanderthalers were short (about five feet tall), but they were strongly built and powerful. The Neanderthal leg bones are curved, which shows that these people were somewhat bowlegged.

Neanderthal man made tools of all kinds—axes, knives, choppers, scrapers, saws, chisels, planes, and tools for punching holes. This shows that man's ideas and thoughts had become more complicated.

Neanderthal men and women were the first to start using decorations. They made designs on bones and on stone tools. They polished stones for jewelry, and scientists think they may have worn flowers.

The Neanderthalers were the first human beings to bury their dead in graves. Homo erectus and all the earlier forms of man had just left dead people to lie where they had

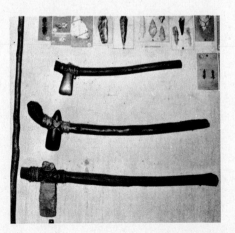

▶ *Man learned that he could wield more effective blows by making hatchets of stone with wooden handles.*

died. Neanderthal man started thinking about death. He began to realize that life ends, and he wondered about what would happen to him after he died. When a Neanderthaler died, the others would arrange his body carefully in a grave. They would put a few tools and some food in with the body. The Neanderthalers probably thought that the dead person would need tools and food to help him in his new kind of life. This is the first sign of man having a religion.

Cro-Magnon—Hunter and Artist

By 35,000 to 10,000 B.C., human beings looked exactly like modern man. They are given the name *Homo sapiens* (wise man). The *Cro-Magnon* people of that time were extremely skilled hunters, and they made thousands of different kinds of tools. They invented the needle with an eye, and began to sew clothes from animal skins.

The most remarkable skill that Cro-Magnon man developed was that of painting. Deep in the caves of France and Spain, archeologists have discovered enormous paintings of animals on the walls. The artwork is beautiful and very true to life.

Scientists think these paintings were used as a kind of magic. Before the men went out to hunt, they would draw a picture of the animal they wanted to catch on the wall of the cave. Having a picture of the animal was almost the same as having the real animal. The picture was a way of helping to catch it, because the animal's spirit was supposed to be trapped in the picture. The Cro-Magnon people also made tiny statues of women which they put in their living places. These were probably goddesses of some kind.

Cro-Magnon people lived in caves or in small huts made of skins and branches. When the weather became cold and windy, they lived in shallow pits in the ground which they also covered with skins and

branches. The Cro-Magnon people had learned how to store food for short periods of time. This was especially important in the winter, when animals were scarce and not much hunting could be done. When good weather came, they picked up their belongings and traveled in search of animals for food.

Modern Man—The Producer and Controller

The greatest change in man's way of life came at about 9000 B.C. Man learned to domesticate plants and animals. He learned how to plant seeds to make crops grow, and he learned how to tame and keep animals to use for food. By planting crops, men did not have to go in search of plants to eat. By taming animals—such as cattle, sheep, and pigs—men no longer had to roam the forests in search of wild animals for meat. For the first time, people started *producing* their own food instead of *gathering* it.

This made a great change in the way people lived. When man was a food-gatherer, he had to live in very small groups and always be ready to move to find more animals to eat. He could not keep very many things, because he had to be able to carry everything with him when he moved. There was no time for man to think of anything much except getting food, protecting himself, and burying the dead.

When man became a food-producer, he lived in one place all the time, because he could not go far from his crops and animals. He could store food and own more things, because he stayed in one place. Since he now produced his own food, he did not always have to worry about hunting for the next meal. He could think about other things.

Modern man settled down and began to form villages. People who lived together in one place had to agree on rules for getting along with each other. This was the beginning of law. People in villages began to trade with each other. Stone tools were replaced by iron and bronze, which could be melted and shaped into all kinds of strong, useful tools. Some villages grew into cities. Nations came into being, with definite areas of land ruled by kings. Writing was developed as a way to keep records of what man was doing and thinking.

People speak of "the races of man" but it is hard to say exactly what a race is. An anthropologist or

▲Iron was used by the very early civilizations. Tools and weapons made of iron were stronger and more useful than those made of stone. An early method of making iron was to heat the ore over a charcoal fire.

◀A prehistoric Indian burial pit near Salina, Kansas, contains more than 140 skeletal remains of men who were at least six feet in height.

a biologist *might* say that a group of people united by heredity and slightly different from other people is a race. To some extent, races differ from each other in how often certain genes occur—genes that control color of eyes and skin and texture of hair, for example. A race is a genetic strain—even a subspecies of man. Races are different from each other in a few ways, but they are alike in thousands of ways. Actually, all men are one species. The few differences among racial groups, such as skin color, can cause violent emotions, but a man's skin is no more important than the shape of

►*When early man came out of his cave homes, he built crude homes in towns. The ruins of such a town in Afghanistan are shown here.*

his toes. An ethnic group is a number of people who share the same background of religion, race, and culture, or some of these characteristics.

Man's life on earth is the history of an amazing creature who is still trying to find new ways to live in and control the world around him.
For further information on:
Man's Body, *see* BRAIN, EYE, FOOD, HANDS AND FEET, SKELETON, SPEECH, TEETH.
Man's Civilization, *see* AGRICULTURE, ANCIENT CIVILIZATIONS, ART HISTORY, BURIAL CUSTOMS, CITY, CIVILIZATION, CULTURE, LAW, RELIGION, SCIENCE, WRITTEN LANGUAGE.
Man's Environment, *see* CAVE DWELLER, CLIFF DWELLER, ICE AGE, LAKE DWELLER, MAMMALS OF THE PAST, STONE AGE.
Man's Evolution, *see* ANTHROPOLOGY, APE, ARCHEOLOGY, EVOLUTION, FOSSIL, MONKEY.
Man's Mind, *see* BRAIN, INTELLIGENCE, LEARNING.

MANATEE AND DUGONG

Manatees and dugongs are mammals that live in the sea all their lives, just like whales and dolphins. They have flippers for arms, and broad, flat tails like walruses and seals. Manatees and dugongs are shy animals. They spend most of their time feeding on seaweed.

Manatees and dugongs must breathe air to live. For this reason they live in shallow water close to the shore. They have special muscles that make it possible for them to close their noses. This allows these animals to hold their breath and stay under water for about fifteen minutes while they eat. Then they swim to the surface of the water, take another deep breath, and return underwater to eat again.

The mermaids of legend and story were probably manatees and dugongs that sailors saw at a distance. The mermaids were sometimes called "sirens." This is why the scientific order of the manatees and dugongs is called *Sirenia.*

Manatees

Manatees are sometimes called "sea cows." They live in the warm waters of the Atlantic Ocean off the North and South American and African coasts. A full-grown manatee is usually between 10 and 13 feet long. It eats 100 pounds of plants a day.

The mother manatee gives birth to her baby under water, but pushes it to the surface immediately so that it can take its first breath of air. The parents are very affectionate. They carry the baby with one of their flippers. The baby manatee is breast-fed just like a human baby, while its mother holds it with her flippers. Perhaps this is why sailors once believed that the manatees they saw were mermaids.

Dugong

The dugong is almost as large as the manatee. A full-grown dugong is usually between seven and ten feet long. The dugong lives in the warm waters of the Indian Ocean, the Red Sea, and the coastal waters north of Australia. Male dugongs have tusks sticking out of their upper jaws. They use their tusks to dig seaweed from the bottom of the sea. The tusks never wear out, however. They keep growing from the dugong's jaw as fast as the points wear away.

ALSO READ: ANIMAL, DOLPHINS AND PORPOISES, MAMMAL, MERMAID, WALRUS.

MANET, EDOUARD (1832–1883)

It is hard to believe that the charming painting by Edouard Manet shown here, *Gare Saint-Lazare* (The St. Lazare Railroad Station), was hated and rejected by art critics at the time it was painted. Today it is one of the most beloved paintings in the National Gallery of Art in Washington, D.C.

Manet was born into a well-to-do family in Paris, France. He wanted to be a painter, but his father wanted him to be a lawyer. Rather than do that, he went to sea. At last he was allowed to study painting—in Holland, Germany, and Italy. He spent much time copying the work of three old masters—Frans Hals, Francisco Goya, and Diego Velazquez. He adopted Hals's way of painting with free, vigorous brush strokes. Manet liked to paint everyday experiences—old beggars, poor children from the streets, bullfights, and horse races. His style of painting was not in fashion. His works were turned down at the big annual *Salon*, an exhibition of paintings in Paris. Manet became the hero of a younger group of painters called the Impressionists,

who liked to paint outdoors in changing light.

Gare Saint-Lazare is simply a moment observed in life. The picture suggests a mother-daughter theme. The mother looks up, as if the artist had interrupted her reading. At the same time the little girl turns to look at a cloud of steam rising in the railroad station.

Manet has painted what the eye would see at a glance—almost what one would catch in an unposed photograph. Notice the bright colors that give the feeling of outdoor lighting, and the bright tones of the woman's face and the girl's arm and neck. Contrasts of light and dark make the painting sparkle. One contrast can be seen in the dark railing against the white smoke. Can you pick out others?

Perhaps you can understand why this painting offended art critics of the day who were used to paintings posed in studios. The girl's back is turned. She's not posing at all. The puppy is sleeping, paying no heed to the painter. It was unusual for an artist in 1873 to paint a picture like this in a railway station! Since then, styles have changed.

ALSO READ: ART HISTORY; HALS, FRANS; IMPRESSIONISM; PAINTING.

▲*A manatee is a mammal that lives in the sea.*

▼Gare Saint-Lazare, *by Edouard Manet. National Gallery of Art, Washington, D.C., Gift of Horace Havemeyer in memory of his mother Louisine W. Havemeyer.*

▲*The keen fisherman has no problem catching something in Manitoba's many lakes and rivers.*

MANITOBA   The province of Manitoba is in the center of Canada. It links the prairie lands of western Canada with the industrial cities of the east. The province of Ontario is east of Manitoba and Hudson Bay is northeast. Saskatchewan borders the west, the states of North Dakota and Minnesota border Manitoba on the south. Manitoba is a region of vast wheatlands, lakes, and forests. The capital city of Winnipeg is one of the largest cities in Canada.

Manitoba is often thought of as flat, prairie country with endless miles of grain fields. Actually, only a small area in the southern part of the province is prairie. The central area lies within the Canadian Shield, a region of rocky hills and forests. The land is studded with hundreds of lakes and rivers, which cover more than 39,000 square miles of the province. Lake Winnipeg is nearly 250 miles long. In the north, the land flattens to the coast of Hudson Bay.

The climate of Manitoba is a typical continental climate—hot in summer (up to 90 degrees) and very cold in winter (sometimes 40 degrees below zero). The land is covered by deep snow in the winter. But the rainfall in summer is light, just enough for grain crops.

History

American Indians of the Assiniboin, Cree, and Ojibwa tribes settled in Manitoba many centuries ago. The origin of the name "Manitoba" is uncertain. It probably comes from the Assiniboin Indian word "Manitobau," which means "the straits of the great god Manitu." But it may also come from Sioux Indian words meaning "prairie waters."

The first European to visit the area was the English explorer, Thomas Button, who explored the western coast of Hudson Bay in 1612. An English trading organization, the Hudson's Bay Company, was given money by the English government to set up fur-trading posts in most of northwest Canada. This region was then known as Rupert's Land. The North West Company from Montreal became a bitter rival, and many clashes occurred between the two companies. The fur traders were against the idea of permanent settlements which might destroy their trapping grounds. But in 1812, a group of Scottish pioneers established a farming colony near the future site of Winnipeg.

When Canada became an independent country in 1867, the Canadian government purchased Rupert's Land from the fur-trading companies. Indians and people of mixed Indian and French-Canadian

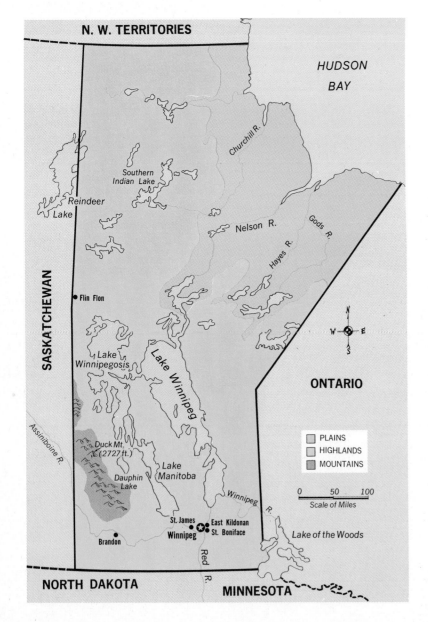

N. W. TERRITORIES

HUDSON BAY

Churchill R.

Southern Indian Lake

Reindeer Lake

Nelson R.

Gods R.

Hayes R.

SASKATCHEWAN

Flin Flon

Lake Winnipegosis

Lake Winnipeg

ONTARIO

Assiniboine R.

Duck Mt. (2727 ft.)

Dauphin Lake

Lake Manitoba

Winnipeg R.

Lake of the Woods

St. James
East Kildonan
Winnipeg
St. Boniface

Brandon

Red R.

PLAINS
HIGHLANDS
MOUNTAINS

0   50   100
Scale of Miles

NORTH DAKOTA   MINNESOTA

parentage (called *métis*) felt that the new settlers were stealing their land. In 1869, they launched a rebellion under the méti leader Louis Riel. The rebellion was suppressed, but in 1870, the métis were given a small region of Rupert's Land. This region became the province of Manitoba. In the 1870s, the first railroads were built across Manitoba and settlement increased. Farmlands were opened up, and by the early 1900s Manitoba had become one of the chief grain-producing regions of Canada.

People

The northern regions of Manitoba are still almost uninhabited, and most people live in the cities, towns, and farms of the south. More than half a million people live in the metropolitan area of Winnipeg, a bustling industrial and transportation center. It has the largest railway yards in Canada. Most of the wheat, oats, and vegetables grown in Manitoba are processed in Winnipeg and then shipped overseas or to other areas of Canada. Winnipeg is also noted as a university city, and a center for the performing arts has recently been opened there.

Most of Manitoba's wealth comes from agriculture. The major crops are wheat, barley, and rye. Cattle, pigs, and sheep are also raised. The fur trade has always been important in this region. And some fur-bearing animals, such as the mink, are now raised on special farms. Fisheries have been set up on several of the lakes. Most of the people work in food processing, the leading industry in the province. Others work in the transportation industry.

The people of Manitoba have come from many different areas of the world, and some have kept alive the traditions of their homelands. A folklore festival is held in Winnipeg every year, and the colorful costumes, songs, and dances are a famous tourist attraction. Tourists also come to Manitoba to camp in the national parks and fish in the trout streams.

ALSO READ: CANADA, FUR TRADER, HUDSON'S BAY COMPANY, OJIBWA INDIANS.

MANN, HORACE (1796–1859) Horace Mann can be called "the father of public education," because of the great educational reforms he started in American public schools.

He was born on May 4, 1796, in Franklin, Massachusetts. He graduated from Brown University and Litchfield Law School. From 1823 to 1837, he served in the Massachusetts state legislature. During this period he helped to establish a state board of education, the first of its kind in the United States.

Soon Mann became active in efforts to improve state schools. Teachers in those days were often untrained, and physical punishment for students was common. Many children attended school only two or three months a year. Mann wanted to improve those conditions.

In 1837, Mann was appointed secretary to the Massachusetts board of education. He brought great changes to the state's public schools by doubling teachers' salaries and raising the minimum time that children must go to school to six months a year. He improved the quality of teaching by starting new training schools for teachers. He believed that religion should be kept out of public schools. He also felt that all children should have a free high school as well as elementary school education. Educators in other states began to adopt his ideas.

In 1848, Mann was elected to the U.S. House of Representatives. In 1852, he became president of Antioch College in Ohio. In his last speech, he made a statement that could sum up his own lifetime, "Be ashamed to die until you have won some victory for humanity."

ALSO READ: EDUCATION.

MANITOBA

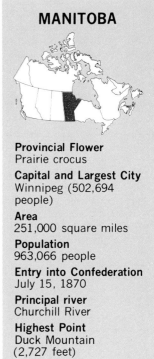

Provincial Flower
Prairie crocus

Capital and Largest City
Winnipeg (502,694 people)

Area
251,000 square miles

Population
963,066 people

Entry into Confederation
July 15, 1870

Principal river
Churchill River

Highest Point
Duck Mountain (2,727 feet)

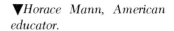

▼*Horace Mann, American educator.*

Airline stewardesses and stewards must have especially good manners in order to make their customers' flights as comfortable and pleasant as possible.

The French word "etiquette" led to the English word "ticket." An etiquette was a note of instructions on behavior given to someone invited to a royal reception.

MANNERS Most people follow certain common-sense rules which help them to get along better with others. These rules are called *etiquette*. When a person is careful about following these rules, we say he has good manners. On some formal occasions, a person must obey most of the rules of etiquette in order to get along well with the people around him. At other times, only a few rules are important.

Years ago, people had rules for almost everything that they did. Oriental countries developed elaborate rules of behavior. Rich people in many countries did very little work, and they spent much of their time deciding which ways of behaving were correct and which were not. They made rules of speech and dress for their servants. Where a person sat at the dinner table was important to them. Today, people are not so formal.

Many of the old rules are not followed at all, but some are still good to remember. No matter where a person is, he should not be rude to other people, and he should not grab things he wants or speak in an unfriendly manner. A polite person usually waits until another person has finished speaking before he begins to talk. He chews food with his mouth closed, says "Please," "Thank you," and "Excuse me." He holds the door open for the person behind him, and uses a knife and fork to eat, not his fingers

Most of the old rules made sense at the time when they were made. For instance, when roads were made of dirt, horses splashed mud and water on the people who were on the sidewalks. A man usually walked on the side nearest the street to protect a lady's fine clothes. Today, most men still walk on the curb side, but this is not nearly so important as treating people politely and kindly in other ways.

Most of the manners followed today make life more comfortable for everyone. If no rules existed, the strongest or the smartest people would always get their way. They would be first in line, grab the most food, and do all the talking. Manners make sure that everyone gets a chance and is treated fairly.

Manners must be learned. Even the person who is now the most polite started life as a crying, kicking baby who screamed when he did not get what he wanted. Slowly, as he grew older, he learned that he must

His classmates listen politely, without interrupting, while a boy speaks to his teacher (right). A police officer escorts a number of well-mannered students across a busy intersection (far right).

take turns and that he did not have to howl to get attention. Small children take time to learn manners, just as they take time to learn to tie their shoelaces. But a child will find it easier to learn good manners if the rest of his family treat each other politely.

Sometimes people find it hard to remember all the things a person supposedly shouldn't do—which fork to use and how to introduce people to each other. But these things are not so important as the simple rule of treating people kindly and courteously—remembering to behave as you would like others to behave toward you. You do not want to listen to others talk with their mouths full. Nor do you like to be left in a room with strangers without being introduced to them. So the well-mannered person does not treat other people this way either.

ALSO READ: INTRODUCTION.

MANUFACTURING Manufacturing means making something. The word comes from two Latin words, *manus* (hand) and *facere* (to make). Before machines were invented, products were made by hand. Today the word "manufacturing" is used in connection with products made by machines. The products made are often called *manufactures*.

For many centuries, people used spinning wheels to make wool and cotton into yarn. The yarn was then woven on looms to make hand-woven cloth. In the early 1700s in England, men and women were paid by merchants to do the spinning and weaving by hand in their own homes.

Between 1733 and 1800, several Englishmen invented machines that could spin yarn and weave cloth. These machines could produce large amounts of yarn and cloth in a short time. At first the machines were operated by water power. Later, they were run by steam engines. The engines and the machines were kept in buildings called *factories*.

Factories were soon built to make other kinds of products. Thousands of people were needed to work in these factories. New stores were opened to sell the products. Other people supplied raw materials, such as wool, cotton, iron, lumber, oil, and paper, to the factories. This use of machines for manufacturing led to the major social and economic changes known as the Industrial Revolution.

Another change in manufacturing began about 1800 in New Haven, Connecticut. Eli Whitney, inventor of the cotton gin, received an order to make thousands of guns, called muskets, for the U.S. government. Up to that time, these guns had been made by hand, one at a time. Whitney wanted to find a way to produce a great quantity of these guns in a short amount of time. First he made a pattern for each part of the musket. The workmen cut out the parts so that each part was exactly like its pattern. Then all the parts were sorted out. All the musket barrels were placed together, all the triggers were placed together, and so on. Each workman was in charge of one part of the gun. The first workman handed his part of the gun to a second man. This second workman attached a part onto the gun and passed it to a third workman, who also attached a part. As the gun passed down the line, the different parts were assembled. At the end of the line, when the last workman had attached a part, the gun was complete.

▲ *Some manufactured products are still made partly by hand. These tennis rackets are being strung by a skilled craftsman.*

▼ *Many products are manufactured on automated machinery. Fewer workers are needed when such machinery is used.*

▲An automobile assembly line. Each worker is assigned a specific job which he must perform before the car passes farther along the assembly line. Thousands of parts are fitted together in the manufacture of an automobile.

This was the beginning of the assembly line. All the parts of the product were *interchangeable*. This means that identical parts were made in exactly the same way. If one part of a gun—such as the barrel—were broken, it could be replaced with another barrel that had exactly the same measurements. In a modern assembly line, a product travels slowly along a conveyor belt. As the product reaches a worker, he adds a piece of equipment, or does a particular task. At the end of the line, the product is complete.

Not only mechanical things are manufactured on assembly lines. Almost all of the packaged food sold in stores is produced on assembly lines. The clothes you wear, the books you read, and the furniture you use are other products manufactured on assembly lines. The use of manufacturing methods that can produce great quantities of a product is called *mass production*.

▲Many products are mass-produced on an assembly line system. Here, cans containing insecticide move slowly along a conveyor belt. Workers remove defective cans and package the remainder.

The lives of people are now being affected by new scientific discoveries. The science of electronics has produced such things as the telephone, radio, television, radar, sonar, and computers. With electronic computers, man can instantly solve complicated mathematical problems that once would have taken him months or even years to solve. Computers are used to guide space ships, forecast the weather, draw maps, and do thousands of other jobs. In manufacturing, computers

are important in *automation*. The word "automation" is a combination of the words "automatic" and "operation." In some factories, machines that were once operated by people are now controlled by computers. The computers can turn the machines on and off at the right time, as well as make sure that each machine is working properly.

An *industry* is a branch of manufacturing. For example, the automotive industry manufactures cars, trucks, and other motor vehicles. There are also the steel industry, the food industry, the clothing industry, and the construction industry, among many others. All of these involve particular kinds or processes of manufacturing.

New manufacturing methods are constantly being developed as new discoveries demand them. Some new ones are nuclear power plants, new and bigger jet aircraft, rocket launchers and space ships, new ways to preserve foods, and new discoveries in the field of medicine. Every day people use some product of modern manufacturing. Manufacturing has encouraged the invention of new products, and manufacturing methods have made more of these products available to a larger number of people.

ALSO READ: AUTOMATION; COMPUTER; ELECTRONICS; ENGINE; INDUSTRIAL REVOLUTION; WATT, JAMES; WHITNEY, ELI.

MAO TSE-TUNG (born 1893) The leader of the People's Republic of China, Mao Tse-tung, sometimes has been called "The Great Dragon." Mao has headed the government of China for more than 20 years, but most Westerners know very little about him.

Mao was born in Hunan province, China. As a student, he read many foreign books that had been translated into Chinese. He worked as a librarian and as a primary school teacher and principal.

MAP   1447

In 1921, Mao helped to start the Chinese Communist party in Shanghai. The Communists joined with the Kuomintang, the Nationalist party, to drive out warlords in northern China. Mao was in charge of organizing the Hunan peasants. Later, Mao felt that the Chinese Nationalist government under Chiang Kai-shek treated the Chinese people badly. The Communists split with the Nationalists in 1927. Mao was elected chairman of the Chinese Communist Party in 1931. In the 1930s, civil war broke out between the two parties. When the Communists were driven from their position south of the Yangtze River, Mao led his small guerrilla army on the historic Long March through the center of China. After a journey of about 6,000 miles, the Communists took up new positions in Yenan in northwest China.

When Japan invaded China in 1937, the Communists joined the Nationalists to fight the Japanese. A civil war among the Chinese broke out after Japan was defeated in 1945. In 1949, the Nationalists were driven from the Chinese mainland to the island of Taiwan (Formosa). Mao became chairman of the new People's Republic of China.

Under Mao's leadership, the Chinese Communists took control of China's land and industries. They established schools where young people studied Communist ideas as part of their school work.

Mao's Great Leap Forward plan in 1958 to improve China's farmlands and industries was not completely successful. The farmers and factory workers had been organized into large collectives, or groups, for working. The plan was changed so that collectives were smaller and farmers could have small plots of land for themselves. Mao stepped down as head of the Republic but continued to be chairman of the Chinese Communist Party. China has become a powerful, united nation.

Selections from Mao's writings have been published in a little red book, *Quotations from Chairman Mao Tse-tung*. Chinese people are given copies of the book to study the ideas of their leader.

In March of 1972, Mao and President Nixon met together in Peking to discuss ways in which relations between China and the United States might be improved.

ALSO READ: CHIANG KAI-SHEK, CHINA, COMMUNISM.

MAP   One day more than 4,000 years ago, a tax collector picked up his "notebook"—a soft clay tablet —and his "pencil"—a pointed stick. This man, who lived in ancient Babylonia, had to write down how much land each person owned, so the government would know how much tax to collect. It would have been a long, hard job to write a description of each piece of land. This man had a better way of keeping his records—he drew a map. This map —which is in an English museum— is the oldest known map. It is not very good, but it was a start. Since then, map-making *(cartography)* has gotten much better.

Going Where You Want to Go
The type of map you probably know best is the "road map." This map is

▲*Mao Tse-tung, a leader of the People's Republic of China.*

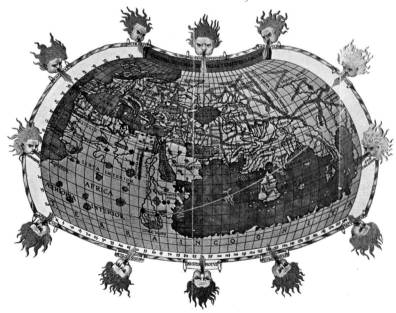

▼*An old map of the known world at the time of Ptolemy II, an Egyptian king who lived in the third century B.C. The blowing heads were meant to show the direction of the winds.*

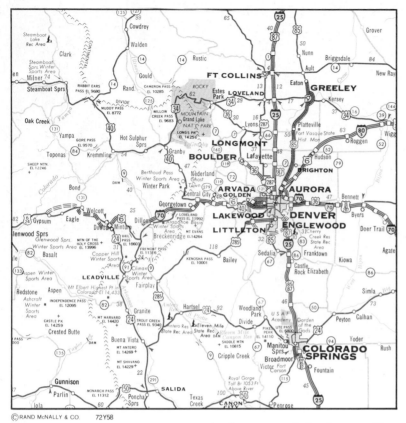

© RAND McNALLY & CO.   72Y58

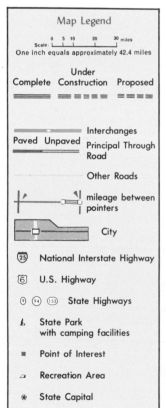

Map Legend

Scale: 0 5 10   20   30 miles

One inch equals approximately 42.4 miles

	Under	
Complete	Construction	Proposed
═══	═ ═ ═	─ ─ ─

Paved Unpaved | Interchanges
Principal Through Road

⎯⎯⎯ Other Roads

⊢⎯⎯⊣ mileage between pointers

▭ City

(25) National Interstate Highway

(6) U.S. Highway

(9) (94) (133) State Highways

⚓ State Park with camping facilities

▪ Point of Interest

⌐ Recreation Area

✳ State Capital

The legend may also show symbols for picnic grounds, airports, and golf courses. Some symbols indicate land forms, such as mountains, highlands, plains, and deserts.

Grids help you locate things on a map. A grid is a pattern of numbered lines that run from side to side and up and down a map. You can tell someone that a town is at the point where a horizontal (side-to-side) line with a certain number crosses a vertical (up and down) line with another number. He can then locate the town by tracing the lines on the map to the point at which they cross. The largest grid of all covers a world map. Its vertical lines are called *meridians of longitude*, and its horizontal lines are called *parallels of latitude*. Navigators on ships and airplanes use this grid for locating their positions.

The legend also tells you one other useful piece of information, the *scale* of the map. Maps reduce the size of the area they show. The scale tells you how much each area is reduced on the map. The scale of a map depends on how large an area is shown and on how large the map itself is. For example, think of four

▼*Maps are useful in many ways. This man is using a map to pinpoint a forest fire. He then directs fire fighters to the fire's exact location.*

mainly for automobile drivers. You can probably get a road map of your state at a gas station, without charge.

What does the road map show? You can see the roads that connect the towns and cities. But the map shows much more than that. The capital city of your state is probably marked with a star on the map. Are some of the city names spelled with bigger letters than others? Or perhaps most of the cities and towns are printed in black, but a few are in red. This tells you that some cities are small and others are large. The smallest towns are printed in the smallest letters.

Legend

The map tells even more than this. On almost every road map there is a small box titled "legend" or "key." The legend shows many symbols, such as colors and figures, and explains what they mean. For example, a thin blue line might mean a dirt road. If you were driving, you could choose another route if you were in a hurry or if it were raining hard.

MAP   1449

maps—a map of your city, a map of your state, a map of the United States, and a map of the world. All these maps are printed on pages the size of this page. Your city is much smaller than your state. One inch on your city map may equal one-quarter or one-half mile. On your state map, an inch may equal 10 or 20 miles. As the area of a map grows larger the scale grows smaller. On the U.S. map, an inch may be 200 miles, and on the world map, every inch may represent 2,000 miles. There is no limit to how many miles an inch might equal.

In the legend of most maps, you will see a *scale of miles*—a thin line marked off in miles (or parts of a mile). On your city map, for example, you may see that one inch equals one-quarter mile. When you measure the distance between two particular streets, you find that it is three inches. What is the real distance? Can you easily walk between the two streets?

Some Kinds of Maps

If you have ever flown in an airplane, or looked down from the top of a mountain or a tall building, you know that everything looks different than it does from ground level. You can guess that an airplane pilot could easily get lost. But pilots carry maps that show cities and towns, rivers and mountains, and many other landmarks, such as railroad tracks. These maps, called *charts*, help pilots steer their planes quickly and safely.

Ships also have special charts, maps of the waters they sail on. Without a chart, a ship might crash into a sandbar or be unable to find its harbor.

Many other types of maps serve important purposes. Many farmers have soil maps made of their farms. A *soil map* shows what types of soil are in an area. A farmer can use this information to decide what kinds of crops will grow well on his farm. If

you wanted to live in a city where the temperature was always around 70 degrees, you could look at a map of average temperatures. If you wanted to live in the mountains, you could look at a *contour map* that shows altitude—height above or below sea level. Businessmen use maps that show railroads, truck roads, canals, sea lanes, and the populations of towns and other areas. These maps help businessmen decide on the best places to sell their products and the best routes over which to ship the goods. Geography students use general reference maps, which show boundaries, cities and towns, mountains, rivers, bays, lakes, and other natural features of the earth. Some maps show the average rainfall in an area. You will find many interesting maps in an *atlas*, a collection of maps.

Globes and Maps

The world is a sphere—a big ball. But maps are printed on flat pieces of paper. This means that a map is distorted (pulled out of shape). You can see this if you draw a picture on a hollow rubber ball. Then cut a piece from the ball and press it flat on a table. What happens to the picture?

Distortion is not a problem on maps showing small areas. But if you want to see what the world really looks like, you must look at a globe—a map printed on a ball. A globe shows every place on Earth in its proper position and size. But a globe cannot show much detail and is much more awkward to carry around than a map.

A map is called a *projection* of the Earth's surface. If you had a transparent globe (one that you could see through) with a light inside it, the light would project, or cast a shadow of, a part of the globe's surface on any flat surface nearby. In a way, a map-maker projects part of the Earth's surface onto the flat paper of his map. One of the oldest

▲*A globe is a map of the Earth in the form of a sphere. It is the most accurate form of map.*

▲*A human head is drawn onto a number of map projections to show the degree of distortion on each one. A globe projection shows the general shape of the continents and the oceans.*

▼*A mercator projection makes polar areas appear larger than they really are. It is used by navigators because it shows accurate compass directions.*

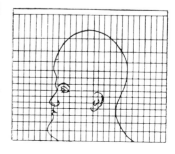

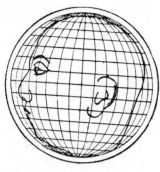

▲*An orthographic projection distorts the sides of the map. But it is useful for making blueprints since it accurately shows general land areas as they would appear when viewed from a great distance above Earth.*

▼*A sterographic projection shows little distortion around the center of the projection. It is used primarily to show land features such as bays and capes.*

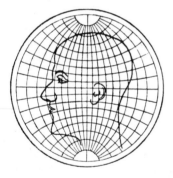

projections is Mercator's. In the 1500s, Gerhardus Mercator straightened out the meridians of longitude so that they ran parallel instead of meeting at the North and South poles. Therefore, on his projection, places near the poles look much farther apart and much larger than they really are. For example, Greenland looks as big as North America on a Mercator projection, although it is actually much smaller.

Map Making

A lot of work must be done to make a map. For thousands of years, map-makers walked, rode horses, or sailed ships everywhere, trying to record all the information they needed in order to make maps. Today, most maps are drawn from photographs taken from airplanes. An *aerial* photograph can show many miles of land, and this makes the map-maker's job easier. But flying airplanes over every part of the world is expensive, so map-makers are using a new tool, satellites. Satellite pictures show even larger areas than airplane pictures. For example, before 1969, only one-quarter of all the land in Peru had been mapped in 50 years. Then a satellite flew over Peru, and in three minutes it took photographs that were used to make maps of three-quarters of the country!

▶*A photographic aerial map being pieced together. Each photo is taken so that it overlaps with the one before it. Nothing is missed.*

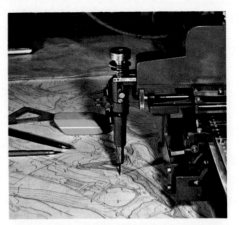

▲*A stereoplanigraph is a machine that draws contour maps based on color changes shown in photographs taken by airplane. Each line follows an altitude measurement. Here, the finishing touches are being applied to a map.*

The maps in the *Young Students Encyclopedia* have been designed especially for young students. With the article on each continent you will find a big *relief map* (one which shows mountains, lowlands, and other heights of land by different colors). The continent maps show the capitals and major cities of every continent, as well as the big rivers. Each continent also has a climate map. Every country has a *pinpoint* map—a guide to finding the country on the big continent map. Each state of the U.S. and each Canadian province has its own map.

Try making a map of your route to school or to a friend's house. Put in streets, parks, large buildings, and any other important features you can think of. Can you show the scale of your map? (Try measuring your steps with a yardstick and counting how many steps you need to get to school.) You will soon discover that map-making is challenging and interesting work.

ALSO READ: ATLAS, EARTH, EQUATOR, GEOGRAPHY, INTERNATIONAL DATE LINE, LATITUDE AND LONGITUDE.

MARBLE see ROCK, SCULPTURE.

MARBLES Like most games which have been played for many years, the game of marbles or "mibs" has a language of its own. Experienced marble players call themselves *hoodlers*. Marbles are usually made of glass, but they can be made of clay, steel, or stone. Boys and girls play with colorful *immies*, small *peewees*, *aggies* made of agate, *commies* made of clay, and *glassies* and *steelies*.

In many cities, sections of the playgrounds are reserved for marble players. In the spring, a series of tournaments for marble players under the age of 15 is held. Each region of the city has its champion player, who may become city champ by beating regional champs.

From two to six contestants may play in an official game of marbles, but for championship matches there are only two players. As in other organized sports, there is a *referee*. In important matches, there is also an official *scorer*.

The standard *ring* in a marbles game is a circle measuring 10 feet in diameter. Thirteen marbles are placed in a cross in the center of the ring. The hoodlers take turns and try to *shoot* the 13 marbles out of the ring. The players hold the *shooter* marble between the thumb and index finger. When he shoots, the player must *knuckle down*. That means that he must keep at least one knuckle in contact with the ground until his shooter has left his hand. The winner must shoot the most marbles from the ring.

In some informal games, the players keep the marbles which they shoot out of the ring. But tournament matches are *for fair*, which means that all marbles are returned to their owners after the game.

MARCH The stormy month of March is the third month in the calendar. March's name comes from *Martius*, meaning "the month of Mars." Mars was the Roman god of

DATES OF SPECIAL EVENTS IN MARCH

1 ● Saint David's Day, feast day of the patron saint of Wales.
 ● United States Articles of Confederation were ratified by the 13 colonies (1781).
2 ● Sam Houston, American political leader, was born (1793).
 ● Texas declared its independence from Mexico (1836).
 ● First nonstop airplane flight around the world was made by Captain James Gallagher in the U.S. Air Force B-50 plane, *Lucky Lady II*. Gallagher and his crew of 13 men made the flight in 3 days, 22 hours, and 1 minute (1949).
 ● First crossing of the Antarctic completed by a team led by Vivian Fuchs (1958).
3 ● First international air mail service began between Seattle, Washington, and Victoria, British Columbia (1919).
 ● "The Star Spangled Banner" was declared the official national anthem of the United States (1931).
4 ● Presidential Inaugural Day in the United States, until 1937.
 ● The United States Constitution went into effect (1789).
 ● Frances Perkins became the first woman appointed to the President's Cabinet. She served as Secretary of Labor (1933).
5 ● Boston Massacre (1770).
6 ● Michelangelo, artist of the Italian Renaissance, was born (1475).
 ● Antonio Santa Anna, Mexican general, captured the Alamo (1836).
7 ● Alexander Graham Bell patented the telephone (1876).
8 ● Justice Oliver Wendell Holmes, Jr., was born (1841).
 ● The *Merrimack* fought the *Monitor* in the Civil War (1862).
10 ● First paper money issued by the United States (1862).
12 ● Girl Scout movement founded in the United States (1912).
 ● First transatlantic radio broadcast (1925).
14 ● Albert Einstein, scientist and developer of the theories of relativity, was born (1879).
15 ● Julius Caesar was assassinated (44 B.C.).
 ● President Andrew Jackson was born (1767).
 ● Russian monarchy came to an end when Czar Nicholas II was overthrown (1917).
 ● American Legion, largest veterans' organization in the United States, was formed (1919).
16 ● President James Madison was born (1787).
17 ● Saint Patrick's Day, feast day of the patron saint of Ireland.
18 ● President Grover Cleveland was born (1837).
21 ● First treaty pledging peace between colonists and Indians (1621).
23 ● Patrick Henry made his famous speech in which he said, "Give me liberty or give me death." (1775).
25 ● British Parliament abolished the slave trade (1807).
27 ● George Washington signed the bill creating the United States Navy (1794).
29 ● President John Tyler was born (1790).
 ● British North America Act created the Dominion of Canada (1867).
30 ● United States bought Alaska from Russia (1867).
31 ● United States bought the Virgin Islands from Denmark (1917).
 ● Newfoundland became the tenth province of Canada (1949).
 ● Daylight Saving Time first used in the United States (1918).

war. March has 31 days. The *vernal* (spring) *equinox* comes in this month, usually on March 21. On the equinox, daylight and night are both exactly 12 hours long in all areas of the world. The vernal equinox marks the end of winter and the start of spring. In southern areas of the world, fall begins in March.

March weather in most northern lands can be very changeable, with icy winds one day and soft sunshine the next. A famous saying about March weather is, "If March comes in like a lion, it goes out like a lamb."

The yellow jonquil is March's flower. Its birthstone is the aquamarine, as blue-green as the ocean. Kelly green is March's color, in honor of St. Patrick, the patron saint of Ireland. St. Patrick's feast day is celebrated on March 17.

ALSO READ: CAESAR, JULIUS; CALENDAR; MONTH; SEASON.

MARCONI, GUGLIELMO (1874-1937)

▲*Guglielmo Marconi, Italian inventor.*

The Italian electrical engineer Guglielmo Marconi is often called the "father" of wireless broadcasting. He invented a telegraph that could *transmit* (send) signals over a longer distance than ever before. These signals were sent without wires, making use of electromagnetic waves in the air.

Marconi was born in Bologna, Italy. He became interested in science, and began to do experiments in electricity and telegraphy. Marconi went to England in 1896, where he set up the first wireless telegraph company. He invented a type of tall aerial, or antenna, to send and receive his wireless signals.

Marconi first thought of his business as an emergency signal company. He set up his equipment in lighthouses and ships so that ships in trouble could send messages asking for help. A ship caught in a storm in 1899 used Marconi's device. All on board were saved.

In 1901, Marconi sent the first wireless signals across the Atlantic Ocean. Wireless broadcasting was then being used only for transmitting emergency signals. The Marconi Trans-Atlantic Service began sending messages for newspapers and other businesses in 1907.

Marconi's wireless broadcasting was later developed into the radio and television that we know today. Marconi shared the Nobel Prize for physics in 1909, and was widely honored throughout the world for his work.

ALSO READ: RADIO, TELEGRAPH.

MARIE ANTOINETTE (1755-1793)

The poor people in France were forced to pay very high taxes during the 1700s. They were hungry and resentful, and they looked with envy at the carefree life of the royal court at the palace of Versailles, outside Paris. The one person they hated more than anyone else was the queen, Marie Antoinette.

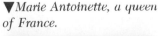

▼*Marie Antoinette, a queen of France.*

Marie Antoinette was born in Vienna, Austria. Her parents were Emperor Francis I and Maria Theresa of Austria. When Marie was only 15 years old, she came to France to marry the heir to the French throne. Her husband became King Louis XVI in 1774, and Marie became queen of France.

Marie was a gay and beautiful young woman. She found her husband slow and boring, and she hated her formal duties as queen. Her enemies accused her of spending too much money at court. She did not seem to care about the poor people of France, and she became very unpopular. Legend says that she was once told that the French people were starving because they had no bread. Her reply was, "Let them eat cake."

The French Revolution broke out in 1789, and an angry mob stormed the palace at Versailles. The king and queen were taken to Paris by force. When the royal family tried to flee Paris, and Marie appealed for help to her family in Austria, the French people accused the royal family of treason. Louis and Marie were thrown in prison in 1792, and were executed the following year.

ALSO READ: FRENCH HISTORY; FRENCH REVOLUTION; LOUIS, KINGS OF FRANCE.

MARIJUANA see MOOD MODIFIER.

MARINE CORPS The Marine Corps is a branch of the armed forces of the United States. The Marines are trained to fight on land, on water, and in the air. The men are usually experts in *amphibious warfare*. "Amphibious" is a word describing something that can survive both on land and in the water, such as a frog. Amphibious warfare is conducted by first attacking from the water and then moving in to hold an area of beach.

▲ *A Marine battalion in battle dress takes part in an amphibious exercise of the U.S. Sixth Fleet off the coast of Spain. Training creates an effective fighting force.*

The U.S. Marine Corps is headed by a commandant who has the rank of general. He is appointed to a four-year term by the President. The Marines work closely with the U.S. Navy. Marines can be found serving on large naval ships and at military bases both in the United States and in foreign countries. The Marines also serve as guards at United States embassies.

The first Marine Corps was organized by a decision of the Continental Congress on November 10, 1775. The Corps was created to defend the American colonies during the American Revolution. After that war, the government decided there

was no more need for the Marine Corps. The present Marine Corps was established in 1798. The Marines fought in the War of 1812, the Civil War, and the Spanish-American War.

During World War I, the Marines served aboard U.S. ships. They also fought in France, and their bravery brought them world-wide fame. The Marine Corps fought in most of the battles in the Pacific during World War II. They became well known for their courage and fierce fighting abilities. The Corps also fought in the Korean and Vietnam conflicts.

The U.S. Marine Corps Women's Reserve was organized during World War I. After the war, it was done away with, but was re-established during World War II. The women were trained to take over some of the non-fighting duties when the men went into battle. The Women's Corps was made a permanent organization in 1947.

ALSO READ: AMERICAN REVOLUTION; BATTLES, FAMOUS; CONTINENTAL CONGRESS; KOREAN CONFLICT; MILITARY CAREER; NAVY; SPANISH-AMERICAN WAR; WAR; WAR OF 1812; WORLD WAR I; WORLD WAR II.

MARINE LIFE Many scientists believe that life began in the ocean and existed there for more than a billion years before moving out on land. Most of Earth's creatures still live in the oceans. The plants and animals living there are called "marine life." The largest animals that have ever lived can be found in the ocean. These are the blue whales, which may grow to be 100 feet long and weigh 150 tons—bigger than the largest dinosaur, the most enormous land animal that ever lived. Marine life also includes animals that are made up of only one cell, 1/25,000 of an inch in length, and many kinds of ocean plants that are even smaller. Marine life may be divided into three groups—*plankton, nekton,* and *benthos.*

▲ *Marines of the U.S.S. Wasp in action against British soldiers aboard H.M.S. Reindeer during the War of 1812.*

▼ *A diver takes samples of marine life on the ocean floor. Samples such as this help scientists to unravel the mystery of life deep below the ocean surface.*

Plankton

Plankton includes all kinds of marine life that cannot swim but only drift with the currents and tides. Plankton comes from the Greek word *planktos*, meaning "wandering." Plankton includes fairly large plants and animals, such as seaweed and jellyfish, as well as plants and animals small enough to pass through the tiny openings of a strainer. There are two main types of plankton—phytoplankton and zooplankton.

Phytoplankton ("plant plankton") includes seaweeds and algae but is made up mostly of *diatoms* and *dinoflagellates*. Diatoms are microscopic, single-celled plants covered by two shells of a glassy material. The shells fit together like a box and lid. Dinoflagellates are tiny plants surrounded by chalk-like shells. The shells have openings for a whip-like organ. The beating motion of these whips moves the dinoflagellates through the water. Phytoplankton also includes green plants, which use sunlight to make their own food. Sunlight cannot go deeper in water than about 300 feet, so phytoplankton cannot live below this depth. Phytoplankton is eaten by thousands of kinds of animals, small and large. For this reason, the water level where phytoplankton live is called "the pasture of the sea."

Zooplankton ("animal plankton") consists of thousands of kinds of very small animals that float and swim on or near the surface of the ocean. The smallest and simplest of these are *protozoa*, consisting of only a single cell. *Copepods* and *krill* are very small members of the same group to which lobsters and crabs belong. Jellyfish, very small worms, and the larva and eggs of fish are also part of zooplankton. Protozoa feed on phytoplankton, and larger zooplankton feed on protozoa and on each other. The smaller zooplankton have bubbles of air inside their bodies. These air bubbles help to keep them afloat.

Plankton is scarce in tropical seas. It is most abundant in the colder waters in the Arctic and Antarctic Oceans, where there may be as many as 10,000 forms of plankton in every inch of water. Rising currents of water in these oceans are rich in minerals, which act as fertilizer for phytoplankton. Plankton provides food for sea birds, shrimp, mackerel and herring, herds of baleen whales, and other animals.

Nekton

Nekton consists of animals that can swim freely and are not dependent on currents and waves. Nekton includes ocean fishes, varying in size from less than an inch long to the size of whale sharks, which may be more than 50 feet long. There are nearly 20,000 kinds of ocean fish known. Nekton also includes ocean-living mammals, such as whales, porpoises, seals, and walruses. Some nekton feed on plankton, the rest feed on other nekton.

Nekton cannot live just anywhere in the ocean. Each kind of nekton must live in a location and at a depth where the temperature, food supply, and saltiness of the ocean are best. Fish that live deep in the water have to withstand the tremendous pressure caused by the weight of the water above. These fish have swim bladders filled with air or other gas. The bladders equalize the pressure inside and outside the fish. If a fish from a lower depth rises above its usual level, its swim bladder expands. This makes the fish so light that it cannot swim down to deeper water. It may have to rise all the way to the surface where less pressure causes the bladder to expand so much that the fish bursts.

Nekton of the middle and lower depths of the ocean live thousands of feet down in constant darkness where light never penetrates. Since there is no light, plankton cannot grow there. Nekton of this region must feed on each other or on the

▲ *A croaker swims in an underwater world teeming with marine life. Croaker fish are a form of nekton.*

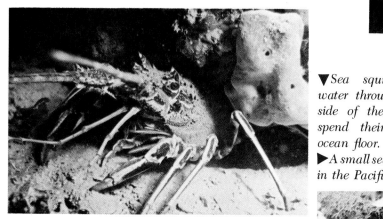

▲ *The spiny lobster lives off the coasts of southern California and Florida. It often hides under rocks on the bottom of the ocean.*

▼ *A rich assortment of marine life can be seen when the tide is out. The plants and animals of tidal pools can survive the periodic loss of water.*

▼ *Sea squirts squirt out water through holes in the side of their bodies. They spend their lives on the ocean floor.*
▶ *A small sea bass swimming in the Pacific Ocean.*

▲ *Sea urchins are spiny-looking creatures that move slowly about the ocean floor. They are dangerous to touch.*

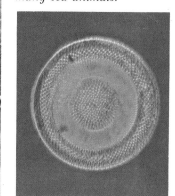

▼ *The tiny diatom is a one-celled plant. It is a form of plankton. Diatoms are an important source of food for many sea animals.*

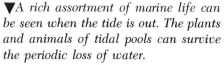

▲ *The seal is a form of nekton. It is an aquatic mammal that spends some of its time in the water and some on land.*

remains of dead plants and animals sifting down from the upper regions. At these depths live the lantern fish and other strange creatures that have huge mouths, long teeth, and luminous organs that give off a dim light. Most of these creatures are small, not much over a foot long, but giant squid feed at the middle depths. Sometimes, sperm whales will dive 2,000 feet down in pursuit of the squid.

Benthos

Benthos includes all the plants and animals that live on the ocean bottom, anywhere from the shallows to the deepest parts. In those parts where light reaches the bottom, a great variety of sea plants grows. No plants grow in the deeper parts of the ocean bottom. Exploration of the deepest parts of the ocean floor has shown that the animals living there are not much different from those living in the shallows. Benthos of the deepest sea includes starfish, worms, brittle stars, clams, oysters, snails, corals, sponges, flounder-like fish, and many others. On the floor of the ocean, the pressure is thousands of pounds per square inch. This pressure is so evenly distributed throughout the bodies of the animals of the benthos that they do not feel any pressure at all. Except for animals that have air spaces in their bodies (such as fish having swim bladders), the benthos can be brought to the surface without injury due to lessened pressure.

Marine Ecology

Marine life provides us with much food. For centuries, people thought the numbers of fish, lobsters, crabs, oysters, clams, and shrimp were endless. Modern ways of fishing have greatly lessened the numbers of these food animals. Many nations, realizing that they are in danger of losing their seafood supply, have agreed with other nations not to take too many food animals from the ocean. Unfortunately, not all nations live up to these agreements.

Marine life is also endangered by polluted waters from rivers that empty into the ocean. Crude oil is cleaned out of or spilled from oil tankers. People dump huge amounts of sewage and garbage into the ocean. All of these things are polluting the ocean water. Many scientists believe that if this pollution is not ended, all marine life will be killed within about 50 years.

ALSO READ: ALGAE, CRUSTACEAN, DOLPHINS AND PORPOISES, ECOLOGY, FISH, OCEAN, PLANT, PROTOZOAN, SEALS AND SEA LIONS, WALRUS, WATER, WHALES AND WHALING.

MARION, FRANCIS (about 1732–1795) The Revolutionary War general known as the "Swamp Fox" was Francis Marion. He was born in Berkeley County, South Carolina, about 1732. He lived on a plantation near Georgetown, and was educated in the country schools. Marion had his first military experiences when he fought in battles against the Cherokee Indians in 1759 and 1761.

Marion was elected to the South Carolina Provincial Congress in 1775. He became commander of a regiment of colonial troops during the Revolutionary War. In October, 1779, Marion led his regiment against British forces at Savannah, Georgia. He was injured in battle but escaped capture.

The colonial army was defeated by the British in South Carolina in

1780. Marion and his soldiers hid in the nearby swamps, where the British could not follow them. Marion won his name, "Swamp Fox," when he and his men attacked the British troops again and again from the safety of the swamps. These attacks helped win South Carolina back from the British.

Marion became commander of Fort Johnson in South Carolina after the war. He also served several terms in the South Carolina Senate. He died on February 26, 1795, and was buried on his plantation at Belle Isle, South Carolina.

ALSO READ: AMERICAN REVOLUTION, GUERRILLA WARFARE.

▼*Francis Marion, American general.*

MARKSMANSHIP Expert shooters are skilled in marksmanship. Many hours of practice shooting are required to become a good marksman, or *sharpshooter.*

Most shooting authorities—whether they are talking about bows and arrows or about firearms—agree that it is best for the beginner to have an experienced shooter with him to give advice. The beginner should also have a thorough knowledge of how to handle a gun safely before he ever begins to fire it.

Beginning marksmen should start with a *short-range* target—one that is placed fairly close to the shooter.

The area behind the target should be a steep bank or hillside where there is no chance of the bullets hitting people, livestock, buildings, or automobiles. Target shooting for *handguns* (pistols and revolvers) is done standing up. There are four positions in rifle shooting—lying flat on the stomach, sitting, kneeling on one knee, and standing.

When he begins to shoot, the marksman must move slowly and take careful aim. He does not jerk his finger on the trigger. He squeezes the trigger back very slowly, at the same time holding his gun sight steady on the target. Then he fires.

A shooter who is able to get *tight groups* is considered a good marksman. Tight groups are bullet holes in the target that are close together. The best marksmen enter shooting contests, including the Olympics.

ALSO READ: ARCHERY, GUNS AND RIFLES, OLYMPIC GAMES.

MARQUETTE, JACQUES (1637-1675) AND JOLIET, LOUIS (1645-1700) These two explorers were the first white men to travel the upper Mississippi River. They made the dangerous trip through the region in canoes and on foot. Their journey inspired other people to explore and settle in the central part of North America.

Joliet was a French Canadian born in the province of Quebec, where he later studied to be a priest. He became a fur trader and explored much of the land near Lake Superior. Jacques Marquette was a French Jesuit missionary sent to Canada in 1666. He founded a mission at St. Ignace, Michigan, on Lake Superior.

In 1673, the two men were sent on an expedition by the governor of New France, to find a route to the Pacific Ocean. They set out in canoes across Lake Michigan, accompanied by five other men. They traveled up the Fox River, almost to

▲*A good marksman never hurries his shot. Before firing he holds his rifle in a correct position, steadies his aim, and concentrates on the target.*

▼*An archery match. It takes constant practice to improve your score and become a good marksman.*

▲ *Father Jacques Marquette preaching to some American Indians.*

the source, and then carried their canoes overland to the Wisconsin River. The men followed the Wisconsin River down to the point where it flowed into the mighty Mississippi. They turned back after they had passed the mouth of the Arkansas River, because they realized the Mississippi did not flow into the Pacific Ocean. They wrote a book about their explorations called *Voyages and Discoveries in some of the Lands and Nations of Mid-America.*

After their trip, Father Marquette returned to mission work and Joliet made further explorations. Joliet explored the region north of the Saguenay River as far as Hudson Bay. He later traveled through part of Labrador. The island of Anticosti, located in the Gulf of St. Lawrence, was given to Joliet in recognition of his services.

ALSO READ: EXPLORATION, MISSIONARY, MISSISSIPPI RIVER.

▲ Giovanni Arnolfini and His Bride, *painted by the Flemish artist Jan van Eyck in 1434. The bride and bridegroom are exchanging their marriage vows.*

MARRIAGE   When a man and woman decide to live their lives together, they marry. Marriage is a legal agreement to care for each other and any children which they might have.

The engagement is a couple's announcement that they intend to marry. The engagement period can be a time when a man and woman decide if they are sure they want to marry. If the couple is still in school or college, they may want to continue their studies after marriage.

Later, the marriage ceremony takes place, often in a church or synagogue. The ceremony is conducted by a minister, priest, or rabbi, or by a judge or justice of the peace.

Each state has its own laws about marriage. A couple must be above a certain age to marry. Many states require health examinations before marriage. Both the man and the woman must wish to marry the other. If it is found out that either the bride or groom was forced into marrying, the law may not consider the couple married at all and the marriage would be annulled.

Sometimes a couple is not happy together. They may decide to *divorce*, which means to end their marriage. Each state has its own laws about divorce. The courts make sure that the children will be cared for. Sometimes the children live with the mother, sometimes the father, or perhaps they divide their time between both parents.

▼*A young bride and her naval officer husband walk under crossed swords, a traditional navy custom, as they leave the church after the wedding ceremony.*

A person who is married cannot marry again unless he gets a divorce or his mate has died. In some states, two people may have a common-law marriage, in which the man and woman may decide to have no ceremony or marriage contract, but simply to begin living together as husband and wife and be considered married by the neighbors.

Different countries have their own marriage traditions and customs. The throwing of rice at the bridal couple is a hope for fertility, or that they will have children. Presents are given to the family of the bride in many American Indian, African, and Melanesian tribes. In many countries, families used to arrange the engagement and marriage of children. In some countries, the bride's parents still pick the man she will marry, and the bride has little choice in the matter. There are some countries in which a man may have several wives (polygyny), or a wife may have several husbands (polyandry). Both these practices are included in the term *polygamy*.

ALSO READ: LAW, WEDDING CUSTOMS.

MARSHALL, JOHN (1755–1835)

John Marshall held office as chief justice of the United States Supreme Court for 34 years—longer than any other chief justice. It was during his long term that the Supreme Court clearly established itself as the "third branch of government."

Marshall was born in Germantown, Virginia. He served with George Washington at Valley Forge during the American Revolution. He became a lawyer in 1780, and began his political career as a delegate to the Virginia legislature two years later. He was elected to the U.S. House of Representatives in 1799. President John Adams appointed Marshall to be secretary of state in 1800 and chief justice of the Supreme Court in 1801.

Marshall supported the power of the Federal Government over individual states in many of his decisions. He also upheld the Constitution as the supreme law of the land. His most famous case, *Marbury vs. Madison* in 1803, established the right of the Supreme Court to decide whether laws made by the legislative branch of government were against the Constitution. President Thomas Jefferson had refused to honor an appointment made by the former President, John Adams. Marshall ruled that a law made by Congress, which would force Jefferson to go ahead with the appointment, was unconstitutional. "A legislative act contrary to the Constitution is not law," Marshall said. "It is . . . the duty of the judicial department to say what the law is."

Marshall's beliefs often brought him into conflict with federal and state officials, but he was always able to defend his ideas. He became well known for his powerful speaking ability and persuasiveness. His decisions were clearly written, and were noted for their balanced reasoning and style. He is remembered chiefly for his efforts to build a strong Federal Government and a powerful Supreme Court.

ALSO READ: GOVERNMENT, SUPREME COURT.

MARSHALL, THURGOOD (born 1908)

Thurgood Marshall was the first Negro to become a member of the United States Supreme Court.

Marshall was born in Baltimore, Maryland. He graduated from Howard University Law School, and began practicing law in Baltimore. Marshall joined the legal staff of the National Association for the Advancement of Colored People (NAACP) in 1936. He later became director of its Legal Defense and Educational Fund. His years at the NAACP were spent defending people who thought they had been denied their legal rights as citizens because of their race. He won 29 of the 32 civil rights cases he tried be-

▲*The marriage certificate of ⬦Napoleon I and Marie Louise, his second wife. In most countries an official paper is needed to make a marriage legal.*

▼*John Marshall, an early chief justice of the United States Supreme Court.*

▲*Thurgood Marshall, first black associate justice of the Supreme Court.*

▲*Karl Marx, founder of Communism.*

▼*Mary, Queen of Scots.*

fore the Supreme Court. His most famous victory came in 1954, when he argued the case *Brown vs. Board of Education* before the Supreme Court. The decision in this case made it illegal for communities to force black children to attend racially segregated schools.

Marshall served as Solicitor General of the United States for two years (1965-1967). In this position, he represented the Federal Government in Supreme Court cases. President Lyndon Johnson appointed him an associate justice of the Supreme Court in 1967.

ALSO READ: CIVIL RIGHTS, NATIONAL ASSOCIATION FOR THE ADVANCEMENT OF COLORED PEOPLE, SUPREME COURT.

MARSUPIAL see MAMMAL.

MARX, KARL (1818-1883) The great series of changes in Europe, known as the Industrial Revolution, brought wealth and comfort to some people. But many workers who labored in the new factories were poor and miserable. Few people in the 1800s questioned these unfair conditions. But one man, the German philosopher Karl Marx, began to speak of a new system of government known as *Communism*, under which the people of a country would together own the industries and means of production.

Karl Marx was born in Trier, Germany. He was influenced as a young man by the ideas of liberty and equality of the French Revolution in the late 1700s. He began to attack the *capitalist* economy, under which a few people owned the industries and ran them in order to make a profit for themselves. Marx traveled to France, where he met another German, Friedrich Engels. The two men agreed that the unequal "class system" should be destroyed. Marx believed that the lives of the workers would become so unbearable that people would finally overthrow the wealthy classes.

They would then set up their own government, and own all property in the name of the people. But this government would not be needed for long, he thought, because the people would live together peacefully without government if no one owned any more than anyone else.

These ideas were written down in the *Communist Manifesto* by Marx and Engels, and in Marx's book *Das Kapital* ("Capital"). Marx was persecuted by the German and French governments for his ideas, and he spent the last half of his life in England. There, he founded the important organization known as the International Workingmen's Association.

Only a small number of people supported Marx during his lifetime. But his ideas have inspired Communist revolutions in several countries of the world since 1900. Some of the countries that now have Communist governments are China, the Soviet Union, Yugoslavia, Poland, Czechoslovakia, Rumania, Albania, Bulgaria, East Germany, Cuba, and Hungary.

ALSO READ: CAPITALISM, COMMUNISM, ECONOMICS, INDUSTRIAL REVOLUTION, SOCIALISM.

MARY, QUEEN OF SCOTS (1542-1587) The tragic life of Mary, Queen of Scots, was ended by the executioner's ax. The beautiful young queen had ruled in the gay, elegant court of France, and in the cold, gray castles of Scotland. She had also spent almost half of her life imprisoned in England.

Mary was the daughter of King James V of Scotland. Her father died six days after she was born, and Mary became queen of Scotland. She was pledged to marry Francis, the heir to the French throne. In 1548, she was sent to France, and ten years later she and Francis were married. Mary was 16 years old at the time.

Francis's father died in 1559, and Mary and her husband were crowned king and queen of France. But Francis died the following year, and Mary returned to Scotland, where she was still queen.

Mary married her cousin, Lord Darnley, in Scotland. But she soon found that Darnley was a weak and vicious man. She began to spend more and more time with her Italian secretary, David Rizzio. Darnley became violently jealous and, in 1566, he murdered Rizzio. Mary then became interested in a Scottish nobleman, the Earl of Bothwell. Darnley was murdered, and Mary married Bothwell. The Scottish people became convinced that Mary and Bothwell had murdered Darnley. They forced Mary to give up her throne. Her one-year-old son became King James VI of Scotland. Mary fled to England to her cousin, Queen Elizabeth I. But many people considered Mary the queen of England, and Elizabeth was afraid Mary might try to seize her throne. She had Mary imprisoned for 19 years. Mary was finally convicted of plotting against Elizabeth. She refused to admit any guilt, but was beheaded. Mary's son became King James I of England.

ALSO READ: ELIZABETH I; ENGLISH HISTORY; JAMES, KINGS OF ENGLAND; SCOTLAND.

MARY, QUEENS OF ENGLAND

Two women named Mary were queens of Britain. *Mary I* (1516–1558) was the daughter of King Henry VIII and his first wife, Catherine of Aragon. They had several children, but Mary was the only one to live beyond infancy. Henry wanted sons, so he had his marriage to Catherine declared invalid. Mary became queen after her half-brother Edward VI died in the year 1553. She then announced that she was going to marry Philip, the son of Charles V, the king of Spain. The English people did not want her to marry Philip because he was a Spanish Catholic. Most of the English had become

Protestants, and Spain was an old enemy. Mary was also a Catholic, and would not listen to her people. After their marriage, she and Philip began to persecute the English Protestants. They had almost 300 people burned at the stake in their attempt to make England a Catholic country again. Mary was given the nickname, "Bloody Mary." Philip soon left her and returned to Spain. Mary had no children. After a long illness she died, bitter and alone. She was succeeded by her half-sister, Elizabeth I.

Mary II (1662–1694), daughter of James II, married William, Prince of Orange, the ruler of the Netherlands, and both became rulers of England in 1689.

ALSO READ: ENGLISH HISTORY; HENRY, KINGS OF ENGLAND; WILLIAM AND MARY.

▲*Mary I, queen of England.*

MARYLAND

"Our flag was still there," say the words of the U.S. national anthem, *The Star-Spangled Banner.* All during that noisy September night in 1814, the huge U.S. flag waved above Fort McHenry. The fort guarded the entrance to Baltimore harbor. Fort McHenry is still standing. Day and night, the U.S. flag is kept flying there. Fort McHenry is visited by many tourists who come to Maryland.

Land and Climate

Maryland is a Middle Atlantic state. It is located between Delaware on the east, Pennsylvania on the north, West Virginia on the west, Virginia

▼*A view of Baltimore from Fort McHenry National Monument and Historic Shrine. During the War of 1812, while the British bombarded the fort, Francis Scott Key composed* The Star-Spangled Banner.

MARYLAND

State flower
Black-eyed Susan

State bird
Baltimore oriole

State tree
White oak

Capital
Annapolis (29,592 people)

Area
10,577 square miles
(ranks 42nd)

Population
3,922,399 people
(ranks 18th)

Statehood
April 28, 1788
(7th of the original 13
states to adopt the
Constitution)

Principal rivers
Patapsco River
Potomac River

Highest point
Backbone Mountain
(3,360 feet)

Largest city
Baltimore (905,759
people)
(7th largest city in U.S.)

and the District of Columbia on the west and south.

Maryland has three sections. They are part of three narrow regions that stretch north and south along most of the eastern United States. The regions are the Appalachian Mountains, the Piedmont Plateau, and the Atlantic Coastal Plain.

Western Maryland is in the Appalachians. The highest point in the state is a ridge called Backbone Mountain, near the border of West Virginia. The Potomac River, with its north branch, forms most of Maryland's boundary with Virginia. The river winds through and out of the Appalachian Mountains. The easternmost ridge of the Appalachians in Maryland is Catoctin Mountain.

Just to the east, in the valley of the Monocacy River, the Piedmont section begins. It is high, hilly land. In Maryland the Piedmont section is from 40 to 50 miles wide. A line drawn from Washington, D.C., through Baltimore will show you about where its eastern edge is.

The rest of Maryland is in the Atlantic Coastal Plain. The land is either gently rolling or flat. Places that are poorly drained are swampy. Maryland's coastal plain is divided by the Chesapeake Bay into the Western Shore and the Eastern Shore, connected by the Chesapeake Bay Bridge. The bay and the Atlantic Ocean enclose the *Delmarva Peninsula*, which contains parts of three states: Delaware, Maryland, and Virginia.

Chesapeake Bay is 200 miles long and is Maryland's most important body of water. Several rivers pour into it. At the northern end, the Susquehanna empties into the bay. (The bay is really the water-filled valley of this river.) The mouth of the Patapsco River provides Baltimore with a good harbor on the bay. Maryland's state capital, Annapolis, is on the south shore of the Severn River where the river flows into the

Chesapeake. Baltimore has a fine location for trade. Ocean-going ships sail up Chesapeake Bay to it, or they go up the Delaware River between Delaware and New Jersey to the Chesapeake and Delaware Canal. The ships then cross the canal, enter Chesapeake Bay, and go down to Baltimore.

Maryland has a climate that suits crops—and people. In the mountainous western part, summers are mild and winters cold. The coastal plain has hot summers and mild winters.

History

The story of Maryland starts in England. It begins with an Englishman, George Calvert, first Baron Baltimore. Lord Baltimore owned land in Ireland, and Baltimore is the name of a small Irish fishing port.

Lord Baltimore was a Roman Catholic. In the 1600s, English Roman Catholics were not allowed the same freedom to worship that most Protestants had at that time. Lord Baltimore asked King Charles I to let him start a colony on Chesapeake Bay. He wanted to form a colony where Roman Catholics and Protestants would enjoy the same rights. King Charles gave him per-

▼*The citizens of Maryland are proud of their state's long and interesting history. Here, the First Maryland Regiment fife and drum corps, dressed in colonial costume, parades past a group of spectators.*

mission to found the colony of Maryland—named for the king's wife, Queen Henrietta Maria.

George Calvert died in 1632. His eldest son, Cecil, became the Second Baron Baltimore. He asked his brother, Leonard, to take the first colonists to Maryland. Some were Roman Catholics, and some were Protestants. Leonard Calvert was their governor.

In March, 1634, Calvert's two ships—the *Ark* and the *Dove*—reached Chesapeake Bay. They sailed a short distance up the Potomac and anchored. Calvert went ashore to make friends with the Indians. The Indians he met belonged to the Piscataway tribe. This tribe was planning to leave the area to get away from the warlike Susquehannock tribe. They were glad to sell their huts and fields to the English. Calvert paid for them with cloth, axes, and other goods. Governor Calvert named the Indian village and the nearby river "Saint Marys." Soon the colonists built houses of the European kind. Saint Marys was the capital of Maryland until 1694, when Annapolis was made the capital.

Maryland had a long, bitter quarrel with Pennsylvania over the boundary line between the two colonies. At times there was trouble between the Protestants and Roman Catholics, but usually Marylanders were peaceful. Farming and trade brought them wealth.

In 1776 Maryland became one of the 13 original United States. Maryland and Virginia gave a 10-square-mile tract of land in 1790 and 1791 to create the District of Columbia. During the War of 1812, there was fighting in Maryland. The British crossed the western shore of the Chesapeake, captured Washington, D.C., and tried to take Baltimore.

Maryland was a slave state. The American writer and lecturer, Frederick Douglass, was born a slave on the Eastern Shore. He escaped in

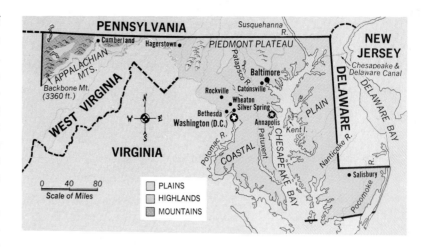

1838. During the Civil War, some Marylanders fought for the Confederacy, others fought for the Union. A bloody Civil War battle was fought in September, 1862, on the banks of Antietam Creek, near Sharpsburg. Both armies had heavy losses.

After the Civil War, manufacturing grew rapidly in Maryland. Its busy seaport, Baltimore, became a great factory center.

Marylanders at Work

The waters of the Chesapeake Bay provide a harvest of fish, crabs, oysters, and clams for Maryland fishermen. Two kinds of manufacturing in Maryland are nearly equal in importance. One is the processing of food products, including seafood and vegetables. The other is the production of metals—chiefly iron and steel. One of the world's largest

▼*A sailboat show draws a crowd to the harbor at Annapolis, the historic capital of Maryland.*

steel mills stands at the mouth of the Patapsco River. Two other kinds of manufacturing—transportation equipment and chemical products—are next in importance. All agriculture put together does not bring in as much money as does one of these four industries. Farms cover more than half of Maryland. Livestock brings farmers more money than crops do. The leading crops are corn, hay, and tobacco.

Tourism is important to Maryland. Many people visit Baltimore and Fort McHenry, and the city of Annapolis where the United States Naval Academy is located. The state capitol building in Annapolis was built in 1772 and is still in use. At the village called Saint Marys City, a replica (copy) of the first statehouse has been built.

ALSO READ: AMERICAN COLONIES; AMERICAN HISTORY; APPALACHIAN MOUNTAINS; CHESAPEAKE BAY; DOUGLASS, FREDERICK; MASON-DIXON LINE; NATIONAL ANTHEM; STAR-SPANGLED BANNER; U.S. SERVICE ACADEMIES; WAR OF 1812.

▼ *These scientists are experimenting with helium-neon lasers. The light moving through a laser becomes one narrow, powerful beam. Regular light spreads out in all directions.*

MASERS AND LASERS If you want to talk to a friend who is standing a block away, you can shout at each other and try to hear the words. But at such a long distance, you will have trouble hearing each other. You will hear better if you *amplify* (strengthen) the sounds. You can do this by cupping your hand to your ear. Your hand scoops up sound waves and gives you better hearing.

Scientists have the same kind of trouble "hearing" the signals sent back from rockets far out in space. Scientists cannot improve their hearing by cupping their hands to their ears, but they do hear the signals better when the signals are amplified. The device scientists use to strengthen such weak signals is a maser. "Maser" is a word made up of the first letters of *m*icrowave *a*mplification by *s*timulated *e*mission of *r*adiation.

Here is how a maser works: substances absorb (take in) and emit (give off) energy all the time. Scientists call these little packages of energy *photons*. Normally, the energy going into a substance is equal to the energy coming out. In masers, the substance is put into a *high energy state* (highly excited). In a high energy state, the atoms of a substance will emit energy at a certain rate when triggered by radio waves. The photons that are emitted help make a stronger radio signal. This is called *stimulated emission*.

The maser is a very sensitive amplifier. In the space program, masers have detected and amplified radio signals 100 times weaker than any other kind of amplifier has.

Making Light Stronger
Light is also made up of photons. These photons have shorter wave lengths than radio signals have, but they behave much the same. If you remember this, and change the "m" in "maser to "l" for light, then you will know what laser means—*l*ight *a*mplification by *s*timulated *e*mis-

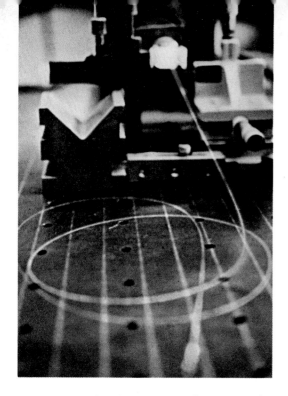

◄ *Tiny glass-fiber filaments can conduct light the way a pipe conducts water (far left). These strands of glass are used to transmit a laser beam.*

◄ *A scientist generates a fan of multi-colored light rays from a beam of light given off by a laser (left).*

sion of radiation. Another name for laser is *optical maser* ("optical" means "pertaining to sight").

Ordinary light—from a lamp or the sun, for example—is made up of many wave lengths of blue, green, and red light. The combination of all these colors looks white.

What happens when a laser is turned on? One kind of laser has a tube with flat ends. The ends of the tube are made into mirrors, and the tube itself is often a ruby. The first thing that happens is that energy (usually light) is pumped into the tube. This energy is absorbed by the atoms of the ruby. Atoms that contain a great deal of energy are said to be *excited*. When a photon travels to the end of the tube, a mirror then turns it around so it must travel through the tube again, knocking loose more photons. All this happens in an instant, and there are millions of identical photons zooming back and forth in the tube. When the light gets very strong, it passes through the mirror as a beam of laser light. The photons of laser light all travel in the same direction and the beam of light is very concentrated —it does not spread out as an ordinary flashlight beam does.

Scientists have bounced a laser beam off the moon. The time the beam needed to travel this huge distance was measured, and scientists were able to check the distance from the Earth to the moon. In industry, lasers are used as drills. A laser can burn a tiny hole with great accuracy. This makes lasers useful tools for doctors, too. In an operating room, a surgeon using a laser can cut away diseased tissue in a fraction of a second, without harming surrounding healthy tissue. Scientists are still exploring uses of lasers.

ALSO READ: ATOM, ENERGY, LIGHT, MIRROR, RADIATION, RADIO, SOUND.

MASK A mask is a covering for the face. A person's face is the most recognizable part of his body. When you see a person, you usually quickly recognize him by his face. A person's face is a very important part of his identity.

People all over the world have used masks to change or hide their identities. In ancient Greece and Rome, masks were worn by actors in plays. By putting on a mask, the actor could change his own identity to that of the character he was playing. The faces on the masks had very exaggerated expressions—funny, comical ones and very sad, tragic ones. Today actors use make-up instead of masks.

▼ *The ancient Greeks used masks in the theater to express various emotions such as happiness, sadness, or anger. What emotion do you think this mask expresses?*

▲This Ceylonese craftsman is carefully putting the finishing touches to a theatrical mask (left). A decorative mask made of carved wood from New Britain. The hair is made of vegetable fibers (center). The devil dancing mask used by Peruvian Indians at fiesta time (right).

▼This wooden mask is used on the island of Borneo during ceremonial dances.

▼Masks can be made out of almost any material. These mask-makers are using paper bags.

In Europe during the 1400s, plays called *masques* became popular. The actors wore masks to represent different characters or qualities, such as patience, love, evil, or jealousy. Since the 1700s, people have enjoyed *masquerades*. These are big parties where all the guests wear masks. When people meet each other at a masquerade party, they try to guess each other's real identity. At a certain time, each guest takes off his mask and reveals who he is.

Masks have been used since ancient times in religious ceremonies. Natives of many countries have made masks to represent various spirits. When these masks were worn, the people believed that the wearer actually lost his own identity and became the spirit itself. Other religious masks were made to look terrible and frightening. These were used to scare away demons, evil spirits, and other dangers. In China

and Japan, actors have used decorated masks. Some of these masks even have hair attached. The actor covers his own face with the mask and becomes the character he is playing.

The most familiar use of masks today is for Halloween celebrations. When you put on a mask to go trick-or-treating, you cover your own identity and try to become a witch, pirate, or ghost. Burglars and thieves often wear a mask to hide their identities so people will not be able to recognize them.

Masks have been made from many different materials—wood, leather, cloth, metal, feathers, and *papier-mâché* (a kind of paper sculpture). You can easily make your own mask. First find a paper bag that will fit your head without tearing. Put the bag over your head and mark the places for your eyes, nose, and mouth. Cut holes at the places you marked, and then try on the bag to be sure the eye holes are big enough to see through clearly. With crayons or paints, decorate the face of your mask. You can make hair for the mask by cutting pieces of yarn and gluing them to the top of the bag. You can make a mustache or beard by gluing more yarn to the areas above and below the mouth. Ears can be made by attaching curved paper shapes to the sides of the bag. You can also make a stand-out nose by cutting a piece of

paper in the shape of a triangle. Fold the triangle in half, and glue it over the nose hole on the bag.

Masks have other uses besides that of hiding or changing a person's identity. Gas masks are used to keep a person from breathing poisonous gases in the air. Baseball catchers and hockey players wear masks to protect their faces from being hit. Skiers wear knitted masks to keep the cold wind and snow from stinging their faces as they race down the slopes.

ALSO READ: DRAMA, MAKE-UP, PAPER SCULPTURE, THEATER.

MASON-DIXON LINE The Mason-Dixon Line is the southern boundary line of Pennsylvania, separating the state from Delaware, Maryland, and West Virginia. It is famous in history as the dividing line between slave states and free states before the Civil War.

The Mason-Dixon Line was *surveyed* (measured) during colonial days. The Calvert family were the owners of the colony of Maryland. For one hundred years they quarreled with the Penn family of Pennsylvania over the border land between the two colonies. The Penn family claimed that the charter given to William Penn by the king of England included the disputed land. But the Calverts also claimed the land as part of the territory of Maryland.

The families made an agreement in 1760 to hire two English surveyors, Charles Mason and Jeremiah Dixon, to determine the boundary line. Their survey took four years, from 1763 to 1767. They set the line at 39 degrees, 43 minutes, 26.3 seconds north latitude. This boundary line has remained the same ever since.

The line was extended westward in 1784, to settle Virginia boundary disputes over land west of Maryland. This land became the state of West Virginia.

The Mason-Dixon Line became the dividing line between the southern slave states and northern free states in the early 1900s. It is still known as a dividing line between the North and the South.

ALSO READ: CIVIL WAR; CONFEDERATE STATES OF AMERICA; PENN, WILLIAM.

MASS see MATTER.

MASSACHUSETTS How many historic events can you think of in connection with Massachusetts? The Boston Tea Party, Paul Revere's Ride, the Boston Massacre, the Pilgrims' landing at Plymouth Rock, and the Salem witchcraft trials are just a few. The state has a wealth of historical landmarks. Eight million visitors come to Massachusetts each year. Visitors outnumber the people who live there!

The Land and Climate

Massachusetts is one of the New England states, located on the Atlantic coast in the northeastern United States. The ocean forms the state's eastern border, Rhode Island and Connecticut lie to the south, and New York is on the west. Vermont and New Hampshire are north of Massachusetts. The state has four natural regions. You can see all of them by driving from west to east on the state's main road, the wide Massachusetts Turnpike.

The first area consists of the Berkshire Hills. They belong to the same range as Vermont's Green Mountains in the north. The Berkshires have many popular summer resorts and ski lodges. Every July and August, thousands of people come to hear the Boston Symphony orchestra perform at the Tanglewood Music Shed near Lenox. This western area is the highest part of the state. East of the Berkshires is the Connecticut Valley. The Connecticut River, bordered with trees, flows from north to south through Massachusetts. The flat valley floor lies on

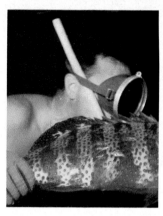

▲*A skin diver's mask allows him to see underwater without getting water in his eyes.*

▼*Surgical masks help keep doctors and their aides from infecting the patients.*

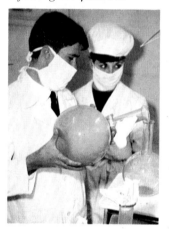

▼*A summer concert at the Tanglewood Music Shed near Lenox, Massachusetts.*

MASSACHUSETTS

State flower
Mayflower

State bird
Chickadee

State tree
Elm

Capital and largest city
Boston (641,071 people)

Area
8,257 square miles
(ranks 45th)

Population
5,689,170 people
(ranks 10th)

Statehood
February 6, 1788
(6th of the original 13
states to ratify the
Constitution)

Principal river
Connecticut River

Highest point
Mount Greylock
(3,491 feet) in the
Berkshire Hills

either side. Its fertile soil makes the valley good farming country. If you drove through this valley, you would see fields covered with cheese-cloth. Cigar tobacco, which needs little sun, grows in the shade under the cloth. Much of the area is divided into neat fields with long, straight borders. The largest town in the valley is Springfield. It is a manufacturing center. Beyond the valley, the land rises again. This highland is part of the mountainous area which extends into New Hampshire in the north. The highland slopes down toward the coast. The principal highland city is Worcester. It is the second-largest city in Massachusetts. It is an industrial city with many factories. Farmers raise dairy cows and chickens and grow crops in the hills around Worcester.

Near Boston, the Massachusetts Turnpike meets another broad highway—Route 128. This highway curves in a large half-circle around Boston. Along it are many electronics plants and research laboratories. The electronics plants made much money during the 1960s, so Route 128 was nicknamed the "Golden Horseshoe."

Following Route 128, you will come to the coast. The Massachusetts coast is low and irregular. It is cut by many streams, dotted with small ponds, and lined with bays, peninsulas, and islands. The most

unusual peninsula is Cape Cod. It looks like an arm bent at the elbow and the wrist. Cape Cod is sandy and produces a few crops. The largest crop is cranberries. More than half the country's cranberries come from Cape Cod. Fishing villages and summer resorts also dot the peninsula where the beaches are excellent.

Winters are cold in Massachusetts. They bring heavy snows, especially in the western part of the state. Summers are mild. Ocean breezes help keep temperatures low near the coast. Winds blow from three directions. Cold, dry air sweeps in from Canada; warm, moist air flows north from the Gulf of Mexico; and cool, damp air comes from the North Atlantic. These winds make Massachusetts weather changeable.

History

Several Indian tribes lived in Massachusetts in the 1600s. One Indian village was called *Massachuset.* The name means "at big hills." (The hills were the Blue Hills south of Boston.) Englishmen used the village's name for the whole tribe, calling its members "Massachusetts." The bay near the tribe's lands was named Massachusetts Bay. This tribe was once a powerful one, but it was almost wiped out by disease in 1670.

In 1620, the English ship, the *Mayflower,* brought Pilgrims to

▶*Fine beaches washed by the Atlantic Ocean line the 192-mile-long Massachusetts coastline.*

Massachusetts. The Pilgrims were *Puritans*, a religious group who suffered persecution in England. They came to America to gain the freedom to follow their religious beliefs. They settled on the coast, on land that belonged to the Wampanoag tribe. These Indians were friendly. The Pilgrims named the new colony Plymouth, after an English seaport. Other Puritans soon arrived in Massachusetts. One of their leaders, John Winthrop, brought more than 900 settlers there in 1630. They established their colony north of Plymouth. It was named the Massachusetts Bay Colony. One of its towns was Boston. The Plymouth Colony and the Massachusetts Bay Colony were united in 1691. Fishing and trade made the colonists prosperous, but they were troubled by wars. They fought with the Indians, and helped the British fight the French colonists. Then, in 1775, the American Revolution began in Massachusetts. The first shots were fired at Concord and Lexington, a few miles west of Boston.

Boston became the country's chief trade center after the Revolution. Sailing ships called *clippers*, carrying rum and tobacco, traveled to Africa and Asia. They returned with rich silks, gold, tea, and spices. The state itself became a leader in the nation's industrial development.

The first American machine for spinning yarn was established at Beverly in 1787. The nation's first power loom (a machine for weaving yarn into cloth) was put to work at Waltham in 1814. Elias Howe invented the sewing machine in Cambridge in 1846. Another Massachusetts man, Lyman Blake, invented a stitching machine for making shoes in 1858. Many textile and shoe factories were established in the eastern part of the state. Whaling, too, was an important economic activity. Whalers brought barrels of whale oil back to the ports at New Bedford and Nantucket.

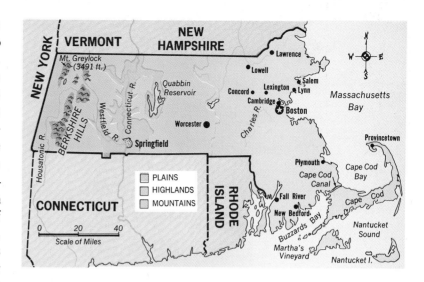

The movement against slavery was in progress at that time. Many of its leaders were men and women from Massachusetts. Frederick Douglass, who was born in slavery in Maryland, started his work against slavery in Massachusetts. More than a century later, in 1966, Massachusetts elected a black man, Edward W. Brooke, to the United States Senate.

Massachusetts also played an important role in America's educational development. The country's first secondary school was set up in Boston in 1635. Free public schools were opened in the state 12 years later. These were the first government-supported schools anywhere in the world. Harvard College, in Cambridge, was chartered in 1636, making it the nation's oldest college. Many other major American colleges, including Radcliffe College (part of Harvard) and the Massachusetts Institute of Technology (MIT), were founded in the state.

Some Massachusetts families moved westward in the 1800s. While they were leaving the state, new Americans were coming in. The Irish came first. They were followed by Italians, Portuguese, and Poles. French Canadians also came.

People at Work in Massachusetts
Massachusetts is no longer the leader in American manufacturing,

The "Sacred Cod," a wooden fish about five feet long, hangs in the Massachusetts State House. Its purpose is to remind the lawmakers who meet there of the importance of codfishing to the state in its early days.

▼ *The Old State House in Boston is one of many historic landmarks in Massachusetts. The building, dating back to 1748, has since been restored.*

▲ *The Fishermen's Memorial in Gloucester honors the fishermen of that city who were lost at sea.*

as it once was. Some textile and shoe manufacturers have moved their factories to southern states. Machinery of all kinds, but especially electronic machinery, is now the state's most important manufactured product. Tourism is far behind manufacturing in the amount of money it earns for the state. Agriculture follows tourism, and fishing follows agriculture. These three industries, however, are still very important. Tourists bring about one billion dollars into the state each year. Milk, chickens, eggs, cranberries, tobacco, hay, and apples are important money-earning farm products. The state's oldest industry, fishing, is still important. The 1969 catch by Massachusetts fishermen was larger than that from any other state on the East Coast.

ALSO READ: AMERICAN COLONIES; AMERICAN REVOLUTION; BOSTON; DOUGLASS, FREDERICK; FRENCH AND INDIAN WAR; INDUSTRIAL REVOLUTION; MAYFLOWER; MAYFLOWER COMPACT, PILGRIM SETTLERS; REVERE, PAUL; WESTWARD MOVEMENT; WITCHCRAFT.

MASSASOIT The settlement of Plymouth, founded by the Pilgrim Fathers in 1620, was on the land of the Wampanoag tribe of American Indians. The chief of the Wampanoag was named Massasoit. He ruled over a large area of the present-day states of Massachusetts and Rhode Island.

The Pilgrims wanted to live in peace with the Indians. Luckily, they met an Indian named Samoset who had learned to speak English from earlier English explorers. Samoset arranged a meeting between the Pilgrims and Massasoit.

If Massasoit had been unfriendly, he could have destroyed the little Pilgrim group. Instead, he came to Plymouth and sat down with Governor John Carver to work out a peace treaty. Massasoit promised not to attack the settlers and the Pilgrims agreed to live peacefully on his land. Later, when a neighboring tribe declared war against the colony, Massasoit fought on the side of the settlers.

The Indians gave the settlers valuable advice on planting crops and hunting for food, and the Pilgrims invited Massasoit to a "Thanksgiving" festival to celebrate their first harvest. Massasoit brought a large group of braves with him. Indians and settlers feasted on venison, roast duck, roast goose, clams, eels, bread, wild plums, and red and white wine.

ALSO READ: INDIANS, AMERICAN; PILGRIM SETTLERS; THANKSGIVING.

MATCH Matches are little things, and they may not seem very important—but what would people do without them? To light a candle or a camp fire, a person would have to spend about half an hour rubbing dry sticks or stone and metal together to produce friction and sparks for a fire. By lighting a match, he can produce fire in a fraction of a second.

The first matches were simple, thin strips of wood dipped in melted sulfur. They lit when a spark was applied, but they could not be struck. Chemical matches were invented in 1812. They were also thin strips of wood coated with sulfur, but they were tipped with potassi-

▼ *The meeting to sign a peace treaty between Massasoit and the Pilgrims.*

um chlorate and sugar. These caught fire when dipped in sulfuric acid. They were developed in France, and were called "instantaneous light boxes." The first striking matches were invented by a British druggist named John Walker in 1827. They were wooden sticks tipped with chemicals that lit when drawn through folded sandpaper.

Today, two different kinds of matches are used—safety matches and strike-anywhere matches. The tips of safety matches are coated with fire-producing chemicals. They will light only when they are rubbed on the specially prepared surface of a matchbox. The secret to safety matches is the phosphorus on the striking surface. When rubbed, this phosphorus gives off tiny sparks which light the tip of the match. The tips of strike-anywhere matches are also coated with fire-producing chemicals. They contain their own phosphorus, however, and can be struck against any rough surface. They are dangerous because they can light accidentally by rubbing together in the box or in a pocket.

Both types of matches are made in factories by machines. Wooden matches are cut from pieces of wood, dipped in chemicals, and packed in boxes. Paper matches are cut from long rolls of cardboard, dipped in chemicals, and stapled into place in matchbook covers. Nearly six billion matches are manufactured in the United States during each year.

Matches are dangerous, and you should never handle them unless an adult is present. When lighting a match, hold the flame end up so you do not burn your fingers. Be sure to close the matchbook cover before you strike a safety match, so that the other matches in the book will not catch fire. Never throw away a used match unless you are sure that the tip is cold and cannot possibly start another fire.

ALSO READ: FIRE, FIRE PREVENTION.

MATHEMATICS You and everyone else in the world use and depend on mathematics all the time. You could not buy a candy bar without counting your money. You could not solve a jigsaw puzzle or make a paper glider without deciding what shapes you need. There would be no buildings if carpenters, bricklayers, and other workmen did not understand shapes, sizes, and numbers. All these activities use mathematics.

History

Mathematics goes back thousands of years. When men first began to farm and to trade with each other, they needed some way of counting and making measurements. They needed to know how much grain they had harvested, or how much land they owned. They had to be able to figure out how many cows or hides a new plow was worth. People first counted on their fingers and toes, and this is probably how we got the number system based on ten numbers. "Eleven" really stands for "ten and one" or "one over ten." "Twelve" stands for "two over." "Twenty" stands for "two tens."

In keeping track of their business, all the ancient civilizations had marks or signs that were used to represent numbers. To do their figuring, many people used an instrument called an *abacus*. The number signs we use today are called *Arabic numbers*. These signs began in India. The Arabs learned them from the Indians, and then introduced them into Europe during the Middle Ages.

Geometry was first used when people needed to measure land surfaces. In ancient Egypt, the Nile River flooded every year. Farmers living along its banks had to find a way to remeasure their fields after the water went down. The ancient Babylonians had also figured out some accurate ways of measuring. The Greeks were the first to describe geometry in an orderly way.

▲*These combs of paper matches will be cut apart to make books of twenty matches each.*

Matches are so inexpensive that they are often given away by restaurants and other businesses. Ivar Krueger, the Swedish "Match King," made a fortune by manufacturing and selling almost all the world's matches in the early 1900s.

MATHEMATICS

▲ *René Descartes made important contributions to geometry and the study of equations.*

▼ *Blaise Pascal invented the first mechanical adding machine.*

▲ *Leonard Euler added to an understanding of algebra, geometry, and calculus.*

▼ *Bertrand Russell, who treated mathematics as a branch of philosophy.*

About 300 B.C., Euclid wrote *The Elements* in which he made geometry into a system of mathematical rules. The Greeks used geometry in surveying, navigation, architecture, and astronomy.

The Arabs first developed *algebra* —a special mathematical "shorthand" that helps describe a problem or give directions quickly and easily. European mathematicians, such as Blaise Pascal, René Descartes, Sir Isaac Newton, and G. W. von Leibnitz, developed and enlarged the rules of algebra and geometry into the sciences of trigonometry, analytic geometry, topology, and calculus. The most recent achievement in mathematics is the invention of the computer. A computer can instantly solve problems that would otherwise take months or even years to solve. With the aid of computers, new mathematical facts and techniques are constantly being discovered.

Mathematics from 1750 to the present time has been filled with thousands of new advances and new areas of study. Some of the great mathematicians were Karl F. Gauss, Leonard Euler, Pierre S. de Laplace, Georg Cantor, and Albert Einstein. In this century, very important work in mathematics has been done by Alfred North Whitehead and Bertrand Russell. Their goal was to organize and develop all the rest of mathematics by using *set theory*. They considered the shapes in geometry, the numbers in arithmetic, and the statements in algebra to be sets, or collections, of mathematical "objects." With their set theory, Whitehead and Russell greatly altered the old ideas about mathematics. Their work was so important that today, textbooks in schools are already using their ideas—calling it "new math." Perhaps you are studying it in school. New math is changing the way mathematics is taught and used from kindergarten up through college, and beyond.

The Basics of Mathematics

Mathematics is a *tool* that can help solve problems and lead to new developments in other fields, such as space flight, medicine, architecture, and so forth. The numerous branches of mathematics include so many ideas that you could spend your whole life studying and only learn a few of them. But all branches of mathematics, from simple arithmetic to complicated calculus, have some things in common.

ASSUMPTIONS. An assumption is a statement that is accepted as being true without proof. Mathematics tries to prove a statement true or false so as to have as few assumptions (or unproved statements) as possible. In mathematics, assumptions are usually called *axioms* or *postulates*. One way of telling the different branches of mathematics apart is by looking at the assumptions. The assumptions of geometry are about shapes, such as lines and circles. The assumptions of arithmetic are about numbers.

DEFINITIONS. A mathematician always wants to understand clearly what a word or symbol means. To do this, he never uses a word or symbol unless it has been clearly defined. Sometimes it is hard to define a mathematical term accurately. For example, the word "point" is very hard to define exactly. A large part of the mathematician's work is the forming of clear and exact definitions for the words and symbols of a problem he is trying to solve.

THEOREMS. A theorem is a mathematical statement that has been proved to be true. In arithmetic, a theorem would be $5 + 2 = 7$. This is a simple theorem, but it can be proved true using the definitions of arithmetic.

LOGIC. A mathematician proves a theorem to be true by using logic. Logic is a way of thinking so as to make as few errors as possible. Studying mathematics can teach a person to think logically about a problem. For example, you may mistakenly subtract instead of add in a problem like 55 + 22 = 77. If you got the answer 33, you know you would have to recheck your calculations. Logical thinking leads you to see that you cannot add one quantity (55) to another quantity (22) and get a result that is smaller than one of the numbers that you added.

WHAT IS MATHEMATICS? Mathematics is a field of study in which theorems are proved using assumptions, definitions, and logic. For this reason, mathematics is very important to the scientist. Over the years, many great scientists have also been mathematicians—Archimedes, Sir Isaac Newton, and Albert Einstein, for example. Mathematics can clarify a complicated scientific problem, and many new discoveries in mathematics have come from other sciences, such as rocketry and genetics.

Working with Mathematics

GEOMETRY. In measuring, the ancient Egyptians worked out a way to make lines meet properly at a corner. You can easily try their method yourself. Get a 12-foot string and tie a knot 3 feet from one end. Tie another knot 4 feet down the string from the first one. Draw a long line in the dirt to show where one edge of your "field" or one wall of your "building" will be. Put the string down on the line so that the first knot is at the end of the line. Use a heavy rock to hold that knot down. Then hold *both* ends of the string and pull them along the line until the short end is taut. Put the ends of both strings together and set them down on the line, keeping the short end taut. Get a rock to hold them. Finally, hold the second knot and walk away from the line (as if making an L shape) until the string is taut in both directions. The short end of the string will be along the line you drew in the dirt. The

part of the string between the two knots shows you where the second "wall" of your building will be. If you do this two more times, you will mark off all four "walls." The L-shaped angle that the string forms is called a *right angle*. It is a very useful angle, as you can see from looking at buildings, roads, furniture, and many other objects.

ALGEBRA. You can see how algebra works by comparing a problem done in both arithmetic and in algebra. *Problem*—A boy goes into a bakery and buys 2 brownies and 1 cookie and pays 26 cents. Another time he buys 3 brownies and 2 cookies and pays 44 cents. How much does 1 brownie cost? How much does 1 cookie cost?

Without algebra, you would have to solve it this way: The second time, the boy paid 18 cents more and got 1 more brownie and 1 more cookie. So 18 cents is the cost of a brownie plus a cookie. Two brownies and 1 cookie cost 26 cents. Subtract 18 cents (the cost of 1 brownie and 1 cookie) from 26 cents, and you get 8 cents (the cost of 1 brownie). Subtract the 8 cents from 18 cents (the cost of 1 brownie and 1 cookie), and you get 10 cents as the cost for 1 cookie.

Using algebra, the solution would be:

$$3b + 2c = 44$$
$$2b + c = 26$$
$$b + c = 18$$
$$2b + c = 26$$
$$b = 8$$
$$c = 10$$

Can you read it? The letter b stands

▲A good way to study geometry is to examine a geodesic dome, a structure made of interlocking geometric figures called polygons. Such a dome is very strong.

▼A basic knowledge of mathematics is needed for many other sciences. These physics students are using mathematics to solve a problem in class.

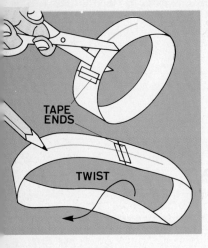

TAPE ENDS

TWIST

for the cost of a brownie, and the letter c for the cost of a cookie.

TOPOLOGY. You know that mathematics contains many ideas. The branch of mathematics called topology is the study of shapes and surfaces and how they change. Here is an interesting topological experiment you can try. Cut out two pieces of paper about 12 inches long and 2 inches wide. Paste the ends of one strip together. If you draw a line along the middle of the outside of this loop, you will come back to where you started. If you cut along the line with scissors, you will wind up with two separate loops.

Now take the second strip of paper, twist it once, and paste the ends together. Try drawing a pencil line on this loop just as you did the other. Your pencil will trace a line on both sides of the paper before you get back to your starting place. Which is the outside and which is the inside? This loop, called a *Moebius strip*, has only one side! The paper it was made from had two sides. What happens if you cut it along your line?

This may seem like a wonderful trick, but it is more than just a trick. It is another example of how mathematics works. Have you ever knotted two pieces of rope together? What makes the knot stay in place? This is the same kind of problem as that of the Moebius strip. You probably never stopped to think about how a simple knot works. But mathematicians think about it.

For further information on:

Mathematical Instruments, *see* ABACUS, CALCULATOR, COMPASS, COMPUTER, GRAPH, SCALE.

Mathematicians, *see* ARCHIMEDES; EINSTEIN, ALBERT; NEWTON, SIR ISAAC.

Study of Mathematics, *see* ALGEBRA, ANGLE, ARITHMETIC, CHANCE AND PROBABILITY, DECIMAL NUMBER, GEOMETRY, MEASUREMENT, NUMBER, PERCENTAGE, SET, STATISTICS, SYMMETRY, WEIGHT.

▼View of Tangiers Seen from a Window, *painted by the French artist Henri Matisse.*

MATISSE, HENRI (1869-1954)

One of the greatest artists of modern times was Henri Matisse, who was born in the French town of Le Cateau. He studied to be a lawyer before he turned to art, which he studied at the Academy of Fine Arts in Paris.

When Matisse began his career, the leading artists were Impressionists, who painted outdoors in daylight, avoiding marked design in their work. Matisse and a few other young painters began to paint using flat planes of brilliant colors. They also used bold designs in their paintings, in sharp contrast to the Impressionists. In 1906, the young painters (as a kind of jest) were given the name *Les Fauves*—the wild beasts—because of the wild colors they used.

Do you get a sudden joy out of picking up a paintbrush and paints and creating a picture on a flat piece of paper? That is how Matisse felt. He said that he was never so happy as when he had a paintbrush in his hand. Look at his painting, *View of Tangiers Seen from a Window.* In this happy scene you can almost feel his joy at painting the picture. He was in Tangiers in North Africa on a happy holiday with two artist friends. See the various tones of blue in the picture—the walls, the sky outside, the horizon. What a strong contrast with the blues the variety of yellow tones make! The lemon yellow rooftops in the distance almost sing out against the sky blue. Note where he has used bright hues in the foreground. As you know from mixing watercolor paints, yellow and blue make green. See how Matisse has mixed those two major colors together to make some green areas. There are no shadows shown anywhere. Matisse eliminated them from his scenes, as he did details. He rearranged nature to suit his paintings.

Someone asked Matisse's advice on how to be a successful painter.

He answered, "One must be a child all one's life." He felt that an artist must see with the fresh eyes of a child. He loved children's art and took a great interest in studying it. He also studied African sculpture and Persian painting.

ALSO READ: ART; ART HISTORY; IMPRESSIONISM; MINIATURE; PAINTING; VAN GOGH, VINCENT.

MATTER Look around you—everything you can see or touch is made of matter. This book is matter. So is a glass and the water in it, and the air you breathe. Matter is anything that has *volume* (takes up space). Scientists also say that matter has *mass*, which is the amount of matter in an object. The mass of an object always remains the same. The pull of the Earth on your body gives you weight, but weight can change. If you could fly to the moon and weigh yourself, you would discover that you weigh only one-sixth as much as you do on Earth. But your mass would still be the same.

All matter is made up of tiny particles called molecules. Molecules are made up of even smaller particles called atoms. And atoms are made up of even smaller particles —protons, neutrons, or electrons. These tiny particles fit together in more than 100 different ways to make the *chemical elements*. Every thing we know is made up of combinations of these elements.

Properties of Matter
These different combinations help us to tell one object from another. We can identify one object by describing it carefully. We say that all matter has properties. A *property* is what you can say about a thing to tell how it looks, feels, smells, tastes, or acts under certain conditions. For example, hardness is a property of stone, lightness is a property of hydrogen gas, and wetness is a property of water. Properties may be

divided into two kinds: *physical* properties and *chemical* properties.

PHYSICAL PROPERTIES. The properties that you can find by direct use of your senses, and by weighing and measuring, are physical properties. Color, shape, odor, roughness, smoothness, sweetness, and saltiness are physical properties. Elasticity (stretchiness or springiness) and tensile strength (how much force is needed to make a thing break) are physical properties that you measure. Another important physical property is *density*, the amount of matter in a unit of volume. Density is found by weighing and measuring. For example, find a rock the same size as a tennis ball. Which has the greater density? Another way of asking this question is, does the rock contain more matter than the ball?

CHEMICAL PROPERTIES. Changing the physical properties of a piece of matter does not change what the matter is made up of. If you cut a piece of wood in half, it is still wood. But if you burn the wood, you cause a chemical change. The matter is no longer wood—it is carbon and a gas which you cannot see. The way matter acts when it undergoes a chemical change is a chemical property of that kind of matter. For example, one chemical property of oxygen is its ability to combine with many metals to form compounds called oxides. Oxygen combines with iron. When this happens, a new substance, called iron oxide, or rust, appears.

▲ *Matter is all around you. Trees are organic or living matter. Mountains are inorganic or non-living matter. The sky, the boat, and the water illustrate the three states in which matter can exist—gas, solid, and liquid.*

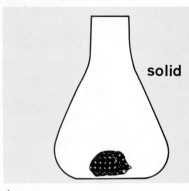 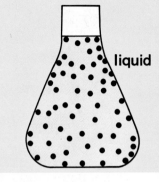 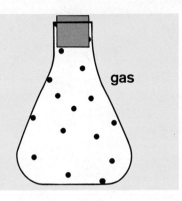

▲ *The three states of matter differ in the closeness of their molecules.*

States of Matter

Matter exists in only three forms, or *states—solid, liquid,* and *gas.* A *solid* has a definite volume and a definite shape. You cannot pour a rock into a glass because the rock's shape does not change. This is so because the molecules of a solid are packed closely together and hold each other in place.

A *liquid* has a definite volume but no definite shape. If you fill a glass with water, the water takes on the shape of the glass. If you pour the water into a bowl, the water takes on the shape of the bowl. The molecules of a liquid are farther apart than those of a solid and do not hold together with such great strength.

A *gas* has no definite shape or volume. The molecules of a gas move about rapidly and do not hold each other in place. When gas is pumped into a container, the molecules fly all over and the gas spreads through the whole container.

Blow up a balloon, but pinch the back half off so that no air can get into it. When the front half of the balloon is full of air, take your fingers away. Does the air stay in the front half? How do you explain this?

When we say that water is a liquid, we mean it is a liquid at room temperature. When water is heated, it turns into steam, a gas. When water is cooled, it turns into ice, a solid. Most gases can be cooled into liquids. Most solids can be melted into liquids. This is important because in all of these changes, energy (the ability to do work) is produced or used up. The relationship be-

tween matter and energy is a very close one.

ALSO READ: ATOM, CHEMISTRY, ELEMENT, ENERGY, GAS, LIQUID, PHYSICS, SOLID.

MAUNA LOA see HAWAII, VOLCANO.

MAURITANIA Mauritania is a republic on the western coast of Africa. It is a very large country, but it lies mainly in the Sahara Desert. The land can support only a small number of people. The country is bounded on the north and west by Spanish Sahara, on the northeast by Algeria, on the east by Mali, and on the south by Mali and Senegal. Part of its west coast reaches to the Atlantic Ocean. Nouakchott is the capital city. (See the map with the article on AFRICA.)

Mauritania has few sources of fresh water. There are some lakes, mainly in the northeast. The Sene-

▼ *The house of a poor family of Moors in Mauritania. This nation has few natural resources because most of it lies in the desert. It is difficult to grow crops.*

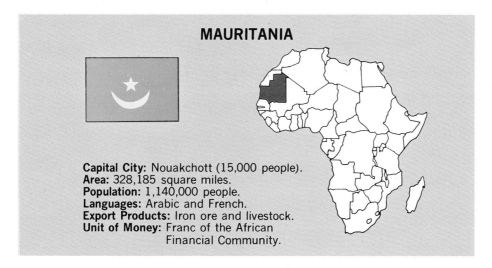

MAURITANIA

Capital City: Nouakchott (15,000 people).
Area: 328,185 square miles.
Population: 1,140,000 people.
Languages: Arabic and French.
Export Products: Iron ore and livestock.
Unit of Money: Franc of the African
Financial Community.

gal River runs to the sea along part of Mauritania's southern border. The river valley and the southern coastal areas are the only fertile regions of the country. Some farming is done there, but livestock raising is the chief industry in this hot, dry land. Iron and copper deposits have been discovered in the northwest, and these two minerals are now the country's major exports. Commercial fishing is a growing industry on the Atlantic coast.

The people who live in the desert areas are Moors. They live in tents, and move frequently to find water and grazing land for their animals. They eat mostly milk, grain, and dates. Camels are very important to them. They travel on these animals and use camel hair to make clothes and skins to make tents. Some black Africans live in the southern part of Mauritania near the Senegal River. They work as farmers and raise millet, corn, rice, and peanuts. French is the country's official language, but most of the people speak Arabic. Almost all Mauritanians follow the Islamic religion.

The area of Mauritania was once part of the powerful ancient African empires of Ghana and Mali from the 600s to the 1000s. These two empires were later overrun by Arab invaders during the 1000s. The Portuguese set up trading posts along the coast in the 1400s, and the region gradually became a center for the slave trade. The territory came under French control in 1903. Mauritania won its independence in November, 1960. It is now governed by a president and an elected assembly.

ALSO READ: AFRICA, CAMEL, DESERT, ISLAM, NOMAD, SAHARA DESERT.

MAURITIUS   The independent nation of Mauritius is on a small island of the same name in the Indian Ocean. It lies about 500 miles east of the island of Madagascar (Malagasy Republic).

Mauritius is thought to be the peak of an ancient volcano. Low mountains rise from the coast to a flat plateau in the center of the island. The capital city, Port Louis, is on the northwest coast. The temperature in Mauritius stays mainly between 70 and 80 degrees. Rainfall is very heavy in the highlands, and the island is often whipped by storms from the sea.

Mauritius is one of the most

▼ *A view of mountainous terrain in Mauritius.*

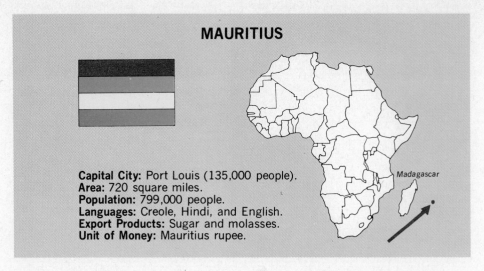

MAURITIUS

Capital City: Port Louis (135,000 people).
Area: 720 square miles.
Population: 799,000 people.
Languages: Creole, Hindi, and English.
Export Products: Sugar and molasses.
Unit of Money: Mauritius rupee.

Madagascar

densely populated areas in the world. Most of the Mauritians are descended from settlers from India. Africans, Chinese, and people of mixed descent also live there. Most of the people are employed in the island's sugar industry. Sugar cane fields cover much of the island, and sugar is the only major export. The sugar industry, however, is not bringing enough wealth to support the growing population of Mauritius. The government is encouraging new industries, including tourism.

Mauritius was visited by the Portuguese in the 1500s. It was later settled by the French, who set up trading posts and plantations. The British captured the island in the early 1800s, and established the colony of Mauritius. They brought many people from India to the island to work on the sugar plantations. Mauritius became independent in March, 1968. It is now governed by a prime minister and a national assembly elected by the people. Mauritius is a member of the Commonwealth of Nations, and the head official of state is a governor-general who represents the queen.
ALSO READ: COMMONWEALTH OF NATIONS.

▼*Matthew Maury, American naval officer.*

MAURY, MATTHEW (1806–1873)
From the study of old ships' *logs*, or records, Matthew Fontaine Maury put together a series of ocean winds and currents charts in the 1800s.

These charts helped advance the science of marine navigation.

Maury was an American naval officer and oceanographer. He was born near Fredericksburg, Virginia, and educated at Harpeth Academy in Tennessee. He entered the U.S. Navy in 1825, but left sea duty in 1839 when he was injured in an accident. In 1842, he became superintendent of the U.S. Depot of Charts and Instruments and of the U.S. Naval Observatory in Washington, D.C. During the next 19 years, he studied both meteorology and oceanography. He wrote *The Physical Geography of the Sea*, the first textbook of oceanography in modern times.

In his charts showing the bottom of the Atlantic Ocean between the United States and Europe, Maury showed that it was possible to lay cables under the sea. Maury was a Navy commander when the Civil War began. He resigned to serve the Confederacy as a diplomat in England. After the war, he was professor of meteorology at the Virginia Military Institute until his death.
ALSO READ: ATLANTIC OCEAN, GULF STREAM, INDIAN OCEAN, OCEAN, PACIFIC OCEAN, TIDE.

MAY May is the fifth month of the year and has 31 days. May was the third month of the ancient Roman calendar. May's name probably comes from *Maia*, Roman goddess of spring. During May, the weather is usually delightfully mild, birds are nesting, and baby animals are being born. Flowers burst into bloom, from the blossoms of fruit trees to the shyest of violets hiding under the brown leaves of last fall.

In most northern parts of the world, May is the last full month of spring. However, the lands south of the equator are entering the early days of winter. The first day of May, called May Day, has been celebrated in northern lands since ancient times. On the first of May, the Romans honored the goddesses Maia and Flora (goddess of flowers). In England on May Day, boys and girls used to go out very early to gather armfuls of "mayflowers," or spring blossoms. With bright ribbons, they would wind these blossoms onto a Maypole as they danced around it. Today in the United States, children often make little baskets of paper, fill them with candy and flowers, and leave them at the doors of friends. May's flower is the lily of the valley, and the birthstone of the month is the green emerald.

ALSO READ: CALENDAR, MONTH, SEASON.

MAYA The Maya Indians lived on the Yucatan Peninsula in what is now southern Mexico, northern British Honduras, and Guatemala. The greatest period of Mayan civilization lasted from about 300 A.D. to about 900 A.D. After the Spaniards conquered Mexico in the 1500s, much of the traditional Mayan culture was destroyed.

The Maya were farmers. Their crops included *maize* (corn), beans, squash, avocados, chili peppers, and cacao beans which they made into a chocolate drink. Mayan harvests were large, and the people had food to spare. Good harvests and extra food helped make the Maya a wealthy and powerful people. They created fine architecture, sculpture, paintings, ceramics, jade engravings,

DATES OF SPECIAL EVENTS IN MAY

1 • May Day. An ancient festival celebrated in many countries. Children dance around the Maypole and make baskets of flowers to hang on the doors of their friends' homes.
• Labor Day in some countries of Europe and in the Soviet Union.
• Law Day in the United States. Lawyers and judges commemorate the rule of government by law.
• Act of Union signed joining England, Scotland, and Wales to form Great Britain (1707).
5 • Christopher Columbus discovered Jamaica (1494).
• Alan Shepard became the first American in space (1961).
6 • Manhattan Island was bought from the Indians for 24 dollars (1626).
7 • A German submarine sank the English ship *Lusitania*, killing many Americans aboard. The incident influenced the United States in its decision to enter World War I (1915).
8 • President Harry S. Truman was born (1884).
• V-E Day marked Allied victory in World War II (1945).
9 • John Brown, anti-slavery leader, was born (1800).
• Richard E. Byrd completed the first flight over the North Pole (1926).
10 • Second Continental Congress met in Philadelphia (1775).
• First transcontinental railroad in the United States completed at Promontory, Utah (1869).
12 • Florence Nightingale, English nurse, was born (1820).
13 • United States declared war on Mexico (1846).
14 • First permanent English settlement in the American colonies was set up in Jamestown, Virginia (1607).
• Israel became an independent nation (1948).
• Lewis and Clark expedition started from St. Louis, Missouri (1804).
15 • United States began first regular air mail service (1918).
16 • Oscar awards to people in the movie industry were first given (1929).
17 • The U.S. Supreme Court ruled that racial segregation in the public schools was unconstitutional (1954).
20 • Homestead Act went into effect, providing free land to people willing to farm it. This encouraged the settlement of the west (1862).
• Amelia Earhart became the first woman to fly solo across the Atlantic (1932).
21 • American Red Cross founded by Clara Barton (1881).
• Charles Lindbergh finished the first nonstop solo flight across the Atlantic (1927).
22 • Sir Arthur Conan Doyle, author of the Sherlock Holmes stories, was born (1859).
24 • Queen Victoria of England was born (1819).
• Commonwealth Day celebrated in the Commonwealth of Nations.
25 • Constitutional Convention opened in Philadelphia (1787).
29 • President John F. Kennedy was born (1917).
• Patrick Henry, American patriot, was born (1736).
• Edmund Hillary became the first man to reach to top of Mount Everest, highest mountain in the world (1953).
30 • Joan of Arc, French heroine and saint, was burned at the stake (1431).
• Memorial Day (now celebrated on the last Monday in May).
31 • Walt Whitman, American poet, was born (1819).
(The second Sunday in May is celebrated as Mother's Day.)

woven fabrics, and featherwork. The Maya had very little metal, so their tools were made from stone, wood, bone, or *obsidian* (a kind of volcanic glass).

The Maya built great cities in the jungles. But most of the people lived

▲*The Mayan Indians built fine pyramids with steps leading to the summit of the structures. This one is still standing at Tikal, Guatemala.*

▼*A modeled head of a Mayan Indian made of stucco. It was found in Palenque, Mexico.*

A baby boy was born on the *Mayflower* during the voyage across the Atlantic. The baby was named Oceanus, for the waters the ship sailed on.

in small villages, and the cities were used mainly for religious ceremonies. The most important building in a Mayan city was a huge pyramid. From the top of the pyramid, Mayan priests led the people in their worship of the gods. People from the villages came to the city for these religious ceremonies, the Mayan noblemen wearing long robes and tall headdresses of feathers and skins.

The greatest Mayan skills were in mathematics and astronomy. They created a calendar almost as exact as the one we use today. The Maya invented the idea of zero and gave it a symbol. They also figured out almost the exact time it takes for the planet Venus to make one orbit around the sun. They wrote down the results of their scientific experiments in a form of picture writing. The Maya were great scientists, but they never invented the wheel.

Descendants of the Maya still live in the Yucatan Peninsula. Some of them closely resemble the statues of the ancient Maya. One group, called the Lacandon Indians, still worships the ancient gods and speaks the ancient language of the Maya.

ALSO READ: ARCHITECTURE; ART; ASTRONOMY; BRITISH HONDURAS; CALENDAR; CENTRAL AMERICA; CORN; GUATEMALA; INDIAN ART, AMERICAN; INDIANS, AMERICAN; MATHEMATICS; MEXICO; PICTURE WRITING; PYRAMID.

MAYFLOWER   A small ship called the *Mayflower* set sail from Plymouth, England, on September 16, 1620. On board were more than 100 passengers. Most of them were Puritans, who had been persecuted for their religious beliefs in England. The Pilgrims, as these people came to be called, had borrowed money from a group of English merchants to cross the Atlantic Ocean. They planned to start a settlement in Virginia Colony, in America, but during the voyage storms blew their crowded little vessel off course.

After sailing for more than two

▲*The* Mayflower *on the high seas of the Atlantic Ocean heads for a strange destination in the New World of America.*

months, the *Mayflower* finally reached land near what is now Provincetown, on Cape Cod. This part of the American coast, called New England, had been explored several years earlier by an Englishman named Captain John Smith. The Pilgrims followed Smith's maps and sailed across Cape Cod Bay to the mainland coast of Massachusetts. There, they founded the colony of Plymouth, in December, 1620. Most of the passengers had suffered terribly from the long voyage. Those who were too sick to be moved stayed on the *Mayflower*, which was anchored in Plymouth Harbor for the winter. The ship sailed back to England the following April.

The *Mayflower* had been a cargo ship and had to be refitted to handle the Pilgrim passengers. It had three masts and a double deck. High wooden structures containing cabins were built above each end of the deck. No one knows for certain what happened to the original *Mayflower* after it returned to England. A ship, resembling the *Mayflower* as closely as possible, was recently built in Britain. This ship, Mayflower II, sailed across the Atlantic in 1957 to commemorate the

Pilgrims' voyage. It is now anchored in Plymouth Harbor.

ALSO READ: MAYFLOWER COMPACT, PILGRIM SETTLERS, PURITAN.

MAYFLOWER COMPACT The agreement known as the "Mayflower Compact" was drawn up by the Pilgrim settlers on their ship, the *Mayflower*. The Pilgrims had received a charter from the English government granting them the right to settle in Virginia. But the first land they sighted in America was Cape Cod. They had not received permission from the government to settle that far north. But by that time, winter had started. The weather was too cold for them to continue their voyage, so they knew they had to start their settlement close by.

Some of the passengers on the ship decided that, because they had no charter for this settlement, they would not be obliged to obey any laws. They boasted that they "would use their own liberty" to do whatever they pleased. But the Pilgrim leaders realized that rules would be needed if the entire company were to live safely in the new land. They drew up an agreement which they read to the passengers at a meeting in the ship's cabin on November 11, 1620.

The Mayflower Compact stated that the settlers would make and obey such "just and equal laws," as might be needed for the "general good of the colony." Most of the men on board signed the agreement. The compact was the first written statement that a group of people intended to govern themselves, in what became the United States.

ALSO READ: MAYFLOWER, PILGRIM SETTLERS.

MAZE A maze is a complicated series of winding pathways. "Labyrinth" is another word for a maze. It is not hard to get inside a maze, but it is difficult to find your way out.

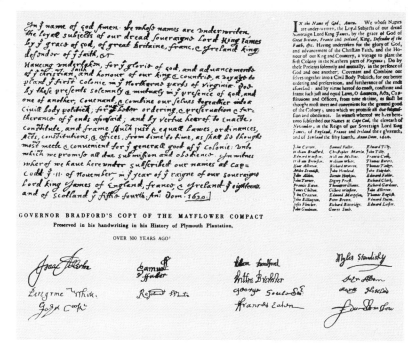

GOVERNOR BRADFORD'S COPY OF THE MAYFLOWER COMPACT
Preserved in his handwriting in his History of Plymouth Plantation,
OVER 300 YEARS AGO!

▲ *The Mayflower Compact. On the left is a copy written by John Bradford with the signatures of the men who signed it below. On the right is a printed version.*

Our word "amaze" comes from the same Latin word as "maze." Maze is a word that can be used to describe any confusing network of passages. A group of puzzling paths in a wilderness can be called a maze. A number of connected, winding streams may be referred to as a maze of waterways.

One of the most famous mazes was a legendary labyrinth on the island of Crete. At the center of this labyrinth lived the Minotaur, a monster with a bull's head and a man's body. King Minos of Crete had imprisoned the Minotaur in the labyrinth. Daedalus, the man who built the labyrinth, made it so complicated that the Minotaur was never able to find its way out.

In England, mazes consisting of paths walled by yew or holly hedges have been built in gardens. People unfamiliar with the maze have a hard time finding their way out. One of the finest mazes in existence is in the garden at Hampton Court Palace, in London.

Scientists sometimes use mazes in research. They run laboratory rats through mazes to test their learning ability. Many children's magazines contain mazes to be traced with a pencil.

▼*Hedges form the walls of this maze. Bushes with small close leaves keep people from seeing through to the next lane.*

▲An enthusiastic crowd watches an early demonstration of the McCormick reaper.

▲Cyrus McCormick, inventor of the reaper.

McCORMICK, CYRUS (1809-1884) Cyrus McCormick invented the most important farm machine, the *reaper*. It looked like a paddlewheel hung out over one end of a horse-drawn wagon. The revolving wheel *reaped* (gathered) a harvest of ripe grain much faster than the grain could be mowed down by hand with a scythe or sickle. Farmers could then take care of many acres of grain instead of only enough for their own families.

The inventor was born in Walnut Grove, Virginia. He was the son of Robert McCormick, a farmer and also an inventor. In 1831, at the age of 22, Cyrus McCormick developed the reaper. It successfully harvested his father's wheat crop that year. But father and son experimented for another three years before they sold any of the machines.

In 1847, McCormick decided that his reaper should be manufactured in Chicago, the young Illinois city that was becoming a shipping center for wheat and other grain crops from prairie farms. He had a hard struggle starting his company, because other reaping machines had been invented. But the McCormick reaper became the most popular, and McCormick became one of the wealthiest men in the West.

The *combine,* which automatically harvests, threshes, and bags grain crops, eventually replaced the reaper. McCormick's firm merged with others to create the International Harvester Company.

When McCormick was 70 years old, he was made a member of the French Academy of Science.

ALSO READ: AGRICULTURE, FARM MACHINERY.

McKINLEY, WILLIAM (1843-1901) William McKinley was President of the United States at a time when great changes were taking place in the nation. American business was growing rapidly. At the same time, people were beginning to demand that the terrible working conditions of workers and laborers be improved. After the Spanish-American War, the nation gained possession of territory overseas, and began to grow into an important world power.

President McKinley, who was known as "the friend of big business," had started life as a poor boy in northeastern Ohio. His father, an iron worker, was ambitious for his children. William attended Allegheny College for one year, but he became ill and was forced to leave. He was teaching in a school when the Civil War began. He joined the Union Army as a private and rose to the rank of major, after taking part in several battles. Following the war, he studied law and opened a law office in Canton, Ohio. His fellow citizens, impressed by his charm and kindly manner, elected him to the United States House of Representatives when he was only 33 years old.

While serving in Congress (1877–1883 and 1885–1891), McKinley suggested certain laws which placed a high protective tariff, or tax, on a number of articles imported from other countries. The purpose was to make those articles cost so much that American industries would be protected from competition. American manufacturers and merchants could then

TWENTY-FIFTH PRESIDENT   MARCH 4, 1897—SEPTEMBER 14, 1901

WILLIAM McKINLEY

Born: January 29, 1843, Niles, Ohio
Parents: William and Nancy Campbell Allison McKinley
Education: Allegheny College, Meadville, Pennsylvania
Religion: Methodist
Occupation: Lawyer
Political Party: Republican
State represented: Ohio
Married: 1871 to Ida Saxton (1847–1907)
Children: 2 daughters (died in childhood)
Died: September 14, 1901, Buffalo, New York
Buried: Canton, Ohio

charge more for products made in the United States. The McKinley Tariff Act (1890) was the highest ever passed by Congress up to that time. The act was very popular with wealthy business leaders. William McKinley was elected governor of Ohio in 1891. In 1896, he was elected twenty-fifth President of the United States and was inaugurated the following year.

McKinley had not wanted to involve the United States in a war with Spain. But in 1898, when the Spanish blew up and sank the U.S. battleship *Maine*, docked at the port in Havana, Cuba, war broke out. In the peace treaty, the Spanish islands of Puerto Rico, in the Atlantic Ocean, and Guam, in the Pacific, were given to the United States. The Spaniards had also been defeated by American naval forces in the Philippine Islands, then owned by Spain. The American government paid the Spanish government 20 million dollars for the Philippines. In the same year, the United States seized possession of the island of Hawaii. McKinley was re-elected in 1900.

In 1901, a Pan-American Exposition was held in Buffalo, New York, to celebrate 100 years of progress in North and South America. William McKinley, in a speech on President's Day (September 5), seemed to have changed some of his ideas about protective tariffs. A country

that expected to sell to other countries, he said, also must buy from them. "No nation," he added, "can be indifferent to any other." At a reception the following day, an *anarchist*—a man who believed that no form of government should exist—shot the President. Eight days later, William McKinley died.

ALSO READ: HAWAII, INTERNATIONAL TRADE, PHILIPPINES, SPANISH-AMERICAN WAR.

◀ *President McKinley* (third man on the right from the seated figure) *watches the signing of a preliminary agreement to end the Spanish-American War in August, 1898.*

MEAL PLANNING Most Americans eat three meals a day and more than one thousand meals a year. It is easy to forget that something as ordinary as a good meal takes planning. *Dietitians* are specialists trained to plan meals for hotels, hospitals, and schools. They also plan menus for people with special health problems.

Everyone needs to know how to plan meals that are healthful and appetizing. The first requirement of meal planning is good nutrition. Your daily diet should include all

▲ *A well-planned meal can be an enjoyable family occasion. It should appeal to the appetite* (above) *and give the important nutrients* (right).

▼ *Calipers are an instrument that can be adjusted to measure thickness as well as length. This scientist is using calipers to measure an ancient skull.*

the foods necessary to good health. One daily food requirement is to eat an orange or other citrus fruit, which provides Vitamin C. You should have one serving (at least) of meat and an egg to provide the protein you need. Your daily diet should also include a green, leafy vegetable, a yellow vegetable, two or more glasses of milk, and two or three slices of bread or other cereal products. All these items provide necessary vitamins and minerals. Try to avoid a lot of sweet desserts and bread made from bleached flour. These foods are not very nutritious. Natural sweets, such as fruit, and whole-wheat bread are much more nutritious.

A good meal planner serves foods rich in vitamins and minerals at every meal. This is not difficult, because Vitamins A, B, and C are found in many good foods. The meal planner also remembers to serve foods that contain iron, the one mineral our bodies cannot store. Spinach (and many other vegetables) and beef liver are rich in iron.

A meal should also look good and tempt the appetite. A dinner of mashed potatoes, cauliflower, and white fish is not appealing to the eye because it lacks color. A potato baked in its brown skin, yellow carrots, and a lemon or parsley garnish for the fish would make a more interesting, colorful meal. Meals are more tempting when each food is served at the proper temperature. Different tastes and textures often make a meal appetizing. Crusty rolls and a crisp salad go well with

soft food, such as an omelet or spaghetti. Spices and herbs provide a variety of tastes in food. Fruit slices and parsley also add color and contrast. A well-planned meal is even more tempting when it is served at an attractive table.

ALSO READ: CITRUS FRUIT, COOKING, DAIRY PRODUCTS, FOOD PROCESSING, FRUIT, MEAT, NUTRITION, SPICES AND HERBS, VEGETABLES, VITAMINS AND MINERALS.

MEASLES see CHILDHOOD DISEASES.

MEASUREMENT Measurement is counting the *units of measure* in whatever you are measuring. Your height is a measurement of distance (from the soles of your feet to the top of your head) in units of feet and inches. Your weight is measured in units of pounds and ounces.

The idea of using units of measure is very old. Units of money, distance, weight, and time were used by very ancient civilizations. These units began in various ways. In England, an *inch* was measured as the length of three barley grains. A *foot* was the length of the king's foot. But some barley grains and some kings' feet were longer than others. To solve this problem, *standard units* were developed. A standard unit is always the same and does not vary. The Bureau of Weights and Measures is the U.S. government agency that makes sure all units of measure used in the United States are exact. The Bureau keeps extremely accurate units of measure with which scientists and manufacturers can check their measuring instruments.

SOME COMMON MEASUREMENTS

Units of Length

Land Measures

12 inches	=	1 foot
3 feet	=	1 yard
5½ yards	=	rod
40 rods	=	1 furlong
8 furlongs	=	1 mile
1 mile	=	5,280 feet

Mariner's Measures

6 feet	=	1 fathom
120 fathoms	=	1 cable's length
6080.20 feet	=	1 nautical mile
1 nautical mile an hour	=	1 knot

Units of Capacity

16 fluid ounces	=	1 pint
2 pints	=	1 quart
4 quarts	=	1 gallon

Units of Weight

16 ounces	=	1 pound
100 pounds	=	1 hundredweight
2000 pounds	=	1 (short) ton

Units of Area

144 square inches	=	1 square foot
9 square feet	=	1 square yard
30¼ square yards	=	1 square rod
160 square rods	=	1 acre
640 acres	=	1 square mile

Units of Volume

1,728	cubic inches	=	cubic foot
27	cubic feet	=	cubic yard
231	cubic inches	=	gallon
2,150.42	cubic inches	=	bushel

Wood Measures

144 cubic inches	=	1 board foot (1 ft. × 1 ft. × 1 in.)
16 cubic feet	=	1 cord foot
8 cord feet	=	1 cord

U.S. System of Weights and Measures

Measurement is done in units. The same thing may be measured in more than one kind of unit. Your height, for example, can be measured in either feet or inches, your weight in pounds or ounces.

DISTANCE. These units are the U.S. measurements for distance.

———————— = 1 inch

1 foot = 12 inches
1 yard = 3 feet = 36 inches
1 mile = 1,760 yards = 5,280 feet

Other units are used for extremely large or small distances. *Angstrom units* measure distances within an atom. It would take more than 250 million angstrom units to make an inch. For very large distances, such as between objects in outer space, *light-years* are used. A light-year is the distance light travels in a year —about six trillion miles!

A ruler or yard stick is the instrument most often used to measure short distances. Another instrument for measuring distance is the *odometer* in a car that keeps track of the number of miles the car has traveled. Things that cannot be easily measured with an instrument can be calculated by using mathematics. The Greek mathematician, Eratosthenes (276–196 B.C.), was able to measure the distance around the Earth by using knowledge of geometry and astronomy.

AREA. These units are the U.S. measurements for area.

1 square inch = the area of a square that measures 1 inch on each side.
1 square foot = 144 square inches, the area of a square that measures 1 foot on each side.
1 square yard = 9 square feet, the area of a square that measures 1 yard on each side.
1 acre = 43,560 square feet

Area is measured according to the number of squares of a certain size that will fit into the area being measured. You can find the area of any rectangle by multiplying the width times the length.

VOLUME. These units are the U.S. measurements for volume. Volume is the quantity or amount that will fit in a container of a certain size.

1 cubic inch = the volume of a cube that measures 1 inch on each edge.
1 cubic foot = 1,728 cubic inches, the volume of a cube that measures 1 foot on each edge.

The volume of a liquid is measured differently from the volume of a non-liquid, such as grain.

Liquid:
16 fluid ounces = 1 pint
1 quart = 2 pints
1 gallon = 4 quarts

Dry:
1 peck = 538 cubic inches
1 bushel = 4 pecks

Volume is measured by filling up a container of the right size, or by using mathematics for huge measurements. The *cup*, *tablespoon*, and *teaspoon* are volume measurements used in cooking.

▲A speedometer is an instrument that measures speed, usually in terms of the number of miles traveled an hour.

WEIGHT. These units are the U.S. measurements for weight.

1 pound = about the weight of a pint of water
16 ounces = 1 pound
1 ton = 2,000 pounds

The system of weight using pounds, ounces, and tons is called the avoirdupois system. A unit of weight called the karat is used in weighing gems and gold.

TIME. Time is one of the first things you learned to measure.

60 seconds = 1 minute
60 minutes = 1 hour
24 hours = 1 day
365¼ days = 1 year, the time the Earth takes to travel around the sun.

Time is measured by the rotation of the Earth on its axis. A month originally meant the time between two full moons.

The Metric System

All units in the metric system are based on a unit called a meter. A meter is one ten-millionth of the distance on the Earth's surface from the North Pole to the equator. This meter length was marked on a platinum rod. The rod was located in Paris, France, and housed in a chamber at a constant temperature and pressure to keep the rod from expanding or contracting. Since

1960, the meter has been measured according to the wave length given off by the element krypton.

The meter is divided into equal parts divisible by ten. The 100 parts of a meter are called centimeters. The 1,000 parts of a meter are called millimeters. A kilometer equals 1,000 meters. The unit for weight in the metric system is the gram. A kilogram, the most common metric unit of weight, is 1,000 grams. The unit for volume in the metric system is the liter.

As you can see, all the metric units are related to each other mathematically. This is an important advantage. Since all the metric units are base ten (multiples or divisions of ten) they fit easily into the decimal system of numbers.

Distance, area, volume, weight, and time are among the usual quantities that are measured. However, there are units and instruments for measuring such things as light, sound, electricity, intelligence, speed, temperature, rainfall, heartbeat, and even brain waves. One of the most important parts of scientific work is accurate measurement. New and more precise measuring instruments are constantly being developed.

ALSO READ: DECIMAL NUMBER, MATHEMATICS, SCALE, SCIENCE, TIME, WEIGHT.

MEAT For most Americans, meat is the main part of a meal. The United States produces over one-fourth of the world's meat, and American families spend about one-fourth of their food budgets on meat.

The word "meat" refers mainly to the edible parts of cattle, sheep, and hogs. The word is also often used for poultry, venison (deer), and game (wild animals). The edible parts of an animal are its muscle tissue and certain internal organs (called variety meats), such as the liver, kidney, brain, and heart. Many people also eat sweetbreads (the thymus gland

Measurements in the Metric and English Systems

Metric to English	English to Metric
Units of Length	
1 centimeter = .39 inches	1 inch = 2.54 centimeters
1 meter = 1.09 yards	1 yard = .91 meters
1 kilometer = .62 miles	1 mile = 1.61 kilometers
Units of Weight	
1 centigram = .15 grains	1 ounce = 28.35 grams
1 gram = .04 ounces	1 pound = .45 kilograms
1 kilogram = 2.20 pounds	1 hundredweight = 45.36 kilograms
Units of Capacity (liquid measures)	
1 centiliter = .34 ounces	1 pint = .47 liters
1 liter = 1.06 quarts	1 quart = .95 liters
1 kiloliter = 264.25 gallons	1 gallon = 3.79 liters

of lambs and calves) and tripe (the stomach of a cow). *Beef* comes from full-grown cattle—steers, oxen, cows, and bulls. *Veal* is the meat of calves (young cattle). *Pork* comes from hogs. *Lamb* meat comes from young sheep, while *mutton* comes from adult sheep.

Meat is a highly nutritious food. It contains large quantities of protein, which is necessary for growth and good health. The proteins in meat are made up of amino acids, which the body uses in almost everything it does. Protein also satisfies your appetite longer than sugars and carbohydrates. Meat contains the B vitamins, such as niacin, and such vital minerals as iron, phosphorus, and potassium. Some meats, especially liver, also contain vitamins A and D. Liver is particularly rich in iron and Vitamin B_{12}. These two substances prevent anemia, a condition in which the body produces too few red blood cells.

Meat must be refrigerated to prevent it from spoiling. It is shipped from the stockyards to grocery stores on refrigerated trucks and railroad cars. Steaks and chops will stay fresh in your refrigerator for two or three days without freezing. Ground meat must be frozen if it is not cooked within 24 hours. Frozen meat should be cooked as soon as it thaws, to prevent bacteria in the meat from spoiling it. Some meats, such as ham and bacon, are preserved through a smoking, salting, or aging process. These meats will stay fresh in refrigeration (without being frozen) longer than untreated meats. Processed meats, such as hot dogs and lunchmeat, have been cooked before you buy them. They also will stay fresh in refrigeration for at least a week. Any cut of meat for sale in a market should carry the purple stamp showing government inspection and grading. Beef is bright red when it is fresh. Fresh veal, pork, and lamb are pale pink. Fresh mutton is dark red. Any dis-

▲ *A young boy cuts a tender, juicy beefsteak. Beef is America's favorite meat.*

coloration in the meat indicates that it is beginning to spoil.

Dry heat or *moist heat* can be used for cooking meat. Tender cuts, such as steaks and rib roasts, can be cooked with dry heat methods, such as broiling or roasting in the oven. Many less expensive cuts, such as chuck roasts, would be too tough if they were cooked by dry heat. These cuts should be steamed, simmered, braised, or baked in a covered container that holds in moisture. Moist heat breaks down the fat and tough connective tissues in meat, making the meat easier to cut and chew. Pot roast is a fairly inexpensive cut of beef which is likely to be tough. It must be stewed slowly to increase its tenderness.

Meat Packing

The meat-packing industry handles the slaughter of cattle, sheep, and hogs; prepares the carcasses (bodies) for sale; and ships the meat to market. The words "meat packing" at one time referred only to the business of packing pork in barrels of salt water to preserve it, but they have come to include all the other parts of the industry.

Farmers and ranchers sell their livestock directly to meat packers or to dealers who then sell the animals to packers. Many animals are put in feeding lots for *finishing*, or fattening, before they go to the meat

▼ *All meat, such as this chicken, is examined and graded by government inspectors before being marketed.*

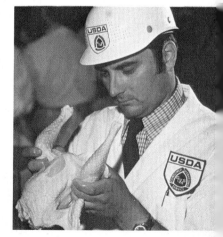

▲Sausage is a popular food which may be made with different kinds of meat. The meat in most sausage is wrapped in a long round casing.

▼A meat cutter sawing huge chunks of pork, a meat that comes from pigs (below). A butcher ties up a piece of meat into a convenient form for roasting (right).

packers. At the packing plant, the animals are first put into pens. They are then stunned (hit on the head) or electrically shocked so that they cannot feel pain. The unconscious animals are put onto an assembly line and slaughtered. Each carcass is hung upside down so that the blood will drain out. After the hog carcasses are softened with hot water, scraping machines remove the hair. The hides on all the animals are stripped off, and the carcasses are split into two pieces (called *sides*) down the backbone. After the internal organs are removed, the sides are washed, inspected, and refrigerated. Then the sides are divided into smaller pieces, called *cuts* of meat. The cuts (and sometimes whole sides) are shipped out in refrigerated trucks or railroad cars.

Most pork is preserved, instead of being sold fresh. Brine (very salty water) is injected into the meat to *cure* it. (The earlier method of curing—packing meat in barrels of brine—took much longer.) Beef that has been treated with brine is called *corned beef*. Many pork cuts, such as ham and bacon, are then *smoked* by being hung in rooms filled with the smoke of certain kinds of wood, such as hickory. Curing and smoking preserve meat and give it a special flavor. Some meats, including beef, are often aged before they are sold.

Trimmings and certain inexpensive cuts of meat are used to make hamburger and sausage. Hamburger, ground chuck, and ground sirloin are all ground-up pieces of beef. Sausage is made from ground pork, beef, and veal, with spices added. Some kinds of sausage contain only

beef or only pork. For example, some brands of hot dogs contain only beef (plus spices, preservatives, and food coloring). Many kinds of sausages are cured and smoked for flavor. Some sausages, such as hot dogs, are completely cooked before they are sold. Sausages are shaped by being put into a skin—either a man-made casing or cleaned animal intestines. The skins are often removed before the sausages are sold.

The U.S. Department of Agriculture inspects all meat that is shipped from one state to another and to and from foreign countries. The meat is inspected to see that it is clean and free from disease. A federal law requires that animals be slaughtered painlessly. Meat that people will eat is also graded by federal inspectors. *Prime*, *choice*, and *good* are the three highest grades.

Other products of meat packing are also useful. Animal fat is used in making lard, soap, candles, plastic, ointments, and cosmetics, among many other things. Hides are used to make shoes, luggage, footballs, and basketballs. Horns, hoofs, and bones are used to make buttons, umbrella handles, gelatin, and bone china. Blood and certain organs and glands are used in making medicines. Insulin (produced by the pancreas) is used to treat people with diabetes. Liver extract is used to treat anemia. Cortisone (produced by the adrenal glands) is used in treating arthritis. Meat packers pride themselves on using "all of a pig but the squeal."

ALSO READ: DOMESTICATED ANIMALS, FISH, FOOD PROCESSING, MEAL PLANNING, POULTRY.

MECHANICAL DRAWING

When an ordinary line drawing is made of a *solid object* (having length, width, and depth), the drawing gives no information about hidden details of the object. What is its real size? How do its parts fit together? What does it look like from different angles? Mechanical drawing, also called *drafting*, is a special method used to show the exact size, shape, and relationship of parts of a solid object (such as a machine or a building).

Draftsmen (people who do mechanical drawings) make several different drawings *(projections)* of an object in order to show it from every side and angle. Projections are not complete in themselves, but when they are considered together, they represent every shape and feature of the object. The front view, or *elevation*, shows the largest side of the object. The *plan* shows the object from directly above. Other views, such as a *side view*, are drawn when the elevation and the plan do not give enough information about the object. The *sectional view* is a drawing of the object with part of its outside cut away to show inside details.

Each line in a mechanical drawing represents a *contour*, or a point where two surfaces meet, such as the line between a ceiling and a wall. Solid lines represent contours that can be seen. Dotted lines represent contours that are "unseen," or must be imagined. For example, in a sectional view of the inside of a building, solid lines represent the outside walls and roof. Dotted lines represent the floors between the levels of the building and the walls between the rooms. These features would not be seen in an ordinary line drawing of the building.

Mechanical drawings are "drawn to scale." For example, one inch in a drawing might represent one foot of the actual object. Someone who looks at the drawing and sees "Scale: 1 inch = 1 foot" knows that

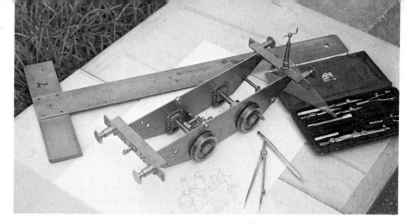

the actual object is 12 times larger than the drawing. Every line of the drawing must be drawn to scale, in order to show each part in its exact relation to every other part. When mechanical drawings are made of a very large object, such as an airplane or an ocean liner, one inch might represent one hundred feet.

Draftsmen use special tools to make sure their drawings are correct in every detail. Some of their tools include a *ruler, compass, T-square, triangle,* and *protractor.* Mechanical drawings can show a cabinetmaker how to built a cabinet, a contractor how to build a house, or an engineer how to build a bridge. Drawing and "reading" mechanical drawings require special training. Many junior and senior high schools and special technical schools provide courses in mechanical drawing.

ALSO READ: DRAWING, ENGINEERING, GEOMETRY, GRAPHIC ARTS, INDUSTRIAL ARTS, MEASUREMENT, MODEL MAKING.

MEDALS AND DECORATIONS

Medals and decorations are awards given to people for doing something especially well. There are three main kinds of awards.

Orders are awarded to people who have done something especially well for many years, rather than to those who have done something great only one time. They are given to heads of state, noblemen, politicians, diplomats, generals, scientists, artists, writers, and so on. Orders are mostly awarded in countries that have—or have had—royal families. A person is said to be a "member of

▲*Mechanical drawing requires special tools, including a T-square and a compass. This drawing is of a locomotive. Part of the model can be seen in the center of the picture.*

▼*A young man has his work checked by his teacher in a mechanical drawing class.*

▼*A Medal of Merit is pinned onto the coat of its proud recipient. This medal honors civilians for outstanding services during wartime.*

▲*Some European orders and decorations,* left to right—*the Order of Merit (West Germany), the Legion of Honor (France), the Order of Lenin (Soviet Union), the Decoration of Honor for Merit (Austria), and the Civil Order of Merit (West Germany).*

▶*A decoration given for outstanding service to Greece is the Order of the Savior.*

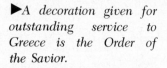

◀*Two awards given by the United States are the Order of the Legion of Merit* (above left) *and the Army's Congressional Medal of Honor* (below left), *the highest military award in the U.S.*

▼*The Order of the Garter, a major British award.*

◀*The Order of the Palmes Academiques is a French award given to educators and scientists.*

▼*The Purple Heart is given to soldiers of the United States who are wounded or killed in war.*

the order" once he receives the award. Members of an order have ranks, or degrees, as in an army.

The United States has only one order, the Order of the Legion of Merit. It is awarded to foreigners who give outstanding help to the United States. Perhaps the best-known order today is Great Britain's Most Noble Order of the Garter, begun by King Edward III in 1348. The Order of the Garter can have only 26 living members at any one

time. One of the 26 members is always the king or queen of England. Women have been awarded orders by many foreign countries for years. The most important order in France —the Legion of Honor—can be given to men, women, and foreigners for outstanding military or civilian service. Women are included in the high orders given by Egypt, Lebanon, Thailand, the Soviet Union, and other countries. Some countries give orders for doing a good job in tourism, postal service, agriculture, writing, and public health.

Decorations are given for a single act, usually heroism in battle. Two of the most respected military decorations today are the British Victoria Cross and the American Congressional Medal of Honor. The Victoria Cross is Britain's highest award. It is above the Order of the Garter. Only 1,347 Victoria Crosses have been given since 1856. The Congressional Medal of Honor has been awarded more than 3,000 times since 1861. It is America's highest military award.

Medals are awarded for anything from acts of heroism to just doing a reasonably good job at something. Governments give medals to the military, to government workers, and to private persons who do something for the government. The highest civilian medal in the United States is the Presidential Medal of Freedom, first awarded in 1957. Medals for outstanding work in science, the arts, athletics, and helping society are awarded by organizations. The gold, silver, and bronze Olympic medals are given for excellent performance in the International Olympic Games.

An order, medal, or decoration is usually presented in the form of a small, flat piece of metal. The metal can have any shape, but usually it is in the form of a circle, star, or cross. The top side is decorated with a picture or inscription that represents the award. In ancient Greece and Rome, coins that represented outstanding people or events were made for currency. In the Renaissance, medals began to be made that were not used for money. Some of the decorations on these early medals were great works of art. Medals for bravery in battle were first given in the 1400s. This custom grew until now there are awards for outstanding achievement in almost all fields.

ALSO READ: NOBEL PRIZE, OLYMPIC GAMES, SPINGARN MEDAL.

MEDICI FAMILY More than 500 years ago, the city of Florence, Italy, was an independent "city-state." Its citizens called it the Republic of Florence, which meant that the citizens of Florence chose their own rulers.

In the 1300s, a family called Medici became important in Florence. The Medici sold wool and loaned out money in the way that a bank does today. The Medici family soon became very rich and powerful. In 1434, the citizens of Florence voted to have the head of the Medici family rule over them. His name was Cosimo de Medici (1389–1464). Once he became head of the Republic of Florence, Cosimo de Medici took away the right of the citizens to choose their rulers. He was a powerful ruler, and he made certain that his son should succeed him.

Members of the Medici family ruled Florence for the next 300 years. They also became rulers of the country around Florence, which is a part of Italy called Tuscany. The head of the Medici family became the duke of Florence and the grand duke of Tuscany.

The dukes of Florence made Florence into a very prosperous and beautiful city. They built magnificent palaces, churches, and museums. Several great artists and architects built the famous private chapels of the Medici family. Cosimo de Medici helped support and encourage many artists, including Brunelleschi, Donatello, Ghiberti, and Fra Angelico. Another member of the Medici family, who was called Lorenzo the Magnificent (1449–1492), supported such great artists as Botticelli, Fra Filippo Lippi, and Michelangelo. Lorenzo was one of the strongest of all the Medici rulers. He held supreme power and allowed the people of Florence very little freedom, but he was a brilliant and cultured man. Through his skillful foreign policy, he made Florence· an important

▲*Lorenzo the Magnificent, ruler of Florence and patron of the arts.*

▼*Marie de Médicis was the wife of King Henry IV and queen of France.*

▲ A color illustration from a medical work published in 1492 shows a lesson in anatomy.

▲Avicenna, an Arab physician (center) surrounded by some of his students.

▼Paracelsus, a Swiss physician, was one of the first to use drugs to treat disease.

power in Italy. The city became a center for many of the most outstanding artists, writers, and thinkers of the great European cultural period known as the Renaissance.

Two leaders of the Roman Catholic Church, Pope Leo X (1475–1521), and Pope Clement VII (1478–1534), were members of the Medici family. Catherine de Médicis (1519–1589) and Marie de Médicis (1573–1642) became queens of France, and adopted the French spelling of their names. The power of the Medici family finally weakened. The last member of the Medici family to rule Florence died in 1737.

ALSO READ: FLORENCE, ITALIAN HISTORY, LEONARDO DA VINCI, MICHELANGELO, POPE, RENAISSANCE.

MEDICINE Medicine is the science and art of healing sick and injured persons, and of helping people avoid sickness. Men have practiced medicine for a very long time. In ancient times, people believed that gods and evil spirits caused sickness. So sick people asked their priests for help. Every priest had secret spells, prayers, and "magic" powders. These things were not really medicines, but priests did learn some useful things. For example, the priests of ancient Egypt learned that certain plants helped cure certain diseases. Other discoveries were made in ancient China and India.

A Greek physician (doctor), Hippocrates, (who lived more than 400 years before Christ), was the first to separate medicine from magic and superstition. He taught that each sickness has its own natural cause which a physician must find by careful observation. Hippocrates is said to have written the *Hippocratic Oath*, the pledge that doctors still take, which tells how they will care for their patients.

Galen, who was born about 600 years after Hippocrates, lived in Rome. He was the first to trace the pathways of nerves, finding what parts of the body they control. He wrote books on anatomy that were used for more than a thousand years. Galen had many good ideas, but he also had some bad ones. For example, he believed that pus, which forms in wounds, was good. This idea was believed by people until about 100 years ago.

During the Middle Ages (from about 500 A.D. to about 1450 A.D.), medicine made almost no progress. Terrible diseases, such as bubonic plague and smallpox, swept through Europe several times, killing millions of people, but the doctors could do nothing.

The Islamic civilization, which began in the 600s A.D., built many hospitals, and Muslim physicians kept alive the teachings of Galen. A Muslim physician, al-Razi, was the first to understand that measles and smallpox are two different diseases. Another Muslim scientist, Avicenna, around the year 1000, gathered together the medical knowledge of his time in a book that was used in medical schools for hundreds of years.

In the first half of the 1500s A.D., Paracelsus, a Swiss physician, used drugs in new ways. He also said that medical schools should not just use the books of Galen and Avicenna, but should study diseases carefully to find new cures. Andreas Vesalius, who taught at the University of Padua in Italy, published the first really accurate textbook of human *anatomy* (the structure of the body) in 1543. For hundreds of years, people had studied Galen's book. But Galen made some mistakes, and Vesalius corrected them. Another important discovery came in 1628, when William Harvey, an English doctor, explained how blood circulates through the human body.

Medicine took a giant step forward when the microscope was invented, sometime near the beginning of the seventeenth century. No one knows exactly who built the first microscope, but one early microscope maker was Anton van Leeuwenhoek, a Dutch merchant. He was the first to see red blood cells and the single-celled living things called *protozoa*.

Another important development came when an English physician, Edward Jenner, made a vaccination against smallpox, in 1796.

Medicine in the 1800s

In the nineteenth century, many important medical discoveries were made. Most of these discoveries we now take for granted. For example, you know that everything in the doctor's office is *sterilized*—kept very clean and free of germs. But for thousands of years, a doctor's office was no cleaner than a carpenter's workshop. Not until the 1800s did doctors try to make things cleaner and safer. This work was led by Joseph Lister of England.

You also know that when a person must have an operation, he is given an *anesthetic*, a drug that makes him sleep. The first anesthetics were used during the 1840s, by William Morton and Crawford Long of the United States and Sir J. Y. Simpson of England.

In the 1860s, Louis Pasteur, a French chemist, and Robert Koch, a German physician, proved that many diseases are caused by germs. Before this, people did not really know how diseases occur. Wilhelm Konrad Roentgen, a German physicist, discovered X-rays in 1895. The X-ray machine is one of the most important tools that doctors have today. They use it to see things inside the body.

Medicine in the Twentieth Century

In the first part of the twentieth century, much work was done on *preventive medicine*. This branch of medicine seeks to *prevent* disease, not cure a person after he becomes ill. Preventive medicine is concerned with *public health*, which includes sanitation, vaccination, and spreading information on good diets and other ways to keep healthy.

Chemists continue to discover life-saving drugs. Among these is penicillin, the first *antibiotic*, discovered by Sir Alexander Fleming.

The pioneering work of the Austrian physician, Sigmund Freud, led to a number of ways to treat diseases of the mind. And medicine developed the idea of *mental health*—the health of the mind—as a goal.

The discovery of vitamins and the role they play in disease and health has also been one of the major breakthroughs of twentieth-century medicine.

Modern surgeons are working to transplant organs and other parts of the body from one person to another. Eye banks have been opened. People will their eyes to the bank when they die. Many blind persons can now see again, thanks to the eyes left by thoughtful donors. Doctors have been successful in transplanting a kidney from one person to another. The newest work is in heart transplants—taking the heart from a recently dead person and giving it to a person with heart disease. These operations are very risky, but they may soon give new life to people whose hearts cannot be made healthy.

Becoming a Doctor

To become a doctor (physician), a student must first take a four-year college course of *premedical* studies. This course includes chemistry, biology, anatomy, and many other subjects. After premedical studies, the student enters medical school, where he studies more detailed anatomy, biology, chemistry, pharmacology (the science of drugs), and physiology (how the body works). In his last two years of medical school, the student works in a hospital, helping the doctors and learning how they treat patients. Then most medical schools award the degree of Doctor of Medicine (M.D.).

▲ *A drawing of the human body from the textbook of human anatomy published by Andreas Vesalius in 1543.*

▲ *Blood-letting was once a common cure for many diseases. The doctor drew the blood from a vein.*

▼ *William Harvey, an English doctor, was the first man to explain correctly how blood circulates through the human body.*

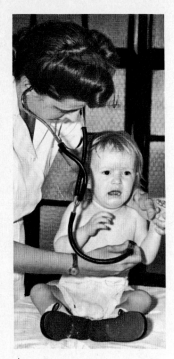

▲ *A doctor examines a baby to make sure all is well. Modern medicine is concerned with preventing as well as treating sickness.*

The first Negro doctor in the United States probably was James Derham (born 1762). As a slave in Philadelphia, he assisted two master doctors. He gained his freedom and practiced medicine in New Orleans, Louisiana.

▼ *The Royal Flying Doctor Service of Australia airlifts patients from outlying areas to the nearest hospital.*

A medical school graduate usually serves a year as a hospital *intern*. He or she works closely with doctors on the hospital's staff. Most interns work a few weeks in each department of the hospital. This way the interns learn many different things from doctors. Some medical schools do not award the M.D. to a graduate until he completes the internship successfully.

Most interns become *residents*, doctors who work in teaching hospitals. A resident still studies with more experienced doctors, but he also teaches interns. At this time, the resident must choose the area of medicine in which he wants to specialize. Then he works in that hospital department. For example, if he wants to work with babies and young children, he spends his time in the pediatrics department.

A young doctor may choose to be a *general practitioner*. Your family doctor, the one you call or go to when you become sick, is a "G.P." He has a wide knowledge of many kinds of sickness, and he must be good at diagnosing—recognizing an illness from signs and symptoms he sees in the patient. If an illness does need special treatment, such as surgery, the general practitioner sends the patient to a specialist.

A *specialist* is a doctor who treats only certain kinds of medical problems. For example, a surgeon is a specialist who performs operations. A cardiologist is a heart specialist, for example, and an allergist treats people with allergies. The list shows some kinds of medical specialists:

Anesthesiologist—gives anesthetics during operations, or directs technicians called anesthetists, who give anesthetics.

Dermatologist—treats skin diseases.

Gastroenterologist—treats conditions of the stomach and intestines.

Internist—deals with diseases that do not require surgery. For example, certain heart diseases can be controlled by regular doses of medicine. The internist prescribes the medicine and checks the patient regularly to make sure the drug is doing its job.

Neurosurgeon—performs surgery on diseased and damaged nerves.

Obstetrician—treats women during pregnancy and then delivers their babies.

Ophthalmologist—treats diseases of the eye and performs surgery on the eyes.

Orthopedist—treats all parts of the skeleton, including bones, joints, and ligaments.

Otolaryngologist—treats diseases of the ear, nose, and throat.

Pathologist—investigates the nature of disease. A clinical pathologist diagnoses disease by means of laboratory tests.

Pediatrician—treats diseases of babies and very young children.

Psychiatrist—treats diseases of the mind.

Radiologist—uses X-rays to picture the inside of the body and makes diagnoses from X-ray pictures; also uses X-rays to destroy tumors.

Surgeon—cuts into the body to repair damaged or diseased organs.

Urologist—treats diseases of the kidneys and other organs that excrete urine.

A doctor may choose not to treat patients at all. He may go into *medical research*. He spends his career seeking new cures for illnesses and seeking new facts about how the human body works. Medical researchers may work only in laboratories, or they may also teach medical students.

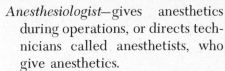

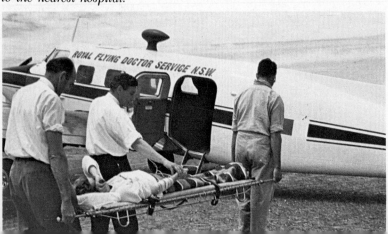

A doctor may choose public health as his specialty. He works to keep whole communities healthy. He sees that a community has proper sanitation, including good sewers and clean water. He tries to prevent epidemics from starting, and if one should start, he directs public officials and other doctors in fighting it.

Numerous different types of activities are all important parts of modern medicine.

For further information on:

Accidents, *see* AMBULANCE, FIRST AID, HOSPITAL, POISON, SAFETY, X-RAY.

Anatomy, *see* BLOOD, BONE, BRAIN, CIRCULATORY SYSTEM, EAR, EYE, GLAND, HAIR, HEARING, HEART, HUMAN BODY, KIDNEY, LIVER, MUSCLE, NERVOUS SYSTEM, NOSE, POSTURE, SKELETON, SKIN, TEETH.

Careers in Medicine, *see* CAREER, DENTISTRY, NURSING, PUBLIC HEALTH, SCIENCE, SURGERY, VETERINARY MEDICINE.

Contributors to Medicine, *see* BANTING, SIR FREDERICK; BARTON, CLARA; BLACKWELL, ELIZABETH; HIPPOCRATES; JENNER, EDWARD; LISTER, JOSEPH; NIGHTINGALE, FLORENCE; PASTEUR, LOUIS; REED, WALTER; SALK, JONAS.

Diseases, *see* ALLERGY, BACTERIA, CANCER, CHILDHOOD DISEASES, COMMON COLD, CONTAGIOUS DISEASES, DISEASE, FEVER, VIRUS.

Drugs and Medicines, *see* ANESTHETIC, ANTIBIOTIC, ANTISEPTIC, DRUGS AND DRUG MAKING, MOOD MODIFIER, NARCOTICS.

Health, *see* EXERCISE, HEALTH, MENTAL HEALTH, NUTRITION, SLEEP.

Life Processes and Physiology, *see* ANTIGEN AND ANTIBODY, BREATHING, COLOR BLINDNESS, DIGESTION, ENZYME, HEARING, HICCUPS, HORMONE, IMMUNITY, METABOLISM, REPRODUCTION, RESPIRATION, SIGHT, SMELL, SNEEZE, TASTE, TOUCH.

Related Sciences, *see* BIOCHEMISTRY, BIOLOGY, CHEMISTRY, PSYCHOLOGY, ZOOLOGY.

MEDITERRANEAN SEA   Now and then an ancient, sunken ship is found at the bottom of the Mediterranean Sea. Such a discovery is a reminder that the Mediterranean has been a busy commercial body of water for many centuries.

The Mediterranean Sea is the largest inland sea in the world. It is surrounded by three continents—Europe, Asia, and Africa. The principal rivers flowing into it are the Rhone, the Ebro, the Po, the Danube, and the Nile. Many islands rise out of the sea. The largest are the Balearics (Majorca, Minorca, Ibiza), Sicily, Sardinia, Corsica, Cyprus, and Crete. Hundreds of smaller islands lie like stepping stones between Greece and Turkey. (See the map with the article on EUROPE.)

The first important voyagers on the Mediterranean were the Phoenicians. These sailors explored most parts of the great sea as early as 1500 B.C. The Egyptian, and later the Greek and Roman civilizations, grew up in the Mediterraneàn Sea region. The Romans called it *Mare Nostrum,* or "Our Sea." Many centuries later, the Suez Canal was built to link the Mediterranean Sea with the Red Sea. The canal was opened in 1869. Since then, vessels have steamed across the Mediterranean, through the canal, and on to Asia. This route is much shorter than sailing around Africa to reach Asia. The Suez Canal has been damaged and blocked by sunken ships

▲*A view of the harbor of Portofino, a resort on the Mediterranean coast of Italy.*

▼*Pleasure boats dot the blue waters of the Mediterranean Sea.*

▲*The Riviera is a European resort area stretching along part of the French and Italian coast of the Mediterranean.*

since the Arab-Israeli War in 1967.

The Mediterranean Sea is more than a commercial path. It provides jobs for many people living along its shores. They catch fish, including sardines, anchovies, and tuna. Divers go underwater, searching for sponges and coral. Other people earn their living by saltmaking. Water taken from the sea is allowed to evaporate in great pans, and the salt is left behind. The climate around much of the sea is warm and mild. Farmers grow grapes, citrus fruits, olives, and tobacco in large quantities.

The Mediterranean has many fine beaches which have become tourist centers employing many people.

Many large European cities, however, have dumped untreated sewage into the Mediterranean. As a result, some parts of the coastal waters have become very polluted.

ALSO READ: EUROPE, SUEZ CANAL.

MEIOSIS see CELL, REPRODUCTION.

MELANESIA The name "Melanesia" comes from two Greek words —*melas* ("black") and *nesos* ("island"). *Melas* refers to the dark skin of many of the people who live on this large group of islands in the southwest Pacific Ocean—the Melanesian Islands. (See the map with the article on PACIFIC OCEAN.)

Land and Climate

The Melanesian islands are scattered over nearly three million square miles of the southwest Pacific, off the northern and eastern coasts of Australia. Some of the islands are *archipelagoes* (clusters of small islands), such as the Bismarck Archipelago. Other islands in Melanesia are New Guinea, New Caledonia, the New Hebrides, the Solomon Islands, and the Fiji Islands.

The Melanesian islands lie just south of the equator and temperatures remain high throughout the year. The hot, damp climate encourages the growth of jungle-like for-

▼*A Fijian of one of the islands of Melanesia wearing a necklace made of whale's teeth.*

▲*Trobriand islanders in Melanesia are building a large wooden frame to hold sweet potatoes.*

ests, but limits farming. During the rainy season, from January to March, tropical rainstorms and cyclones cause much damage. Most of the land is mountainous or volcanic.

The People

Although Melanesia covers a very large territory (more than 400,000 square miles of land), there are similarities among the people of the islands. They are generally sturdy, fairly tall, dark skinned, and have tightly curled hair. Some of the Melanesians, especially in Fiji, are taller and lighter skinned. Most Melanesians speak some version of the Austronesian language. Many also speak a simple form of the English language, known as "pidgin English."

Life in Melanesia

The life of the Melanesians is based on *subsistence agriculture* (growing just enough to live on) and fishing. Trade is carried on between the islands by canoe. Coastal fishermen trade dried or salted fish with the inland farmers, who grow bananas and yams and also raise pigs and chickens.

Metal and its uses were not known in Melanesia until about 400 years ago, when Europeans began exploring the islands. Tools, weapons, and other objects were made with blades of stone and shell. Chromite, cobalt, copper, gold, lead, nickel, and zinc are now being mined on many of the islands.

The largest Melanesian island is New Guinea, which also has the largest population. The people have had little contact with advanced civilizations. In some parts of the dense jungle interior, people still live in much the same way as stone age man. They hunt with bows and arrows and gather wild fruits and vegetables in the forest.

In New Caledonia, cattle are raised on farms. The most important crops are coffee and copra (dried coconut meat used to make coconut oil). Large amounts of nickel, chromite, cobalt, and manganese are mined for export.

The Fiji islands are the most developed of the Melanesian group.

MELANESIA

Country or Territory	Status	Area in Square Miles	Capital	Population
Fiji	Independent 1971	7,036	Suva	519,000
New Caledonia	French overseas territory	7,201	Nouméa	98,000
New Guinea	Australian trust territory		Port Moresby	1,695,000
New Hebrides	British and French condominium	5,700	Vila	80,000
Papua	Australian territory	90,600	Port Moresby	620,000
Solomon Islands (except Bougainville)	British protectorate	11,500	Honiara	140,000
West Irian	Indonesian province	161,514	Djajapura	800,000

Planes and ships traveling across the Pacific stop at Fiji to refuel and get supplies. The islanders raise cacao, citrus fruits, cotton, rice, rubber, and sugar. In both Fiji and New Caledonia, there are some European-owned coffee plantations.

The favorite form of recreation among the Melanesians is a combination of singing or chanting, dancing, and feasting. These activities are often part of a religious ceremony. Most New Caledonians and Fijians have been converted to Christianity. Some islanders continue to worship their native gods and spirits, and many of the men belong to secret religious societies.
ALSO READ: NEW GUINEA, PACIFIC ISLANDS.

MELODY see MUSIC.

▼Pieces of bamboo of varying lengths make fine musical instruments for Fiji Islanders. Each piece makes a different sound.

MELVILLE, HERMAN (1819-1891) *Moby Dick*, one of the greatest books ever written, was the work of Herman Melville, an American writer. Melville was born in New York City. He spent most of his early years at sea, sailing on whaling and trading vessels as a cabin boy. After his return to the United States, he taught school for several years. In 1841, he set sail for the South Seas on a whaling ship. He "jumped ship" (deserted) and spent a month as a prisoner of the natives

▼Herman Melville, American author.

on the Marquesas Islands in the Pacific Ocean. He escaped aboard an Australian ship, which he deserted in Tahiti. In 1843, he enlisted as a seaman in the U.S. Navy. In 1846, Melville moved to Massachusetts and devoted his time only to writing for the next 20 years.

Melville's first books were based on his colorful experiences in the South Seas. Two books, *Omoo* and *Typee*, were very successful, but his popularity lessened after the publication of *Moby Dick*. This work seemed to be too difficult for people to understand. In 1866, in financial difficulty, Melville accepted a position as a custom house inspector in New York City.

Moby Dick, or The White Whale was published in 1851. It is an exciting tale told by Ishmael, a crew member on the doomed whaling ship *Pequod*. Captain Ahab, who has lost a leg in a past fight with Moby Dick, is determined to find and kill the great white whale. Although it is an excellent sea-going story of action and revenge, it is also full of information on whales, religious meaning, and poetic description of people and places. The book was seldom read for many years after Melville's death, but it was finally accepted as one of the great books.

Melville's last book, *Billy Budd*, is a short novel about an innocent and likeable young sailor (Billy) who is hanged for accidentally killing an evil officer aboard his ship. This tragic story of good and evil is considered one of Melville's best. It was published long after Melville died.
ALSO READ: LITERATURE, NOVEL.
MEMOIRS see AUTOBIOGRAPHY.

MEMORIAL DAY Memorial Day, which is also called Decoration Day, is a legal holiday created to honor members of the American armed forces who have been killed in wartime. On this day, their graves are decorated with flowers and flags. There are parades in many cities and towns, and patriotic speeches are often made. Memorial Day is celebrated on the last Monday in May in most states. (It was observed on May 30 until 1971.) Many southern states, however, have set aside their own days for honoring Confederate soldiers who died in the Civil War.

The custom of honoring those killed in wartime was officially begun in 1868 by the Grand Army of the Republic, an organization of Civil War veterans. They originally honored only the Union soldiers and sailors who died in the Civil War. Today, many people bring flowers to the graves of all their loved ones on Memorial Day.
ALSO READ: TOMB OF THE UNKNOWNS.

MEMORY You can probably repeat your name, address, telephone number, and the names of your teachers and friends without looking them up. They are in your memory. *Memory* is the ability to bring to mind past events you have experienced or information you have learned. You might also call this process "remembering."

Scientists have many different ideas about how the memory works, the relationship between memory and learning, and how and why "forgetting" occurs. Some scientists believe that everything that has ever been learned or experienced by someone will always be "stored" in that person's mind—in a kind of "memory bank." But these things will only be brought to mind under certain conditions. You might see a picture of Thomas Jefferson on a nickel, and immediately remember "Monticello"—Jefferson's home. This is called *association*. You saw a picture and "associated" it with something else. How did the word "Monticello" come to you? You might have heard the sound of the word—in your mind—as it was spoken by a teacher. You might have had a picture—in your mind—of how

▼*On Memorial Day in 1958, the remains of the unknown servicemen who died in World War II and the Korean Conflict were taken from the U.S. Capitol to a lasting burial site in Arlington National Cemetery.*

the letters of the word looked as you wrote it in your notebook. Or you may have once seen an actual photograph of Monticello in a book and you "saw" the picture again—in your mind. This kind of memory is called *recollection*.

You remember skills in a slightly different manner. Every time you ride a bicycle, you remember how to balance yourself, how to turn the pedals, and how to steer. But you don't remember every direction that was given to you while you were learning to ride, every single time you get on a bicycle. This kind of memory is *recall*.

A memory may be *concrete* (a picture in your mind of a person, object, or event) or *verbal* (a picture in your mind of the letters of a word). With a "concrete memory" you may have a mental picture of an object, or the sound of someone speaking, or of someone actually moving and doing something. If someone said "Remember that diving contest last summer?" you might "see" the entire scene again—in your mind. The picture was stored in your memory. With "verbal memory" you picture the letters in a word representing an object (as in a spelling test), you "hear" the sound of the word, or you remember how you move your mouth or hand to speak or write the word.

If things can be brought to mind in so many different ways, why do you remember some things and forget others? Pleasant experiences are remembered more easily than unpleasant experiences. You would be constantly unhappy if you remembered every detail of every unpleasant experience you ever had. This is what is referred to when someone says "that is best forgotten."

Some things are forgotten because the person had nothing with which to associate the new information. If someone told you to use ($V = \frac{\Delta x}{\Delta y}$) for figuring the speed of a moving bullet, you would forget it very

▲ *A memory machine stores knowledge. Machines such as this can "remember" much more information than the human mind. The technician is pointing to the reading and writing arm of the machine.*

quickly because you had no previous memory with which to connect the mathematical terms. But if someone explained a science experiment to you, step by step, using information you already have, you are not likely to forget it.

There is a definite relationship between memory and learning. Just as something is learned more easily if it is important to you, something will be remembered more easily if you consider it to be important. If too much is learned at once, most of the later information will be forgotten. If you are given a list of things to remember, you will remember the first few items on the list much better than the others. Something can also be remembered more easily if it is learned just before you go to sleep. Perhaps the mind needs time to "digest" and store information.

Some people use "memory aids" to increase their ability to remember. Any method used to aid the memory with words and pictures is called *mnemonics*. One method is to combine the first letters of a series of words to be remembered to form a new word. For example, if you use the first letters of each of the Great Lakes—*H*uron, *O*ntario, *M*ichigan, *E*rie, and *S*uperior—you can form the word "HOMES." It might be easier to remember the word "homes" and work from there, than to remember all five names.

Another method may be used to remember names. When you meet someone for the first time, you should try to use his or her name several times in your conversation. This repeating is called *reinforcement.* You are "reinforcing" the name in your memory. When you study a lesson to review new information, you are reinforcing your memory of the lesson.

Someone who has a "good memory" is usually someone who has developed some helpful memory aids. Sometimes the person is not even aware that he or she has done so. How do you remember? Do you use any memory aids?

Look at the objects in this picture for one minute. Now close the book. With a pencil and paper, write down the names of as many of the objects as you can remember. Open the book again and compare your list with the picture. Or you might have a friend look at the book while you tell him what is in the picture. Did you remember all the objects? What methods did you use to remember? Did you "see" the pictures in your mind? Did you "hear" the words naming the pictures?

ALSO READ: BRAIN, INTELLIGENCE, LEARNING.

MENDEL, GREGOR (1822-1884) The Austrian monk, Gregor Johann Mendel, discovered the laws of heredity. These laws govern the ways in which living things inherit size, color, shape, and other characteristics from their parents.

Mendel was born at Heinzendorf, Austria, and was named Johann. He was educated at the University of Vienna and became a Roman Catholic priest. In 1843, he entered an Augustinian monastery and took the name Brother Gregor. He taught natural history at schools in and near the town of Brünn. In 1860, he became the *abbot*, or head, of his monastery.

In the late 1850s, Mendel began experiments in the breeding of peas. From these experiments, he concluded that there was something in the sex, or reproductive cells, of living things that pass on characteristics from parents to offspring. He worked out rules that explained how characteristics are inherited. By using these rules, it was possible to tell what the offspring would probably look like. These rules, known as *Mendel's Laws*, are the basis of the scientific study of heredity. Mendel's findings were published by the natural history society of Brünn in 1865, but they were ignored by scientists until the 1900s.

ALSO READ: GENETICS, PLANT BREEDING, REPRODUCTION.

MENDELSSOHN, FELIX (1809-1847) The German composer, Felix Mendelssohn, was one of the leading musicians of his day. He wrote music in the romantic style, with beautiful melodies and poetic themes. He was also a popular pianist and conductor, and he gave many concerts.

Mendelssohn was born in Hamburg, Germany. His cultured, wealthy family provided every advantage for his musical training. He appeared in public as a pianist at the age of nine, and was soon composing music. He wrote the overture, or opening orchestral music, for William Shakespeare's play *A Midsummer Night's Dream*, at the age of 17. This overture, and his

▼*Gregor Mendel, Austrian scientist.*

famous "Wedding March" for the same play, are among his best-known works today. He conducted Johann Sebastian Bach's *St. Matthew Passion* in 1829 and renewed people's interest in Bach's music.

Mendelssohn traveled widely on concert tours in Great Britain, Italy, and Germany. His *Scotch* Symphony and the "Hebrides," or "Fingal's Cave," Overture were inspired by a trip to Scotland. Among his other great works are his *Songs without Words* for piano, and the oratorios (religious choral works) *St. Paul* and *Elijah*.

ALSO READ: BACH FAMILY.

MENTAL HEALTH A person's body can be healthy or sick, and so can his mind. A person who is satisfied with his life and who gets along with other people has good mental health. A person who has trouble getting along with others and who is always unhappy may suffer from mental illness.

Just as cave men probably got stomach aches and sore throats, they also probably had some kinds of mental illness. In other words, like sicknesses of the body, mental illness has been around as long as man has lived on Earth. But while doctors were trying to help people with body illnesses, those people with mental illnesses were not so lucky. For thousands of years, people who had mental illness were starved, beaten, or just locked up in dark cells. Mentally ill people were punished for being witches and were said to be controlled by devils.

Not until about 200 years ago did doctors realize that people with mental problems were sick. Doctors began to study mental illness and to try to treat it, as they did other illnesses. During the late 1800s, Sigmund Freud worked out his psychoanalytic theory, which says that unconscious ideas can affect health.

Treatment of mental illness is better now than ever before, but study

of this illness is very new, and we do not know very much about it. Experts have many different ideas about how to treat mental illness.

Some medical doctors specialize in mental illnesses. These men are called *psychiatrists*. For the most part, they use *psychotherapy* ("psycho" means "mind" and "therapy" means "treatment"). In psychotherapy, the psychiatrist listens to the patient talk about his troubles and then helps the patient understand what is disturbing him. Medical techniques, such as drugs and electroshock therapy are also used by psychiatrists to treat mental illnesses. Some psychiatrists, and a few other persons, receive special training and learn to use Freud's ideas in treating mental illness. These people are called *psychoanalysts*.

Clinical psychologists are not medical doctors, and they do not use drugs. But they spend many years studying *psychology*—the science of the mind.

In addition, there are people called *counselors* and *psychiatric social workers* who are also trained in psychology. They do not study theories for so long a time as psychologists. But they do study ways to help people with mental illnesses get better. All of those who are trained in some branch of psychiatry or psychology can help people with mental illnesses. A psychiatrist, for example, gets most of his training in a mental hospital, so he is most familiar with the worst mental ill-

▲*Felix Mendelssohn, German composer.*

Moses Mendelssohn, the composer's grandfather, was an important Jewish philosopher, known as "the German Socrates." His translation of the Bible into German helped many Jews learn the German language and become part of the European community.

▼*In an effort to determine the causes of the patient's illness, a doctor listens to a disturbed patient talking about his problems.*

▲*This little boy scarcely talks and finds it difficult to play with other children. But with the help of his doctors and the love of his parents, it is hoped he will soon be on the way to complete mental health.*

▼*The members of a family who enjoy doing things together are most likely to have good mental health.*

ness. A counselor might not know how to treat such a case. But the counselor knows a lot about what causes some children to get angry at their parents—or some parents to get angry at their children—for no apparent reason.

Kinds of Mental Illness

There are two main kinds of mental illness, organic and functional. *Organic* mental illness is caused by damage to the brain. The cause can be a high fever, an accident, or a change in the amount of hormones (chemicals) the body produces.

Most mental illness, though, is *functional.* Experts cannot find damage to the brain, but the mind does not function (work) properly. The causes of functional mental illness are not well understood. Most experts say that if a child is not loved and cared for, he or she will develop mental illness. But this is not always true. Experts say that a shocking experience, such as a horrible accident, may cause mental illness. But this is not always true, either. Much research still needs to be done to determine the causes of mental illness and to find cures.

A common type of mental illness is *neurosis.* A neurotic person's thoughts or actions can upset his relations with other people or make him unhappy. A less common—and much more serious—type of mental illness is *psychosis.* A neurotic person knows what is real and what is not. But a psychotic person may think imaginary people and events are real. Psychotics may also be overactive, or they may sit without moving for long periods of time.

Many experts are studying mental illness. Some of these people are trying to find better ways to treat mentally ill people. Others point out that any person can become mentally ill if there is too much stress (hardship or worry) in his life. These people are looking for ways to reduce stress and thus to reduce mental illness.

ALSO READ: DREAM; FREUD, SIGMUND; GUIDANCE; HORMONE; PSYCHOLOGY.

▲*A Norwegian freighter in the Lake Erie port of Toledo, Ohio. The merchant marine handles much of the world's trade in ships such as this.*

MERCHANT MARINE If you were going to take an ocean voyage, you would probably travel on a ship that belongs to some nation's merchant marine. Non-military passenger and cargo ships make up a merchant marine. The people who manage and operate these ships are called merchant seamen. They are civilian employees of the companies that own the ships.

Many different kinds of ships are used by the merchant marine to transport different types of cargo. *Tankers* transport liquids. They can carry anything from delicate French wine to crude oil. *Freighters* usually carry dry cargo, such as automobiles or grain. They sometimes carry a few paying passengers, too. Most passengers, however, prefer to travel on the more luxurious *ocean liners. Bulk carriers* transport heavy dry cargo, such as iron ore.

Merchant marine ships usually fly the flag of the countries of their owners. Most merchant marine ships are engaged in foreign trade, but some travel only from port to port along the coast of their own country. The United States government regulates the U.S. merchant marine. The Coast Guard examines all merchant seamen for fitness, and inspects ships to make sure they meet international safety standards. The Public Health Service supervises ship building, to make sure health regulations are observed. The Maritime Administration of the U.S. Department of Commerce designs programs to aid the development and operation of the merchant marine. The Federal Maritime Board regulates merchant marine shipping. Because the government recognizes the importance of having a strong merchant marine, it helps pay for the building and operation of some merchant ships. It also operates the U.S. Merchant Marine Academy at Kings Point, New York.
ALSO READ: OCEAN LINER, SHIPS AND SHIPPING, TRANSPORTATION.

MERCURY PROGRAM see SPACE TRAVEL.

MERMAID In the harbor at Copenhagen, Denmark, perched on a rock, waves gently lapping around her, sits a statue of a mermaid. She has the body of a beautiful maiden down to her waist. Below that, she has the body and tail of a fish, glittering with shiny scales. She combs her long hair with a golden comb.

The mermaid is a creature from ancient European legend. Mermaids are imaginary beings. They are supposed to live under the waters of oceans and rivers. Occasionally, mermaids are said to appear on land, dressed like humans. They can easily be recognized, as part of their clothing will be wet. The legends

▲*An officer demonstrates a model of a ship's controls in the U.S. Merchant Marine Academy located in Kings Point, Long Island, New York.*

say that mermaids sometimes lure sailors to their deaths. They sing so sweetly that the bewitched sailors let their ships crash against the rocks. A rock in the Rhine River in Germany is the legendary haunt of a mermaid called the Lorelei.

Many songs, stories, and poems have been written about mermaids. The Danish author Hans Christian Andersen wrote a popular fairy tale called *The Little Mermaid.*

Scientists believe that the legends about mermaids may have been inspired by types of sea mammals called *dugongs* and *manatees.* These animals have long bodies, rounded heads, and fish-like tails. Ancient sailors, seeing female manatees or dugongs off in the distance, nursing their babies, probably thought these mammals were mermaids.
ALSO READ: ANDERSEN, HANS CHRISTIAN; MANATEES AND DUGONGS.

MERRY-GO-ROUND Very few people can own a real horse, but anyone can pretend—and that is the best part of riding a merry-go-round. Around and around and up and down go the fiery, handsome horses with bared teeth and proud tails. Gay music fills the air. All too soon, the music and the horses stop, and the ride is over.

A merry-go-round is a ring of wooden or metal animals, usually horses, all set upon a platform which *revolves* (goes around). The riders sit on the backs of the horses.

It can be dangerous to be a merchant seaman during wartime. Enemy forces sank 775 U.S. merchant marine ships during World War II.

▲ *A happy little girl on a merry-go-round waves to her parents.*

The horses are attached to poles, and as the merry-go-round revolves, the horses glide gently up and down. The circular roof overhead, the horses, and the seats all glitter with bright paint and gilt. There is a tradition that the child who catches the brass ring from a holder that hangs just outside the merry-go-round frame gets a free ride.

No one knows for certain where merry-go-rounds began. They were probably invented to imitate the *carousel*, a kind of tournament, or sports contest, in the Middle Ages in Europe. At a carousel, knights on horseback would run races and compete with one another in sports and games. The first "pretend" carousel, or merry-go-round, is thought to have been made in Paris in the late 1700s. Merry-go-rounds have been enormously popular ever since. Large merry-go-rounds are favorite rides in amusement parks and small ones are set up at most traveling fairs and carnivals.

ALSO READ: CARNIVAL, CIRCUS.

MESOPOTAMIA The region of southwest Asia known as Mesopotamia is now part of the modern country of Iraq. Mesopotamia has a very ancient history. Several great civilizations of the ancient world flourished in the region, beginning at about 5000 B.C.

"Mesopotamia" is a Greek name, meaning "the country between the rivers." The rivers are the Tigris and the Euphrates, which flow south-eastwards to the Persian Gulf. Mesopotamia is part of the so-called Fertile Crescent, which curves around from the Mediterranean Sea. Scientists believe that agriculture first developed in this area. Two groups of farmers and traders, the Sumerians and Akkadians, were living in Mesopotamia around 3000 B.C. They built up one of the earliest civilizations in the world. The Sumerians invented an early form of writing known as cuneiform.

Mesopotamia became the center of the mighty Babylonian Empire after about 2000 B.C. The Babylonians were an extremely advanced people. They had laws and writing, and had knowledge of farming, irrigation, and even science. Powerful invaders called Hittites overran Mesopotamia around 1550 B.C. After the 1200s B.C., Mesopotamia was ruled by a succession of neighboring powers. These rulers included the Assyrians, the Persians, the Greeks, and the Romans. The Arabs drove the Romans out of the region in the 600s A.D. The Ottoman Turks became rulers of Mesopotamia in the 1500s. They kept control until they were defeated in World War I (1914–18). In 1921 Mesopotamia became a region of the independent nation of Iraq.

ALSO READ: AGRICULTURE; ANCIENT CIVILIZATIONS; BABYLONIA; GREECE, ANCIENT; IRAQ; OTTOMAN EMPIRE; PERSIA; ROMAN EMPIRE.

METABOLISM All living things, both plant and animal, change food into living tissue and energy. The process by which this is done is called *metabolism*.

Metabolism can be divided into two parts: *anabolism*, or constructive metabolism, builds up new cells and tissues and repairs worn out tissues; *catabolism*, or destructive metabolism, breaks down tissues to release energy.

Metabolism begins with digestion. Food contains three main kinds of

▼ *The royal standard (flag) of Ur, an ancient city of southern Mesopotamia. At one time Ur was the most powerful of all the city states in the country of Sumer.*

materials—*proteins, fats,* and *carbohydrates.* These materials are complicated chemical compounds that are broken down into simpler compounds during digestion. Metabolism eventually uses digested proteins (amino acids) to make muscle tissue. Most fats are stored in the cells of the body, and then used to provide energy. Some carbohydrates are changed to fats and stored, while others are changed to a simple sugar, glucose, the main source of energy.

Amino acids and glucose pass through the walls of the intestine and into the blood stream. Fats are collected by the *lymphatic system.* These food products are carried to all the cells of the body. In the cells, the food is stored or used.

Food materials cannot be used to provide energy without the process of *respiration.* Part of this process is breathing, which brings air into the lungs. Oxygen from the air passes from the lungs into the blood stream. The blood takes oxygen to the body cells. The cells use the oxygen to burn sugar which is often called "fuel." The burning produces energy. Some of this energy is heat that keeps the bodies of people and other warm-blooded animals at the proper temperature. The rest of the energy is used to move muscles, to send messages along nerves, and to build new tissues. These activities produce carbon dioxide and nitrogen-containing wastes. Carbon dioxide is carried to the lungs and exhaled. The nitrogen-containing wastes are carried to the kidneys by the blood and are excreted.

Metabolism goes on more rapidly at certain times, such as just after a meal and during exercise. If a person remains at rest for several hours after a meal, his metabolism settles down to its lowest rate. This rate is his *basal metabolism.* The rate of basal metabolism is an important sign of a person's health. Doctors can measure this rate.

Metabolism is not the same in all living things. Plants and most kinds of animals do not keep a constant body temperature. And plants combine the energy of sunlight with water from the soil to produce starch. No animal can do this. But this process, called photosynthesis, is part of plant metabolism.

ALSO READ: CARBOHYDRATE, DIGESTION, FATS AND OILS, HORMONE, HUMAN BODY, LIVER, MUSCLE, NERVOUS SYSTEM, PROTEIN, RESPIRATION, SUGAR.

METAL "See a pin and pick it up, and all the day you'll have good luck." A superstitious saying, but people living many years ago had good reason to take care of their metal pins, nails, and needles. Since steel was scarce and expensive, early American settlers straightened their bent nails so they could be used again and took good care of their precious needles for sewing.

Metal plays a big part in our lives. Metals have been taken out of the earth and processed to be used in small articles such as nails, and large ones such as automobiles, buses, trains, and airplanes. Electricity is carried by wires made of metal. Large buildings—skyscrapers, apartment houses, factories, airplane hangars, and sports arenas—are built on metal framework. Water is brought into cities, and then into houses and other buildings through metal pipes. Although there are nearly 60 metals, only about 20 are important in industrial use.

▲*Metal is used for electrical cables. This wire cable is going to be buried underground.*

▼*Girders made of steel, a metal alloy of iron and carbon, are used to construct the framework of large buildings.*

▲*Antimony is a hard and lustrous metal that is usually mixed with another metal, such as lead, to form an alloy. Antimony-lead alloys are used in batteries, paints, and ceramic products.*

William A. Burt, a surveyor, discovered iron ore near Lake Superior in 1844. Earlier, Indians in that area had found copper and made many articles with that metal.

▼*An ancient copper pot. Copper is a malleable metal that can easily be beaten into various shapes.*

Characteristics of Metals

Metals vary, but a majority of metals share certain characteristics.

LUSTER. Most metals are lustrous, or shiny, when polished. Knives, forks, spoons, new pennies, and hub caps show the luster of metal. Some metals remain shiny for a very long time. Others soon get a dull surface, because the metal combines chemically with the oxygen in the air. When metals become dull for this reason, we say that they *tarnish* and need polishing. Put a shiny new penny where it will not be touched for a few weeks. You will see it gradually become dull, as it tarnishes. Iron combines very rapidly with oxygen when there is moisture in the air. The iron gets a covering of reddish-brown scales on its surface —called *rust*.

COLOR. Metals vary in color. Most are white, silvery white, or bluish white. Bismuth is pinkish white. Several are grayish white or steel gray. Cobalt is reddish gray. Copper is red, while gold and strontium are yellow.

MALLEABILITY. You can hammer or bend most metals into any shape you want. You can beat or roll them into thin sheets. Metals which can be shaped are called *malleable*. Gold is the most malleable metal. It can be hammered into sheets of *gold leaf* only 1/300,000 of an inch thick. Aluminum and silver are the next two most malleable metals.

On the other hand, a number of metals are brittle. They cannot be hammered, bent, or rolled without shattering. Among the brittle metals are bismuth, cobalt, and arsenic.

DUCTILITY. Some metals can be drawn out or stretched into wire. Such metals are *ductile*. Almost all the metals that are malleable are also ductile. Gold is the most ductile, and silver is second. Copper and aluminum also are ductile, and are used for making wire because they are more abundant and less expensive than gold and silver.

TENACITY. Most metals are *tenacious,* which means that they strongly resist being pulled apart. They are said to have *high tensile strength.* Tungsten and nickel are very tenacious, while lead, zinc, silver, and gold are not tenacious.

FUSIBILITY. Most metals are *fusible*—they can be melted fairly easily. One metal, mercury, melts at 38 degrees below zero and so it is found as a liquid at ordinary temperatures. Cesium and gallium will melt in the heat of your hand. Some metals have very high melting points, and are not considered to be fusible. One of these is tungsten (wolfram) which melts at 6,100 degrees.

CONDUCTIVITY. Most metals are good conductors of heat. This means that heat passes through them very well. The metals that conduct heat best are silver, copper, gold and aluminum. Because aluminum conducts heat well and is cheap, pots and pans are made of it. Poor conductors of heat are bismuth, mercury, and antimony.

Most metals are good conductors of electricity. Almost all metals are better conductors of electricity than are nonmetals. Silver is the best conductor of electricity. Aluminum and copper also are good electrical conductors and are less expensive than silver.

HARDNESS. Metals vary quite a lot in hardness. Nickel, osmium, iron, and chromium are very hard metals. Lead, gold, potassium, and sodium are soft metals.

Metal Ores and Refining

All metals are taken from the earth's crust. Some are very abundant. Aluminum makes up eight per cent of the earth's crust, iron five per cent, and calcium four per cent. There is very little silver, gold, platinum, and iridium in the earth's crust. That is why these metals are rare and expensive. Metals as they are found in the earth with surrounding material are called *ores*.

▲*Molten pig iron is being poured into a mixer, as part of the process of making cast iron, one of the most useful metals developed.*

A small number of metals are found pure in the earth. Gold, silver, and some copper are three of these metals. This fact explains why gold, silver, and copper were used by man in prehistoric times, long before he knew how to get any other metals.

Most metal ores consist of a metallic element combined with elements that are not metals. Oxygen is the main nonmetal with which ores combine. Iron ore is made up of iron and oxygen, or iron, carbon, and oxygen, or iron and sulfur. Tungsten ore consists of tungsten, iron, and oxygen. *Metallurgy* is the science of extracting or taking metals from their ores and *refining* them for use in manufacturing. There are several ways of refining ores. The one most used is *smelting*, in which the ore is melted. In smelting iron, heat causes carbon to combine with the oxygen of iron ore, leaving pure iron. This process was discovered at least 4,000 years ago.

To remove sulfur from metal ore, the ore is *roasted* in air. The oxygen of the air combines with the sulfur, forming a gas and leaving pure metal. This is how the iron-sulfur ore is refined.

Leaching is another way to get metal from ore. A chemical is used to dissolve the metal out of the ore.

In a second step, the metal is removed from the chemical in which it is dissolved. Leaching is used to remove gold from certain gold ores.

Still another way of getting metal from ore is to use an electric current. The current is run through a solution of the ore. The atoms of the metal, which have a positive electric charge, move through the solution and collect on a negatively charged metal plate hung in the solution. This is how aluminum is separated from its ore.

Alloys

Most metals are not used in their pure state. The usefulness of metals can be very much improved by combining them. This is done by melting the metals, and dissolving one in another. The result is an *alloy*. From two to seven metals may go into the making of an alloy. Man learned to make alloys at least 6,000 years ago, when he learned to make *bronze*. Bronze is an alloy of copper and zinc. For more than a thousand years, men made arrowheads and spearheads, axes, swords, cooking pots, fishhooks, ornaments, and many other things from bronze. Bronze is still used for statues, coins (pennies), bells (such as the Liberty Bell), metal jewelry, and fittings for salt-water boats.

The most important modern alloys are those of iron, aluminum, and magnesium. Steel is an alloy of iron and carbon (which is an nonmetal). The most important alloys of aluminum are *Duralumin* (aluminum plus copper, magnesium, and manganese), and *magnalium* (aluminum plus a small amount of magnesium). Both of these alloys are used for crankcases of automobiles.

To make useful objects, a metal such as iron is *forged* or changed from a bar into shapes by heating and molding or *casting*. A simple example of forging is the way that a blacksmith makes a horseshoe. He heats iron and hammers it into

▲*A pitcher made of pewter, a metal alloy of tin, antimony, copper, and lead. Pewter was once commonly used for making fine tableware.*

▼*Aluminum rolls lie ready for shipment to manufacturers of aluminum products. Aluminum is used to make many light but strong metal products.*

▲ *Some metals, such as aluminum cans, may be recycled or reused to lessen pollution of the environment. The discarded metal is collected in a local place and taken from there to a recycling plant.*

shape. Iron can be twisted and bent into shapes, such as *wrought iron* railings, or melted and poured into molds.

Micrometallography has helped scientists study what metals are made of and how they change when treated. This process is the photographing of a small section of a metal, magnified by a microscope.

ALSO READ: EARTH, EARTH HISTORY, MINERAL.

METAMORPHOSIS   Did you know that a caterpillar turns into a butterfly? That a tadpole becomes a frog or toad? Many insects and amphibians go through a series of changes during growth, called metamorphosis. As the young animal grows into an adult, its whole body form changes. The adult body form is usually very different from the younger body form.

Insect Metamorphosis
Insect metamorphosis has three stages—*larva*, *pupa*, and *adult*. Insects that must go through all three stages are said to go through *complete metamorphosis*.

LARVA. The larva is the insect form that hatches from the egg. The outer skin of the larva dries and hardens within a few hours after hatching. This skin is made of a tough material called *cuticle* that protects the larva's soft body. The larva crawls around in search of food. Its mouth is made for feeding on leaves or grasses. As the larva grows, it sheds its skin three to nine times. This is called *molting*. The

hard cuticle material cannot grow or stretch with the body of the larva. The larva must shed the old skin that has become too small and grow a new skin that will fit.

If you watch a fly egg hatch, you will see the fly larva (called a *maggot*) appear. The maggot looks like a squirming worm rather than like a baby fly. The larva of a moth or butterfly is called a *caterpillar*. You can see that these larvae are very different from their adult forms.

PUPA. When the larva has grown to a certain size, it is ready for the pupa stage. At this time, the insect stops moving about and looking for food. Some larvae, such as caterpillars, spin cocoons around themselves. Others, such as cutworms, burrow into the ground. During the pupa stage, the insect does not move or eat. It spends the whole time changing into its adult form. The wings, legs, eyes, antennae, and other parts of the adult body develop.

Silkworms spin cocoons that are valuable to man. Special glands in the silkworm secrete threads of sticky fluid which the insect uses to make its cocoon. Man can steam and unwind these silk threads and weave them into cloth.

If you find a cocoon or other pupa in the fall, you can take it home, keep it in a cool place, and watch for the adult insect to come out in the spring. Then let it go.

ADULT. The adult form of an insect is called an *imago*. When the pupa is fully developed, it breaks out of its cocoon or its underground burrow. As it comes out, the insect's wings are often crumpled and soft. The insect's body fluids are pumped into the wings to make them unfold. The insect exercises its new wings until they become dry and stiff. Then it is able to fly away.

INCOMPLETE METAMORPHOSIS. Wingless insects and other types (such as grasshoppers, locusts, and dragonflies) do not go through all

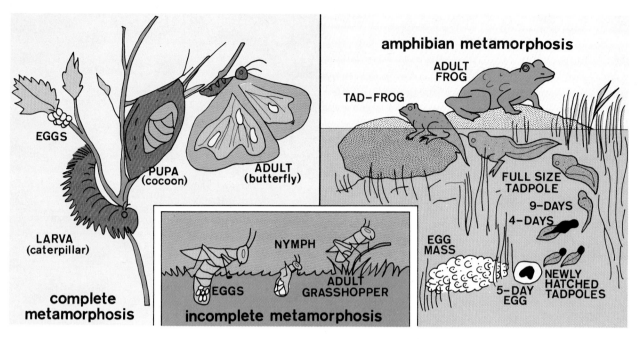

three stages of complete metamorphosis. They go through *incomplete metamorphosis.* The larva of an insect that goes through incomplete metamorphosis is called a *nymph.* Nymphs are very similar to the adult forms, but they are smaller and their wings and other body parts are not fully developed. The nymph gradually changes into an adult by growing and molting. The nymph looks different and more like an adult each time it sheds its skin. When it molts for the last time, the adult insect appears.

Seventeen-year locusts have an unusual metamorphosis. After the nymphs hatch, they live underground for 17 years. They eat roots and grow, molting every so often. They tunnel out of the ground in the spring of the seventeenth year when they are ready for their last molt. They attach themselves to tree trunks or other surfaces, molt for the last time, and fly away. Every seventeen years you can see many empty nymph skins that the adult locusts have left behind.

Amphibian Metamorphosis
Frogs and toads also go through a metamorphosis. Eggs are laid in the water, and they hatch into larvae, called *tadpoles.* A tadpole has a round body with a tail, and breathes through gills like a fish. It lives in water and feeds on algae and other plants. As it gets older, the gills and tail disappear and lungs develop. A pair of hind legs grows and then a pair of front legs. Finally the adult frog or toad comes out of the water and can live on land. Amphibians do not go through a pupa stage. Instead, they gradually change from a tadpole larva to an adult.

ALSO READ: AMPHIBIAN, BEE, BUTTERFLIES AND MOTHS, FLY, FROGS AND TOADS, GROWTH, INSECT, MOSQUITO, SILK.

METEOR The "shooting star" that streaks across the sky is a tiny piece of matter from out of space traveling at a speed of many miles a second. When the particle enters Earth's atmosphere, its friction with the air causes the particle to glow white hot and then to turn to gas. Most of these particles, or meteors, are smaller than a grain of rice.

On a dark night, you can count six or seven meteors an hour. On special nights, though, you may see a *meteor shower.* Then you can count 60 or more meteors an hour! The second week in August is a good time to see a meteor shower.

Scientists are not certain where meteors come from, but many of

▲ *A meteorite composed of iron and titanium.*

them seem to be fragments of planets that crashed into one another. Other meteors are tiny particles from the tails of comets. Some meteors are iron and others are stone.

Once in a while, an extra bright meteor, or *fireball*, appears. Fireballs can sometimes be seen during the day and may even be as bright as the full moon. Some meteors survive their fall through the air and land on the ground. These are called meteorites, and—surprisingly—they are usually cool enough to touch when they land.

▲ *The Great Meteor Crater of Arizona was probably created by a huge meteorite that struck there about 50,000 years ago and made this enormous hole. The crater is located near Flagstaff.*

Most meteorites are small. But big meteorites hit the Earth sometimes. These huge meteors explode when they hit the ground, and dig out craters. The most famous—but not the biggest—crater is in Arizona. The crater is 4,200 feet across and 600 feet deep, and its sides are 150 feet higher than the ground around the hole. The moon is covered by such craters because it has no air to burn up meteors in.

ALSO READ: ASTRONOMY, COMET, MOON.

METEOROLOGY see WEATHER.

MEXICAN WAR The war between the United States and Mexico lasted from 1846 to 1848. It started when the United States was trying to gain more territory in the West. This territory belonged to Mexico and included what is now Texas,

New Mexico, Arizona, Utah, Nevada, California, and parts of Wyoming and Colorado. The Mexican government could not defend this territory well because it was too far away from the capital and centers of population in the southern part of the country.

During the early 1800s, many U.S. settlers had moved into Mexico's land (especially into Texas) because it was unoccupied and undefended. In 1836, Texas settlers defeated Mexican troops and made Texas an independent republic. Texas was granted statehood in 1845. The United States claimed that the Rio Grande River was the southern boundary of Texas. The Mexicans said the boundary was farther north, at the Nueces River. Mexico and the United States both claimed the land between the two rivers.

President James Polk wanted U.S. territory to extend all the way to the Pacific Ocean. He wanted California and all the land between it and Texas. He decided to go to war for it when peaceful arrangements did not work out. He ordered General Zachary Taylor to move some troops to Corpus Christi, Texas. Corpus Christi was on the land that both the Mexican and U.S. governments claimed to own. The Mexican government claimed that General Taylor had invaded Mexico. A Mexican army, led by General Mariano Arista, attacked Taylor's troops. War had begun.

Antonio Lopez de Santa Anna was a former president of Mexico who wanted to get back into power. He agreed to sign a treaty giving the United States the Mexican land it wanted, if Polk would help him get back into power. Santa Anna regained the presidency in 1846, but he refused to give any Mexican lands to the United States. Instead, he strengthened his army in order to defend Mexico's territory.

Polk decided that the only way to make Mexico give up its land was to conquer Mexico City, the capital. Orders were given to General Winfield Scott to attack Mexico City from the port of Veracruz. Many of Scott's men were soldiers borrowed from General Taylor's forces. This left Taylor with only 5,000 men to defend the Texas border. Santa Anna decided to take 20,000 soldiers north and attack Taylor's forces. This, he hoped, would keep General Scott from going to Veracruz by forcing him to come and help Taylor out. At a place called Buena Vista, Taylor's forces beat off Santa Anna's attacks without General Scott's help. Scott landed at Veracruz and moved inland to take over Mexico City on September 13–14, 1847.

On February 2, 1858, the Peace Treaty of Guadalupe Hidalgo was signed. The agreement gave the United States the territories of California, Arizona, Nevada, Utah, and part of New Mexico. It also set the border of Texas at the Rio Grande. In return, Mexico received 15 million dollars.

ALSO READ: AMERICAN HISTORY; ARIZONA; CALIFORNIA; COLORADO; MEXICO; NEVADA; NEW MEXICO; POLK, JAMES KNOX; RIO GRANDE; TAYLOR, ZACHARY; TEXAS; UTAH; WYOMING.

MEXICO The United States of Mexico is the southern neighbor of the United States of America. Mexico is about three times the size of Texas. It is the land of the ancient Maya and Aztec Indians. In Mexico today you can see modern cities, volcanoes, snow-capped mountains, and beautiful beaches. The country is divided into 29 states, 2 territories, and a Federal District. The capital, Mexico City, is located in the Federal District, as Washington is in the District of Columbia.

Land

Mexico has the Pacific Ocean to the west. On the east are the Gulf of

▲*An American captain leading a charge against the Mexicans on May 9, 1846. The charge, near Matamoros, just below the Texas-Mexico border, resulted in a Mexican defeat. On May 13 war was formally declared on Mexico.*

Mexico, the Caribbean Sea, and parts of the Atlantic Ocean. On the north, its border with the United States is 1,600 miles long. The Rio Grande flows along part of the border. The small nations of Guatemala and British Honduras lie to the south of Mexico.

Mountains cover two-thirds of the country. Twenty-two Mexican mountain peaks are more than two miles high. The highest of all are three peaks, Orizabe, which is 18,855 feet, Popacatepetl, and Iztaccihuatl. Many are volcanoes. Popacatepetl means "the hill that smokes" and Iztaccihuatl means "the sleeping lady" in the Aztec language. One Mexican volcano, Paricutin, began to take shape in 1943 in a farmer's field in the state of Michoacan.

The Sierra Madre Occidental mountains run down the west side of Mexico, and the Sierra Madre Oriental run down the east side. The

▼*Old colonial churches are numerous in the Mexican countryside. Most of them were built in the 1600s.*

MEXICO

UNITED STATES

SOUTH AMERICA

Capital City: Mexico City
(3,484,000 people).
Area: 760,373 square miles.
Population: 48,933,000 people.
Language: Spanish.
Export Products: Silver, coffee, and cotton.
Unit of Money: Peso.

▲*Mexican pottery and ceramics are beautiful and colorful. This craftsman in Guadalupe is painting a design on a large vase.*

land between is high and flat. Most Mexicans live on this central plateau, and nearly all large Mexican cities are at least 5,000 feet above sea level. Three exceptions are Monterrey, a major industrial city near the Texas border, and the two seaports on the Gulf of Mexico, Veracruz and Tampico.

Narrow, sandy coastal plains separate the mountains from the sea. Baja California, a narrow mountainous peninsula, extends southward from the state of California. The Yucatan peninsula is a low, level region on the Gulf of Mexico. The Mayan Indian civilization was centered in Yucatan.

On the central plateau, Guadalajara, Mexico's second largest city, is

noted for its mining and agriculture and its pottery and glassware. Cuernavaca, which means "the horn of a cow," has a splendid palace built by Cortes, the Spanish conqueror of Mexico. Murals by the modern Mexican painter, Diego Rivera, now decorate the palace. Taxco, a high mountain town known for its silver, is located south of Mexico City.

Climate

South and southeastern Mexico and the seacoasts have a hot, humid climate. The beach resorts of Acapulco and Puerto Vallarta are on the Pacific coast. In the north, much of the land is desert—scorching hot and dry in summer, sometimes freezing cold in winter. The climate of the

▶*Acapulco is a tourist playground on the Pacific coast of Mexico.*

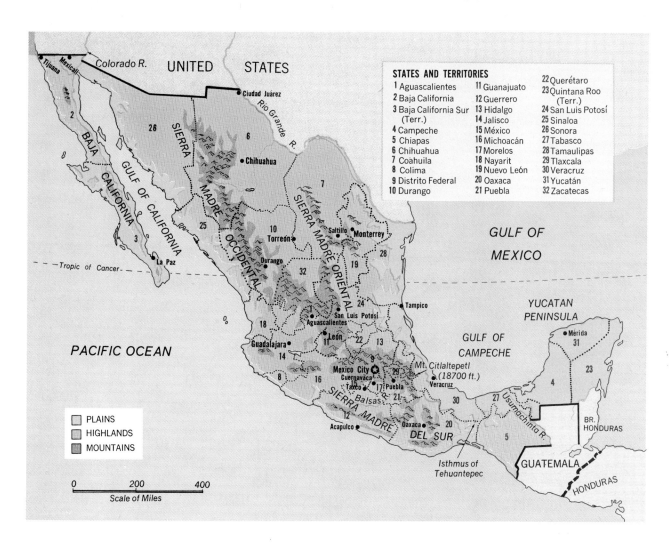

STATES AND TERRITORIES

1 Aguascalientes	11 Guanajuato	22 Querétaro
2 Baja California	12 Guerrero	23 Quintana Roo
3 Baja California Sur	13 Hidalgo	(Terr.)
(Terr.)	14 Jalisco	24 San Luis Potosí
4 Campeche	15 México	25 Sinaloa
5 Chiapas	16 Michoacán	26 Sonora
6 Chihuahua	17 Morelos	27 Tabasco
7 Coahuila	18 Nayarit	28 Tamaulipas
8 Colima	19 Nuevo León	29 Tlaxcala
9 Distrito Federal	20 Oaxaca	30 Veracruz
10 Durango	21 Puebla	31 Yucatán
		32 Zacatecas

PLAINS
HIGHLANDS
MOUNTAINS

0   200   400
Scale of Miles

central part of the country is not so harsh. The altitude keeps the weather mild and temperate. Most of the rain falls in the summer. The year-round average temperature is from 60 to 65 degrees.

Natural Resources

Mexico is rich in natural resources, but until recently only gold, silver, and oil had been developed. Since the 1940s, copper, lead, zinc, tin, mercury, uranium, and iron have been mined.

One-sixth of Mexico is forest country, where lumbering is an important industry. Mahogany comes from the tropical forests. Fig trees and coconut palms grow along the coasts. Oak, ash, walnut, poplar, and gum trees grow in the plateau forests, while pines, cedars, and firs grow abundantly on the mountainsides.

Mexico has 6,000 miles of coast, where much ocean fishing is done. Swordfish and sardines, sharks and catfish, red snappers and octopus, lobster, shrimp, and clams are favorite seafoods.

Corn is the most important grain raised in Mexico. Other grain crops are wheat, rice, and barley. Sugar cane, coffee, tobacco, and bananas also are grown. Mexico is one of the world's largest suppliers of sisal, used for making rope. Cattle and sheep are Mexico's main livestock.

Factories in Mexico produce textiles and paper, as well as leather goods, cement, pottery, and glass. Food and tobacco are processed, and sugar is refined.

One of the most important industries in Mexico is tourism. This fact is not surprising, because Mexico is a land of beauty and excitement, and easy to get to from the U.S.

▼ *A statue of a goddess of the Totonac Indians, a people whose culture prospered between 300 and 900 A.D.*

A woman loaded with her wares in the market of Oaxaca, a city in southern Mexico.

A wall mural of a religious ceremony painted by the ancient Mayans who lived in Mexico.

MEXICO

The very ancient and the very modern stand side by side. You can see the temples and pyramids of ancient Indian civilizations, as well as recently built apartments, hotels, and office buildings.

People

One-half of all Mexicans live in big towns and cities, the other half in villages, farms, and ranches. In the cities many people live and work in modern buildings and carry on a busy industry. About one-third of the Mexican people still live as the poorer Indians did before the Spanish conquest. Their diet is largely corn, chili, and beans. They wear *huaraches* (sandals) or go barefoot, and sleep on *petates* (straw mats) on the floor.

History

In the area called Oaxaca, long before the birth of Christ, early Indian people constructed magnificent palaces, temples, and pyramids. They studied the stars and developed fine arts such as sculpture, painting, weaving, and pottery.

By the time the Spanish arrived from Europe in 1519, other Indian people, called the Aztecs, had built a large capital, called Tenochtitlan, on the site where Mexico City now stands. The Aztecs welcomed the Spanish as guests and considered the Spanish leader, Hernando Cortes, a god. Cortes captured and killed the Aztec leader, Montezuma. War broke out, and Cortes and his men barely escaped. They returned later with a stronger force and conquered the city. Mexico became a Spanish colony. Spanish settlers married Indian women. As a result, most Mexicans today are of mixed Spanish and Indian descent. The people speak Spanish and most are members of the Catholic church.

The Mexicans first rebelled against Spanish rule in 1810, but were unsuccessful. In 1821, the Spaniards signed a treaty granting

Few Mexicans in small towns own automobiles. The burro still provides transportation in many villages.

the Mexicans their independence. Shortly afterward, the Mexican General Santa Anna seized control of the country. American settlers in Texas (which was then part of Mexico) broke away from Mexico and soon joined the United States. War broke out between the United States and Mexico in 1846. Mexico lost and signed a treaty, giving up half of her territory. This territory became the states of California, New Mexico, Arizona, Nevada, Utah, and parts of Wyoming and Colorado.

Santa Anna fled from Mexico in 1855 during a revolt. An Indian, Benito Juarez, became the country's new leader. A constitution, passed in 1857, gave men the right to vote

In November, 1519, Hernando Cortes and his Spanish conquistadors were welcomed to Mexico by Montezuma, emperor of the Aztecs.

and people the right of free speech. Such changes frightened the landowners and church leaders, who felt that they would have to give up their land and powers. The wealthy Mexicans asked Emperor Napoleon III of France for help. French troops arrived, took over the country, and an Austrian nobleman named Maximilian was crowned as emperor of Mexico in 1864. Eventually, the French withdrew their troops, and Maximilian missed his chance to leave with them. In 1867, he was captured and executed by Juarez, who became president again.

After Juarez, there was a period of dictatorship that lasted over 30 years. Francisco Madero started another revolution in 1910 that led to a republican form of government. Through the years, the Mexican government has split up the large land holdings of the church and wealthy people and given land to the poorer Mexicans. All Mexican children are now required to attend school. During the revolutionary period, Mexican artists worked to help Mexicans understand and value their heritage. Diego Rivera and José Clemente Orozco, both well-known painters, were leaders.

Today the government of Mexico is divided into three branches. The president is elected for one six-year term. The legislature consists of a Senate and a Chamber of Deputies, similar to the U.S. Senate and House of Representatives. The Mexican Supreme Court forms the judicial branch of the government.

ALSO READ: ALAMO; AZTEC INDIANS; CORTES, HERNANDO; HOUSTON, SAMUEL; JUAREZ, BENITO; MAYA; MEXICAN WAR; MEXICO CITY; POLK, JAMES KNOX; TEXAS.

MEXICO CITY Mexico City is the capital and largest city of Mexico. It is built on the site of an ancient Aztec Indian city. Mexico City's altitude, 7,800 ft. above sea level, makes it the highest major city in the world. Its population is more than three million.

Wide avenues and flowing fountains add to the beauty of Mexico City, where operas and folklore ballets are often presented. Ancient and modern paintings and sculptures fill the city's museums and galleries. The great Diego Rivera's murals (wall paintings) at the National Palace show many scenes in the history of Mexico. Public buildings share in the artistic glory of Mexico, with murals painted on many of their walls. Aztec art designs decorate the new subway.

The University of Mexico is located in a spectacular university city. Large and colorful ceramic murals brighten the outside walls of some of its buildings. The National Museum of Anthropology has displays of ancient Indian culture, and the Museum of Flora and Fauna shows exotic plants and animals from all over Mexico. Chapultepec Castle is the home of the National Museum of History. The Aztec capital, Tenochtitlan, where modern Mexico City stands, was built on an island surrounded by lakes.

Hernando Cortes, the Spanish conqueror, captured the city in 1521, and it became the capital of the Spanish colony of New Spain. The Spanish built many handsome structures, including a cathedral. "La Catedral" is the oldest cathedral on the American continent.

As the city grew, the lakes surrounding it were drained and the water level in the soil dropped. Many buildings started to sink and today seem decidedly lopsided.

Mexico City was taken by the Americans in the U.S. war with Mexico, and later by the French. Mexican patriots recaptured Mexico City, and it has remained the capital and major city of Mexico.

ALSO READ: ALAMO; AZTEC INDIANS; CORTES, HERNANDO; HOUSTON, SAMUEL; JUAREZ, BENITO; MEXICAN WAR; MEXICO; POLK, JAMES KNOX.

▲The library of the University of Mexico is one of the most impressive buildings in Mexico City. The huge stone mosaics show episodes in Mexican history.

▲Moses, *a marble sculpture by Michelangelo.*

MICHELANGELO BUONARROTI

MICHELANGELO BUONARROTI (1475-1564) Some of the greatest achievements in art during the Renaissance were made by Michelangelo. He was both a painter and an architect, but his first love was sculpture. He thought of sculpture as the making of men—cutting solid, human bodies from hard stone.

The statue of *Moses* with this article shows how Michelangelo gave life to his "men of stone." Moses was the leader of the Hebrews—the man chosen by God to go up Mt. Sinai and receive the Law (Ten Commandments) from God. In Michelangelo's statue, Moses has just come down from the mountain. He has turned his head and seen the Hebrews worshiping a golden calf instead of God. Moses, ashamed, is getting ready to break the stone tablets of the Law (Exodus 32:19).

Can you see Moses getting ready for action? His expression is one of concentration. His leg is pulled back. His hand reaches across his lap to the tablets. The beard being pulled back and the heavy drapery over the knee give a feeling of tension—a feeling that something is about to happen. Moses' strong body seems to be made of real flesh and blood. Michelangelo had spent many years studying the human body and how it works. Can you see how his knowledge revealed itself in the statue of Moses? Michelangelo created a powerful body for Moses to show the greatness and power of Moses' spirit and character.

Michelangelo was born in Caprese, Italy. His family moved to Florence, a city state ruled by the Medici family. Michelangelo first studied painting, but soon switched to sculpture. Lorenzo the Magnificent, head of the Medici family, was so pleased with Michelangelo's art that he brought him to live and work at the Medici palace.

When Lorenzo died, Michelangelo went to Rome where he sculpted the *Pieta* (a statue of Mary with the crucified Christ across her lap). At the age of 26, he returned to Florence and won the right to carve the "Giant." The "Giant" was the name people had given to a damaged, 18-foot slab of marble. No one thought it possible to carve a statue from it using the entire piece of stone. But Michelangelo carved from the "Giant" his great statue of *David*, the slayer of Goliath.

In 1505, the Pope asked Michelangelo to design a huge tomb. The *Moses* statue was to have been part of it, but the tomb was never completed. The Pope asked Michelangelo to paint frescoes on the 10,000 square feet of ceiling in the Sistine Chapel of the Vatican. Michelangelo created hundreds of giant figures on the wet plaster, showing the creation of the world and hundreds of biblical characters and events. He worked for four years, lying on his back in a cramped position at the top of a 60-foot scaffold. The light was dim. His arms ached. Plaster and paint dripped into his eyes. He became ill several times, but he kept working and completed the magnificent frescoes by himself.

Twenty years later, Michelangelo created an enormous fresco for the 60-foot wall behind the altar of the Sistine Chapel. This fresco of the *Last Judgment* shows a powerful figure of Christ ruling the world. Michelangelo also designed the dome for the great Church of St. Peter in Rome—one of the greatest achievements of the Renaissance.

▲Atlas, *a sculpture by Michelangelo. The figure seems to be struggling to free itself from the marble that imprisons it.*

▶*Michelangelo did this portrait of himself.*

Michelangelo had tremendous energy and he rarely stopped working. Art was his whole life, but he was happiest when carving a piece of marble—shaping and putting life into his "men of stone."

ALSO READ: ARCHITECTURE, ART, ART HISTORY, LEONARDO DA VINCI, MEDICI FAMILY, PAINTING, POPE, RAPHAEL, RENAISSANCE, SCULPTURE, VATICAN CITY.

MICHIGAN "If you seek a pleasant peninsula, look about you." This sentence, in Latin, is the motto of the state of Michigan.

Michigan actually has two peninsulas. One is the Upper (northern) Peninsula. The other, more than twice as large, is the Lower (southern) Peninsula. Each of these two parts of Michigan is almost surrounded by the water of the Great Lakes. Our word "Michigan" comes from an American Indian word meaning "big lake." The Straits of Mackinac separate the two parts of the state. A bridge five miles long crosses the straits. The middle section of the bridge is 200 feet above the water.

The Land and Climate
The Upper Peninsula has Lake Superior on its northern coast. Lake Michigan and a little of Lake Huron form its southern coast. A narrow, winding strip of water separates it from Canada on the northeast. Michigan's neighbor on the southwest land side is the state of Wisconsin.

The Upper Peninsula is twice the size of the state of Massachusetts. But only a small number of Michigan's people live in this area. It is difficult to earn a living here. The soil is poor and the forests were almost all cut down by lumbermen years ago. The lumbermen left no seed trees standing. So the forests are only now beginning to grow up again. Mines in the peninsula offer a few jobs. But copper ore is no longer mined. Some iron ore is mined,

but the iron industry does not need a very large number of workers. The Upper Peninsula is visited mainly by people who enjoy a rugged out-of-doors life. The peninsula has plenty of open country, and wonderful places for woodland camping. There are streams for fishing and boating, and—if you don't mind cold water—for swimming.

The western half of the Upper Peninsula is highland, with ranges of hills. The land in the east is low, and swampy in places. Henry Wadsworth Longfellow's story-poem *The Song of Hiawatha* is set in the eastern part of the Upper Peninsula. "The scene of the poem is among the Ojibways on the southern shore of Lake Superior," wrote Longfellow. The Indian hero, Hiawatha, launched his canoe on Michigan's Tahquamenon River.

The Lower Peninsula of Michigan is sometimes called the "Mitten." On the map, it looks like a mitten. Lakes Huron, Saint Clair, and Erie are on the eastern coast. Canada is just across the rivers that connect these lakes. Lake Michigan is on the west coast of the Lower Peninsula. Indiana and Ohio lie to the south.

The northern part of the Lower Peninsula is a broad, flat tableland. The tableland slopes down toward the lakes that border it. Much of the region is woodland and it is dotted with many small lakes. But where forests have been cut down, there are open patches of wasteland.

Most of the people in Michigan live in the southern part of the Mitten. All the state's big cities are in this region, including the capital, Lansing. The area also has some of the best agricultural land in the state. Cattle, pigs, and poultry are raised. Dairy farming is important. The principal crop is corn. Other crops are hay, beans, soybeans, and wheat. Much fruit is grown along the Mitten's Lake Michigan coast. Apples, cherries, and peaches grow in big orchards.

MICHIGAN

State flower
Apple blossom

State bird
Robin

State tree
White pine

Capital
Lansing (131,546 people)

Area
58,216 square miles
(ranks 23rd)

Population
8,875,083 people
(ranks 7th)

Statehood
January 26, 1837
(26th state admitted)

Principal river
Grand River

Highest point
Mount Curwood (1,980 feet) in Upper Peninsula

Largest city
Detroit (1,511,482 people)
(5th largest city in U.S.)

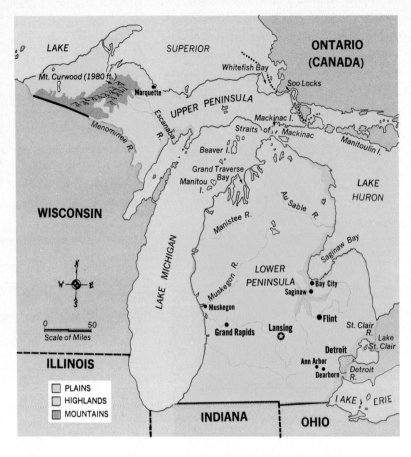

The Great Lakes have an important effect on the climate of Michigan. In the fruit-growing region, cold breezes from Lake Michigan keep the tree buds from forming too soon in the early spring. When the lake finally warms up, the danger of frost has passed.

In summer, the lakes help to keep Michigan cool. But they also make the warm season longer. As winter nears, the land becomes cold more quickly than the water. Winds from the Great Lakes, therefore, still warm the land in late fall. Winters in Michigan are fairly cold. Snows are heaviest in the Upper Peninsula.

History

The "Ojibways" (Ojibwa) mentioned by Longfellow were a major tribe of American Indians in Michigan. Other tribes were the Ottawa, Menomini, and Potawatomi.

French missionary-priests and fur traders were the first Europeans to visit Michigan. Michigan's earliest permanent settlement was a mission

▼A garden of beautiful tulips in Centennial City Park in Holland, Michigan, reminds visitors of the city's Dutch heritage.

founded by Father Jacques Marquette in 1668. At the mission, Father Marquette gathered the local Indians together to teach them Christianity. A French army officer founded the city of Detroit in 1701. His name was Antoine de la Mothe Cadillac. He could not guess how famous his name—and Detroit's—would later become after the invention of the automobile.

Britain defeated France in the French and Indian War, which ended in 1763. But the British were driven out of the region during the American Revolution. Michigan became a state of the Union in 1837.

▲Greenfield Village is a restored historical town near Detroit, Michigan. Tourists may ride through the town in an open carriage.

Michigan had by this time become an important lumber area. Big steam sawmills were built. Thousands and thousands of tree trunks were fed to the whirling saws. The mills turned the logs into timbers for ships and houses. Before long, much of Michigan was a dreary wasteland of stumps. The mining industry brought much wealth to the state in the late 1800s. For many years, half of all American copper came from Michigan. Iron ore was also found there in large quantities. Even today, Michigan is second only to Minnesota in mining iron ore.

People at Work in Michigan

The principal industry in Michigan today is manufacturing. The most important product is automobiles (and their parts). The American automobile industry grew up in the city of Detroit. Other major products manufactured in Michigan are machinery, metal goods, steel, and chemicals. The other principal industry in Michigan is agriculture.

Tourism is an important business in the state. Crowds go to Detroit and Flint to see automobiles being made. Dearborn is the birthplace of the American automobile manufacturer Henry Ford. It is also the site of Greenfield Village, a series of American historical buildings which Ford collected and restored.

Michigan is best-known as a busy industrial state. But it is also a lively cultural center with many libraries and museums, including the famous Detroit Institute of Arts. The impressive scenery of Michigan is preserved in several national forests.

ALSO READ: DAIRY FARMING; DAIRY PRODUCTS; FORD, HENRY; FRENCH AND INDIAN WAR; FUR TRADER; GREAT LAKES; LONGFELLOW, HENRY WADSWORTH; MARQUETTE, PIERRE, AND JOLIET, LOUIS; OJIBWA INDIANS.

MICROFILM

Storing books, magazines, and other papers has become a serious problem in libraries and offices. These materials take up a lot of space and can be completely destroyed by fires or floods. Microfilming can put an end to these difficulties. Microfilming is a way of photographing papers and recording their contents on very small pieces of film. The film is then stored in labeled metal boxes. These boxes take up only five per cent of the space that printed material does. Microfilming also keeps the recorded information safe from fire and water damage.

Special cameras are used to photograph printed material on microfilm. Images of the pages are

▲The skyline of Detroit, Michigan, the automotive capital of the world.

printed one after another on the film. The images are so small that they cannot be read clearly without magnification. The film can be read by inserting it into a desk projector, which operates like a movie or slide projector. The copy is projected onto a screen at normal size. or 1½ times the normal size.

Your local library probably has microfilm and a desk projector that you can use. Ask the librarian to help you select something you will enjoy reading. She will also show you how to load the machine.

ALSO READ: LIBRARY, PHOTOGRAPHY.

MICRONESIA

Scattered over the southwest Pacific Ocean are many small islands that are often grouped together under the name Micronesia ("little islands"). The Micronesians, as the islanders are called, are mainly farmers and fishermen today. But the ruins of great stone fortifications on Ponape, one of the Caroline islands, may be the remains of the buildings of an ancient people.

The Micronesian islands lie north of the equator and east of the Philippine Islands. There are more than 2,000 Micronesian islands. They include more than 1,100 square miles of land spread over about three million square miles of ocean—an area greater than that covered by the continental United States. Micronesia is part of a larger group of Pacific islands known as Oceania. The two other groups in Oceania are Melanesia ("black islands") and Polynesia ("many islands"). (See the map with the article on PACIFIC OCEAN.)

Micronesia is composed of several archipelagoes, or clusters of islands.

▼The men's house, a kind of social club for males, on the atoll of Woleai in the Caroline Islands of Micronesia.

MICRONESIA

Country or Territory	Status	Area in Square Miles	Capital	Population
Bonin and Volcano Islands	Part of Japan		Omura	205
Caroline Islands	U.S. trust territory	525	Saipan	62,000
Gilbert Islands	British colony	166	Bairiki	45,000
Guam	U.S. territory	209	Agana	102,000
Mariana Islands (except Guam)	U.S. trust territory	142	Garapan	11,000
Marshall Islands	U.S. trust territory	61	Majuro	18,000
Nauru	Independent 1968	8	Uaboe	7,000
Wake Island	U.S. territory	3	—	1,000

These include the Caroline Islands, the Gilbert Islands, the Mariana Islands, and the Marshall Islands. Many of the Micronesian islands are coral *atolls*. An atoll is a ring-shaped coral reef, or ridge, that surrounds a *lagoon*. A lagoon is a shallow body of water, like a pond. A shallow channel often leads across the reef to the open sea beyond. The most famous of these atolls, both of them in the Marshalls, are Bikini and Eniwetok, where the United States has carried out nuclear tests. The Gilbert Islands are also coral atolls.

The Marianas and some of the Carolines rise from sea level to form tall volcanic mountain peaks. The scenery of Micronesia is varied and beautiful. There are lush forests and thick mangrove swamps, black sandy beaches, and rocky islands. All of the islands are tropical. Average temperatures range between 70 and 80 degrees. Micronesia has a long rainy storm season—from May to December.

The people of eastern Micronesia are tall with light skins. In the western islands, the people are smaller and darker-skinned. The islanders live in small villages of palm-thatched houses. Fishing is their major activity. The men sail out to the fishing grounds in their swift and graceful outrigger canoes. Coconuts are the most important crop.

Micronesia was visited by the Portuguese explorer Ferdinand Magellan in 1521. After that time, the islands were colonized by Spain, Germany, Great Britain, and Japan. Much of Micronesia was the scene of bitter battling during World War II. After the war, the United Nations gave as a Trust Territory to the United States the Carolines, the Marshalls, and the Marianas (except for Guam, which was already a United States possession). The other main archipelago, the Gilbert Islands, is a British colony. Nauru, a small island west of the Gilbert Islands, is an independent nation.

The government of the U.S. Trust Territory of the Pacific Islands is supervised by the U.S. Department of the Interior. The chief official on the islands is a high commissioner, chosen by the U.S. government. The islands are widely scattered and very different. But in 1964, a Congress of Micronesia was set up under American guidance. Law and order are maintained by trained police in each district. Local judges and sheriffs are all Micronesian. The islands' economy depends on *copra* (dried coconut meat).

ALSO READ: PACIFIC ISLANDS.

▶A group of dancers in gay headdress await the beginning of a celebration on Yap Island (right).

▶ Many people in the islands of Micronesia earn their living from working the land and raising livestock. Brahman bulls are raised on Ponape Island (far right), Caroline Islands.

▲*A microscope is used to inspect the ridges cut into the surface of a phonograph record by an automatic cutting machine.*

MICROSCOPE There is a wonderful device that lets you see very tiny things. It opens up a whole new world of things you cannot see with your eyes alone. It is called a *microscope.* "*Micro*" means "small" in Latin and "*scope*" means "to see." The simplest kind of microscope is an ordinary magnifying glass, which has only one lens. If you read this page with a magnifying glass, the words look larger when you hold the glass a certain distance from the page. A magnifying glass would be of no use to you if you wanted to see all the details of a hair from your head. To see these ordinarily invisible details, you would need a *compound* microscope.

Compound Microscopes
The main parts of a compound microscope are the base, arm, and tube. The tube contains two kinds of lenses. The lens at the bottom of the tube, close to the object that is to be viewed, is called the *objective.* One kind of microscope has a rotating mount that holds several objective lenses, each with a different magni-

fying power. The top of the tube has an *ocular* lens, or eyepiece. The bottom of the arm of the microscope is attached to the base. The top of the arm holds the tube.

The base of the microscope has a platform called the stage, on which the *specimen*—the thing to be viewed—is placed. The stage has a small hole in it. The hole allows light to be reflected on the specimen from a mirror mounted on the base. To view a specimen, such as a hair, through a microscope, you place the specimen on a small glass strip called a *slide.* Another glass strip, called a cover glass, is then placed over the specimen. Some specimens are stained so that they will be easier to see. When a slide is placed on the stage, you look through the eyepiece to view the specimen. You *focus*, or get a sharp image, by turning a *coarse adjustment knob* on the arm of the microscope, and then turning a *fine adjustment knob.* The knobs move the tube up and down to place the objective lens at the

▼*A binocular microscope has two eyepieces instead of one. A person who uses a microscope often will suffer less eyestrain by using a binocular microscope.*

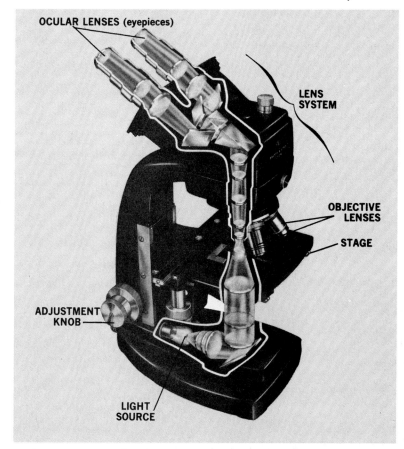

OCULAR LENSES (eyepieces)

LENS SYSTEM

OBJECTIVE LENSES

STAGE

ADJUSTMENT KNOB

LIGHT SOURCE

▲*This microscope, made in the 1700s, has a graceful design.*

▼*An electron microscope uses electrons to magnify very small objects.*

▼*Apollo, the god of music, gives Midas ass's ears after Midas ruled against Apollo in a music contest.*

correct viewing distance from the specimen.

When you look through a microscope, you see a specimen that has been magnified first by the objective lens and then again by the ocular lens. If the objective lens magnified the specimen 50 times, and the ocular lens magnified the objective image 10 times, the image you see is 500 times larger than the specimen looks to the naked eye. The best compound microscopes can make an object look 2,000 times larger than its real size.

The compound microscope was probably invented by Zacharias Janssen, a Dutch eyeglass-maker. The first person to see germs through a microscope, a few years later, was Anton van Leeuwenhoek, who also lived in Holland. This was one of the first of thousands of scientific discoveries made possible by the microscope.

Pictures of specimens in a microscope can be taken by a process called *photomicrography*. In this process, a camera is mounted directly above the eyepiece. The camera usually does not contain a lens, because the microscope itself acts as the camera's lens system.

Electron Microscopes
The most advanced and most powerful kind of microscope is the *electron* microscope. Many things are too small to be seen even when they are magnified 2,000 times by an ordinary microscope. These tiny things, such as viruses, may be magnified more than 100,000 times in an electron microscope! An electron microscope uses beams of electrons, instead of light rays, to "visualize" an object. The "lenses" of an electron microscope are magnetic. They focus the electronic beams in the same way the glass lenses of a compound microscope focus light beams. The image produced by an electron microscope is recorded on photographic film or

projected on a screen covered with a *fluorescent* substance that glows when the beams of electrons hit it.
ALSO READ: EYE, GLASSES, LENS, LIGHT, PHOTOGRAPHY, TELESCOPE.

MIDAS The myths and legends of ancient Greece tell about a great king named Midas. He ruled the country of Phrygia, in Asia Minor. Midas once did a favor for Dionysus, the god of wine. As a reward, Dionysus gave Midas the ability to turn everything he touched into gold. At first, Midas was overjoyed, but then he realized that when he touched his food and wine, they turned into gold, too. Even his little daughter turned into a golden statue when he touched her. Desperate, he begged Dionysus to take back the wish. Dionysus told him to bathe in a nearby river. Midas jumped into the river and broke the spell. Ever since, according to the legend, that river has contained sands of gold.

Another legend says that Midas was once asked to judge a musical contest between Pan, the god of the fields, and Apollo, the god of music. Midas stupidly chose Pan as the winner. Apollo, in a fury, changed Midas's ears into the ears of an ass (donkey). Midas wore a turban to hide the ears, and only his barber knew the secret. One day the barber, unable to keep the secret, dug a hole in the ground and whispered into it the story of the king's ears. Then all the reeds growing in that place whispered to everyone who passed, "King Midas has ass's ears."
ALSO READ: LEGEND, MYTHOLOGY.

MIDDLE AGES The years between the end of the Western Roman Empire and the beginning of the Renaissance (476–1450 A.D.) are known as the Middle Ages. During the 400s, tribes of people lived in northern Europe. These people were being attacked by Huns (tribes from the East) and being pushed across the borders of the Roman

Empire. They came in huge numbers, escaping from the Huns and at the same time fighting the Romans for a place to live. The Roman Empire could not stand up against the fierce warfare waged by these northerners. The Empire was destroyed by tribes called the Franks, Goths, Visigoths, Ostrogoths, Alemmani, Burgundians, Jutes, Teutons, Angles, Saxons, Lombards, Avars, Magyars, and Bulgars. The northern invaders were good warriors, but they had neither the education nor the skills to keep the Empire going.

Village Life

During the next 500 years, the northern tribes mixed with the Roman population. The Roman Empire no longer existed, so there was no main government to enforce laws. A person's only safety was to live close to a nearby chieftain who was powerful enough to fight off an enemy. These chieftains became rulers or lords of small areas. In return for a lord's protection, a person would become a *serf*. Serfs had to promise to serve their lord for their entire lives.

People lived in little huts and cottages clustered close to the big house of their lord. In exchange for protection, the people had to farm their lord's land. Farming was the main way of life for most people. Great distances separated the lands of one lord from those of another. People did not travel much, because they had to stay home and work the land. That meant that there was very little communication between one village and another.

Agriculture and the need for protection became the basis for a system of government called *feudalism*. In feudalism, every person had a rank—from serf (the lowest rank) to baron or king. Each person had obligations to people of higher and lower rank. Higher ranking nobles would give pieces of land to lower-ranking nobles or serfs. These peo-

ple were then required to provide soldiers, arms, or food for nobles of higher rank. In this way, everyone was protected and fed.

The Church

Monks were religious men of the Christian faith who lived in small groups in abbeys or monasteries. Their three main occupations were work, study, and prayer. Monks believed in the value of education, and almost all of them could read and write. Monks provided services that people were not able to get from their lords. The monks ran schools and hospitals, helped the poor, set up libraries, and provided a peaceful place for people to get away from the hardships of their everyday lives.

Monasteries began in Italy and then spread to all parts of western Europe. Wherever monks went, they converted the people to Christianity. By the year 1100, Christianity was the religion of all western Europe. The Pope in Rome was head of the Church. Bishops were assigned certain areas, and priests were in charge of the local churches. The Church taught that anyone who lived a good life would be rewarded by God. Men were afraid of being punished by God if they did wrong. The Church and its teachings helped bring peace to Europe during the Middle Ages. People looked to the Church for education, medicine, and help in hard

▲*The lord of the manor was the judge of his people during the Middle Ages. He held court to decide cases and give out punishments (left). Most people worked on the land. Many were serfs who had to farm the lord's land as well as their own (above).*

▼*Monks preserved the knowledge of the time by copying manuscripts and storing them in libraries.*

▼*Large, lofty cathedrals were built during the Middle Ages, such as this one in Bruges, Belgium, which was finished during the 1100s.*

▲ *A battle charge during the Middle Ages. The knights wore heavy armor and fought with swords and lances.*

times. Since everyone in western Europe was Christian, people thought of their religion as *catholic* —universal, a faith for everyone.

The Crusades

In the year 1095, the Pope announced that the Holy Land (in what is now Israel) was being ruled by Arab Muslims. The Europeans thought that the Muslims had no right to rule the Holy Land since they were not Christians. Europeans organized Crusades—long marches to the Holy Land where they planned to overthrow the Muslims.

Some of the crusaders who went to seize the Holy Land discovered that they liked the Muslims. The Arabs had built a great civilization. The crusaders admired the Arabs' beautiful carpets, graceful furniture, and spicy food. They also admired Muslim literature and philosophy as well as their discoveries in mathematics, astronomy, and medicine. The crusaders took back to Europe some of the ideas and products of Muslim civilization.

Towns and Businesses

During the early Middle Ages, traders traveled from one place to another selling their goods. They would meet to exchange goods and get products that their customers wanted. These meetings developed into large trade fairs. Booths displayed pots and pans, leather goods, fabrics, armor and weapons, tools, and many other things.

The trade fairs became towns where traders and craftsmen had

▲ *Art in the Middle Ages was devoted to religion. The Virgin Mary holding the Christ Child was a popular subject for painters.*

their businesses. Guilds were formed. The merchants' guild controlled all the businesses in a town. Each craft—such as weaving, candle-making, and baking—had its own guild. No one could practice a craft unless he belonged to a guild. In the late Middle Ages banks were established where people could borrow money, which they had to pay back with interest. As business grew, towns became larger and stronger. Town councils were set up, and the nobles (on whose lands the towns were located) allowed the towns to govern themselves.

Education

The Church provided the only education during the Middle Ages. Students went to cathedral schools to be taught by master teachers in subjects such as language, philosophy, mathematics, medicine, and astronomy. Often masters and students formed themselves into a guild, called a *universitas,* and set up rules to guide their schooling. Universities in the Middle Ages had no special buildings. Masters rented rooms, and students sat on the floor. Each student was given a test about halfway through his training. If he passed, he became a *baccalaureus,* and was able to be an assistant teacher. When he finished his education, he became a master and was allowed to teach on his own.

The Arts

Art in the Middle Ages was almost always connected with religion. Architects created giant cathedrals to honor God. Sculptors decorated cathedral walls with statues and carvings of biblical figures. Glassmakers created brilliant stained-glass windows showing scenes and symbols of the Christian religion. Some monks were artists at *manuscript illumination* (drawing pictures and designs to illustrate or decorate a book). Artists painted pictures to be hung in churches. Religious plays, called *masques*, were performed. Church music was sung in Latin by choirs of men in the great cathedrals. Popular songs were sung by everyone and were often accompanied by a lute or harp.

The End of the Middle Ages

By the 1500s, the printing press had been invented. More people were able to read and learn. Merchants were traveling throughout the known world, bringing back new products and knowledge. Kingdoms and city-states had developed. Western Europeans could now learn about the past through books, and begin to explore the world around them. The Renaissance had begun.

ALSO READ: ART HISTORY, BANKS AND BANKING, CASTLE, CATHEDRAL, CHRISTIANITY, CITY, CRUSADES, DRAMA, EDUCATION, FEUDALISM, GOTHIC ARCHITECTURE, GUILD, ISLAM, KNIGHTHOOD, MONASTERY, POPE, RENAISSANCE, SCULPTURE, STAINED GLASS.

MIDDLE EAST The Middle East has been called "The Cradle of Civilization." Here great empires developed more than 5,000 years ago, while primitive tribes roamed over most of the rest of the world. We know about these ancient empires because their people left written records. The Sumerians, who lived on land between the Tigris and Euphrates rivers (in what is now Iraq), were the first people to develop written language. Today, this ancient land has become an area of conflict in a struggle for change—a struggle between old and new.

The People

In the Middle East live people of different races, nationalities, cultures, education levels, and religious sects. Most of the people are Arabs, and most of the Arabs are Muslims—followers of the Islamic religion.

CHRISTIANS, JEWS, AND MUSLIMS.

Christians, Jews, and Muslims can be found in almost every Middle Eastern land. Christian Arabs form about half the population of Lebanon. The modern Jewish state of Israel, made up largely of people who recently came from Western Europe, is very different from its Muslim-Arab neighbors. Israel also includes about 300,000 people who are not Jewish—mainly Christians and Arabs. In Turkey and Iran are many people descended from Indo-Europeans. Most of the Turkish people are Muslims, but not Arabs. They speak Turkish, not Arabic.

STRUGGLE BETWEEN OLD AND NEW. The Middle East is not a unified culture area. Turkey, for instance, long ago cast off many Mus-

lim customs, such as the wearing of veils by women. Israel is influenced much more by Western ideas than her neighbors are. Yet all of these lands (Arabia, Egypt, Iran, Iraq, Israel, Jordan, Lebanon, Syria, and Turkey) are involved in the current problems of the world crossroads that we call the Middle East.

The Land

The Middle East is a land mass forming an important crossroads

▲*A street in Aleppo, Syria. The city is located between the Mediterranean Sea and the Euphrates River—a region of the Middle East that is historically important.*

◄*The beautiful Majid-i-Shel mosque in Isfahan, Iran. Most people in the Middle East are Muslims.*

▼*All kinds of fascinating objects are on sale in the bazaars of many Middle Eastern cities. This one in Turkey sells copper and brass goods.*

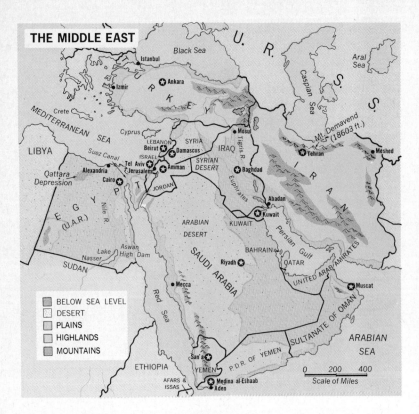

THE MIDDLE EAST

BELOW SEA LEVEL
DESERT
PLAINS
HIGHLANDS
MOUNTAINS

Scale of Miles
0   200   400

way of life. Since gaining independence in 1948, Israel has made remarkable progress in using modern techniques of conservation to bring fresh water south from the Jordan River. By laying pipelines, they have managed to make the rocky Negev Desert "bloom." Syrian and Jordanian farmers also use water from the Jordan to irrigate their fields. Neither the Arabs nor the Israelis can increase their use of water from the Jordan River without depriving their rivals. The struggle over the Jordan River's limited flow is a source of rising tension.

History

The Middle East has been a target for conquest since ancient times because of its location, culture, and wealth. During the Middle Ages, the Europeans thought that the Muslims, who were not Christians, had no right to rule the Holy Land. A long series of wars, the Crusades, were fought between Christians and Muslims from the 1000s to the 1200s to capture the holy city of Jerusalem for Christianity.

After World War II, a part of Palestine became the Jewish state of Israel. The Arab nations claimed that the land belonged to almost a million Arabs who lived there. They also felt that the Western nations, which had voted for the establishment of the state of Israel in the United Nations, had broken their promise of complete self-rule and independence for the Middle Eastern Arabs. Although the Arab states now govern themselves, many Arabs still distrust the Western countries. Border clashes, acts of sabotage, and outright warfare have been the general state of affairs between Israel and the Arab states since 1945. The United Nations has so far been unsuccessful in making peace.

Oil and Trade

Industry is increasing in the Middle East. The land is rich in oil, holding

between Asia, Africa, and Europe. It has coastlines on the Caspian, Black, Mediterranean, Red, and Arabian seas. Great deserts, where nomadic tribes still herd sheep, cover much of the land. Mount Demavend, in northern Iran, is 18,603 feet high. The Dead Sea in Jordan is the lowest point on Earth—1,287 feet below sea level.

SEARCH FOR WATER. Living in one of the hottest and driest regions of the world, Middle Easterners have had to find ways to bring water to their lands for drinking and irrigation. Searching for water has influenced much of their history and

MIDDLE EAST			
COUNTRY	AREA IN SQUARE MILES	CAPITAL	POPULATION
CYPRUS	3,572	Nicosia	630,000
EGYPT	386,000	Cairo	32,501,000
IRAN	628,000	Teheran	27,892,000
IRAQ	116,000	Baghdad	8,840,000
ISRAEL	7,978	Tel Aviv	2,822,000
JORDAN	34,750	Amman	2,160,000
LEBANON	3,475	Beirut	2,645,000
SYRIA	72,587	Damascus	5,866,000
TURKEY	296,185	Ankara	34,375,000

two-thirds of the world's known supply. Western companies drill for the oil, refine it, and ship it to all parts of the world. The companies share the profits with the Middle Eastern countries that have given them the oil rights. The man-made Suez Canal, which connects the Mediterranean Sea to the Red Sea, has been a great help for world trade. But the canal has been closed since 1967.

Today the Middle East is divided into many independent states. Some countries, such as Lebanon and Jordan, are ruled by presidents and elected parliaments, or kings with limited powers. Others, such as Syria, are ruled by military dictatorships with absolute power over the people. Clashes among the Arab states, because of their many differences, are common. The Middle East is an area of constant concern to other countries of the world.

For further information on:

Middle Eastern Cities, *see* ABU SIMBEL, CAIRO, JERUSALEM.

Middle Eastern Countries, *see* ARABIA, CYPRUS, EGYPT, IRAN, IRAQ, ISRAEL, JORDAN, LEBANON, SYRIA, TURKEY.

Middle Eastern Geography, *see* BLACK SEA; CASPIAN SEA; DEAD SEA; DESERT; GALILEE, SEA OF; IRRIGATION; MEDITERRANEAN SEA; NILE RIVER; SAHARA DESERT; SUEZ CANAL; TIGRIS-EUPHRATES RIVER.

Middle Eastern History, *see* ANCIENT CIVILIZATIONS; ARCHEOLOGY; ASSYRIA; BABYLONIA; BYZANTINE EMPIRE; CRUSADES; EGYPT, ANCIENT; JEWISH HISTORY; MESOPOTAMIA; OTTOMAN EMPIRE; PALESTINE; PERSIA; PHOENICIA; SUMER.

Middle Eastern Religions, *see* CHRISTIANITY, ISLAM, JUDAISM.

MIGRATION Many animals travel at certain times of the year. They leave one area and go somewhere else for part of the year. Later, they return. Migrating animals usually return to the same place

▲ *A dam in the Negev Desert, a region in Israel. Irrigation projects such as this have made part of the desert suitable for farming.*

each year when it is time to have their young. Birds are the best-known migrating animals, but many other animals migrate, too. Whales, caribou, bats, fish, and seals are migrators. Some insects also migrate.

Mammals

Migrating mammals usually follow the same paths year after year, and they always migrate at the same seasons. Usually mammals migrate in order to find food and water. Caribou, for example, raise their young in the far northern parts of Canada and Alaska. As summer ends, thousands of caribou leave the *tundra* (northern plains) and head for the shelter of forests to the south. Their swift-trotting migrations take them hundreds of miles. In the spring, they return to the tundra.

The American buffalo, or bison, once migrated in enormous herds. They traveled between summer feeding grounds on the northern Great Plains and winter pastures in the lower Mississippi Valley, always using the same trails. The bison, by changing their feeding grounds regularly, did not overgraze the land. New grass had a chance to grow strong before the herds returned.

Many seals, whales, and other sea mammals are migratory. The Alaska fur seals spend the cold winter months off the coasts of Mexico and Japan. In spring, they swim north through the Pacific Ocean and do not stop until they reach the Pribilof

The white beluga whale lives in the Arctic and migrates south in the summer and north in the winter. No one knows why it follows this upside-down path.

▲*These young elk are migrating from night feeding grounds to shelter and rest in the forest.*

Islands near Alaska. There, the baby seals are born. In winter, thousands of seals go southward again.

Lemmings—small, mouse-like animals—migrate whenever food becomes scarce. Hundreds of them travel together, always moving in one direction. They swim lakes and rivers and cross over high mountains, eating as they go. Finally they reach the ocean. They try to swim across it, but eventually they drown.

Man has also been a migrator. Thousands of years ago, the ancestors of man traveled from Africa to all parts of the world. Man was a hunter. He followed the migrating animals north in summer and south in winter to obtain food.

Birds

Every part of the United States has some migrating birds. Most of the bird population east of the Rocky Mountains stays around only during certain seasons. In autumn they leave, and in spring they return to build nests. West of the Rocky Mountains there are more *resident birds*. Resident birds do not migrate.

Many migrating birds are able to stand cold temperatures and could probably find enough food in winter. This means they do not migrate just to find food or escape the cold.

Many scientists think that migration is a habit. Birds probably began to migrate during the Ice Age, when the northern regions of the world were much colder than they are now.

Some birds fly great distances when migrating. North American warblers, for instance, spend the winter in South America. The Arctic tern migrates farther than any other bird. In summer it lives in the most northern parts of Europe, Siberia, and North America. In winter, it migrates to the most southern area of the world, the Antarctic. An Arctic tern's round-trip journey may be as long as 22,000 miles. Not all birds migrate long distances. Some fly only from fresh water to salt water, or from high mountains to the valleys below.

Many birds, when they are migrating, fly only at night. If you could shine a big light into the night skies during migratory months, you might see warblers, flycatchers, vireos, orioles, tanagers, and most of the shore birds. Hawks, swallows, ducks, and geese migrate during the day.

How do birds find their way? Why do they travel along certain routes? Nobody knows all the answers. Some scientists think that birds learn to recognize landmarks—certain mountains, coastlines, and rivers. Experiments have shown that night-flying birds use the stars to help them.

Migrating birds are born with a *homing instinct*. With this instinct they can tell when to migrate, where to go, and how to return. In experiments, birds have been taken far from their nests and set free. They always return.

Insect-eating birds usually migrate farther than those that eat seeds. One insect-eater, the black-polled warbler, travels between 3,500 and 7,000 miles in migration. Some seed-eaters, like bob-white quails, do not migrate at all.

▶*Canadian geese flying in the formation common to ducks, geese, and swans. During the wintertime Canadian geese have been known to migrate as far south as northern Mexico.*

Insects and Fish

The migrations of butterflies and some locusts are the best-known examples of insect migration. About 50 kinds of butterflies migrate each autumn. Their delicate wings carry them a thousand miles or more. Each year they move to the same places their ancestors used. Some locusts are migratory and fly great distances in search of fresh food.

The salmon is probably the best known of the migratory fish. Unlike the birds, these fish migrate only twice during their lives. Their migration is caused by the breeding instinct. Salmon lay their eggs in freshwater rivers and streams. After they lay their eggs, the salmon die. The young then hatch out and swim downstream to the oceans and seas. Later they struggle against currents, rapids, and waterfalls to return to the very place where they were hatched. They lay their eggs, then die, and the process is repeated.

ALSO READ: ANIMAL, ANIMAL MOVEMENT, BIRD, BISON, BUTTERFLIES AND MOTHS, FISH, INSECT, MAN, REPRODUCTION, SEALS AND SEA LIONS, WHALES AND WHALING.

MILITARY CAREER The first men to land on the moon were U.S. military officers. Our astronauts have come from the United States Army, Navy, Air Force, and Marine Corps. Not everyone can become an astronaut, but all the military services give young people a chance to learn skills that can help them build good careers. A soldier, sailor, Ma-

◄A salmon leaps out of the water as it attempts to spring over a fall while migrating upstream to its spawning grounds.

rine, or member of the Air Force can be trained as a mechanic, a surveyor, a photographer, a printer, or a radio broadcaster. He can get training as a cook, baker, computer programmer, electrician, accountant, plus hundreds of other careers. Of course, special training is also offered in weapons.

All of the military services have programs to help young people get a good education. A boy or girl who graduates from high school and joins the armed forces can arrange to study for a college degree. Even if a young *recruit* (person who joins an organization) didn't graduate from high school, the services will show him how to finish his education.

Studying and training for the kind of work he wants to do can help the recruit prepare for a good future in civilian life or in the military service. He may have opportunities to travel to many parts of the world. His family receives free medical care, and he is given regular in-

MILITARY OFFICERS IN U.S. ARMED FORCES

ARMY	AIR FORCE	MARINES	NAVY
Chief of Staff	Chief of Staff	Commandant	Chief of Naval Operations
General	General	General	Admiral
Lieutenant General	Lieutenant General	Lieutenant General	Vice Admiral
Major General	Major General	Major General	Rear Admiral (upper half)
Brigadier General	Brigadier General	Brigadier General	Rear Admiral (lower half)
Colonel	Colonel	Colonel	Captain
Lieutenant Colonel	Lieutenant Colonel	Lieutenant Colonel	Commander
Major	Major	Major	Lieutenant Commander
Captain	Captain	Captain	Lieutenant
First Lieutenant	First Lieutenant	First Lieutenant	Lieutenant (junior grade)
Second Lieutenant	Second Lieutenant	Second Lieutenant	Ensign

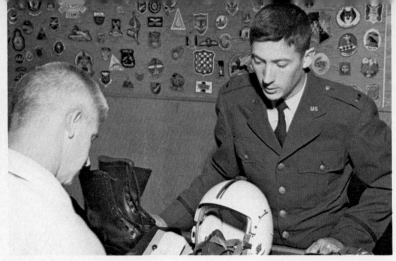

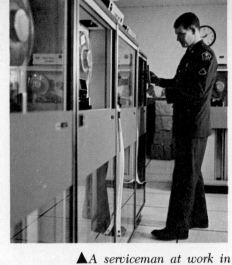

▲An air force pilot receives some of the equipment he needs for the job. Many of the different insignia (badges) worn by the military are shown in back.

▼The huge naval aircraft carrier U.S.S. Enterprise. Even aboard this one ship, there is a wide variety of careers available for the men of the Navy.

▲A serviceman at work in an army computer center. He will be able to use the skills he obtained here when he leaves military service to work in civilian life.

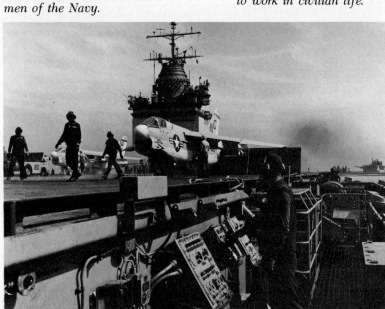

▲Two female marine officers in dress uniform. The white uniform is worn in the summer and the blue uniform in the winter.

creases in pay. If he performs his duties well, a young recruit has a chance to become an officer. Officers are given responsibility for commanding others. Many recruits become officers by attending special training schools, but men and women can become officers in other ways. *Warrant* officers hold rank as experts in various technical fields. *Noncommissioned* officers earn higher grades for skill and length of service. *Commissioned* officers are appointed by the President.

ALSO READ: AIR FORCE, ARMY, CAREER, COAST GUARD, MARINE CORPS, NATIONAL GUARD, NAVY, U.S. SERVICE ACADEMIES.

MILK see DAIRY PRODUCTS.

MILKY WAY If you have ever looked at the sky on a moonlit night, away from the glaring lights of a city, then you have probably seen the Milky Way—a faint, shining band of light across the sky.

The Milky Way is a galaxy, a huge collection of billions of stars. The sun is one of these stars. The Milky Way is what astronomers call a *spiral galaxy*. It is shaped something like a wheel. This wheel is at least 100,000 light-years across, but only about 10,000 light-years in thickness.

This wheel shape that is shown in the drawing helps to explain why our galaxy looks like a band of light. The blue dots are the stars of the Milky

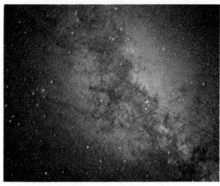

The wheel shape of the Milky Way (far left), *and the trail of* Echo, *a space research satellite, passing through the Milky Way* (left).

Way, and the black dot is the Earth. If you look toward the faces of the wheel (at the top and bottom of the drawing) you see only a few stars. In those directions in the sky, you see only scattered stars. But if you look to the left or the right (the front or the back, you see so many stars that they look like a continuous strip of light.

ALSO READ: ASTRONOMY, STAR, SUN, UNIVERSE.

MILNE, A. A. (1882–1956) The British writer A. A. (Alan Alexander) Milne is known all over the world for his stories about the toy bear Winnie-the-Pooh. Milne was born in London. After studying at Cambridge University, he worked for eight years as an editor for *Punch,* a British humor magazine. He wrote several novels and many plays, including *Mr. Pim Passes By* and *Wurzel-Flummery.* He also wrote *The Red House Mystery* and *A Table Near the Band,* a collection of short stories. His autobiography, *It's Too Late Now,* was published in 1939.

Milne wrote four books for his small son, Christopher Robin. *When We Were Very Young* and *Now We Are Six* are collections of delightful poems about childhood. *Winnie-the-Pooh* and *The House at Pooh Corner* are stories about some very lovable toy animals. Pooh, who belongs to Christopher Robin, is a bear "with a Pleasing Manner but a Positively Startling Lack of Brain." Pooh loves honey ("hunny") more than anything else and often gets into difficulties trying to get more of

it. (Pooh often feels it necessary to stop for a "little Something" from his hunny jar.) He lives in a forest with his friends, Piglet, the gloomy donkey Eeyore, Owl, Kanga and little Roo, Rabbit, and a playful, bouncing Tigger. Milne's endearingly funny characters, drawn by the British artist Ernest H. Shepard, are fun to read about. Once you have met the "Bear of Very Little Brain," you will never forget him.

ALSO READ: CHILDREN'S LITERATURE.

MILTON, JOHN (1608–1674) Religion and politics were the major forces in the life of the English poet John Milton. As one of the leaders of the Puritans, a strict Protestant group, he disagreed with many of the practices of the Church of England. He expressed his religious and political convictions in his writings.

John Milton was born in London, England, and was educated at Cambridge University. When he became involved in the growing Puritan movement, he wrote several *pamphlets* (booklets) criticizing the practices of the English church and government. During this period, he wrote *Areopagitica* (a demand for freedom of the press) and *Of Education,* two of his most famous prose works. He supported the Puritans during the English Civil War, and he was active in the Puritan government until the monarchy was restored in 1660.

Milton wrote much of his best poetry after his retirement from public life, although he had become

Some Indian tribes, such as the Iroquois and the Algonkins, believed the Milky Way was the trail to a world beyond this one. The flickering stars were seen as campfires along the long trail.

▼*A. A. Milne, English author and playwright.*

▲ *John Milton, English poet and political writer.*

blind by this time. Religion is the major theme in most of his poems. His long epic poem *Paradise Lost* tells the dramatic story of how Satan, once an angel, rebels against God and convinces Adam and Eve to reject God's commands. *Paradise Regained,* a somewhat shorter epic poem, describes Christ's coming to save mankind from the mistakes of Adam and Eve.

ALSO READ: ENGLISH HISTORY, LITERATURE, POETRY, PURITAN.

MIMICRY see BUTTERFLIES AND MOTHS, PROTECTIVE COLORING.

MINERAL Many people think a mineral is anything that is neither animal nor vegetable. To a prospector or a miner, a mineral is an *ore*—something found in the earth from which metals or other useful materials can be made. To a physician or a dietitian, minerals are very small amounts of certain metals (such as iron and copper) that are found in foods and are needed by the human body for good health. To a scientist, a mineral is a chemical element or compound found in or on the earth. Gold, iron, quartz, and salt are examples of minerals. Scientists have discovered more than 2,000 minerals. All minerals are solids, except for mercury and water.

The Structure of Minerals
The elements that make up any mineral are always the same. Quartz is always made up of the elements silicon and oxygen and nothing more. The gem mineral, beryl, is always composed of beryllium, aluminum, silicon, and oxygen. Because the elements of a mineral are always the same, scientists say that the mineral has a *constant composition of elements*.

In quartz, there is always one atom of silicon for every two atoms of oxygen. Quartz can never have three atoms of silicon and one of oxygen, or any other combination of silicon and oxygen atoms. Because

▼ *Sulfur is a common non-metallic yellow mineral. It is often found in combination with other minerals. Here it is combined with celestite.*

the amount of each element in a mineral is always the same, scientists say that the mineral has *definite proportions*.

Some substances taken from the ground seem to be minerals, but really are not. Coal, lignite, and asphalt look like minerals, but they do not have a constant composition. Their elements are not always the same. Coal is made up of carbon from decaying plants that died hundreds of millions of years ago. Along with the carbon are various amounts of sulfur, and some compounds of carbon, hydrogen, and oxygen. Lignite is very much like coal, but has less pure carbon. Asphalt, the black material that is used to pave streets, comes from petroleum that seeps to the surface of the earth. The lighter parts of the petroleum evaporate, leaving almost solid asphalt.

True minerals are *crystalline*. This means that they are made up of crystals. A crystal is a combination of atoms that join together to form a definite, orderly shape. The outer shape of a perfect crystal (one that is not broken) shows the arrangement of the atoms. The crystals that make up a mineral may be very tiny or hundreds of feet long.

Minerals and Rocks
Rocks are not minerals. Rocks are mixtures of minerals that have been formed by heat or pressure in the earth, or by the action of water. A few kinds of rocks, such as marble, are made up of only one mineral.

Suppose you find some rocks that are made up of a mixture of two minerals—quartz and mica. Some of your rocks may be mostly quartz and very little mica. Others may be half quartz and half mica. And still others may be made up of much more mica than quartz. This shows that rocks do not have a constant composition, as do the minerals that make up the rocks.

A pure mineral has a *constant weight*. A rock does not. One cubic

▲*Amethyst is a variety of quartz. It is of gemstone quality. Amethyst has very large crystals. It is transparent with a pale purple color.*

▲*Calcite is the second most common mineral. It is usually found mixed with other minerals.*

▲*Chalcopyrite is the most common copper mineral. It is brass yellow with a metallic luster.*

▲*Essonite is a variety of garnet. It has a brownish color Most essonite is of gemstone quality. It is also called cinnamon stone.*

▲*Lapis lazuli is a lovely blue, transparent mineral. Since ancient times it has been highly prized as a decorative mineral.*

▼*Molybdenite is a gray colored mineral with a metallic luster. It occurs naturally in thin layers or veins.*

▲*Agate is a pretty mineral made up of layers or bands of quartz. Agate varies in color, and it is always cloudy looking.*

▶*Pyrite is a mineral that looks like gold. It is therefore also called fool's gold. It is made of iron sulfide. Pyrite is opaque with a metallic luster.*

inch of any mineral weighs exactly as much as all other cubic inches of the same mineral. The weight of a cubic inch of rock depends on the amounts of light and heavy minerals in the rock. If you weigh two pieces of the same rock, each a cubic inch in size, you will see that their weights differ. The heavier piece contains heavier minerals.

▲ A pudding stone, or conglomerate, is a number of pebbles or rocks cemented together. Many different minerals can be found in a single pudding stone.

How Minerals Form

At one time in its early history, the Earth was a hot mass of melted substances. All the elements that made up the Earth were liquid. These liquid elements mixed. Some combined chemically, forming compounds. The elements that combine easily with other elements (such as silicon, aluminum, iron, and oxygen) formed the most compounds. Other elements (such as gold, silver, and platinum) formed very few compounds, or remained pure. Both kinds of elements became minerals.

Metallic and Nonmetallic Minerals

There are two main kinds of minerals, *metallic* and *nonmetallic*. Metallic minerals may be pure metals, such as gold and silver. They may also be compounds containing elements that are metals, such as *galena*, which is composed of lead and sulfur. Nonmetallic minerals contain no metal elements. Quartz is a nonmetallic mineral, because the silicon and oxygen elements are not metals.

▲ An opal is a noncrystalline mineral that can be polished to become a gem.

Identifying Minerals

Minerals can be described by their characteristics. Each mineral has a different set of characteristics. By describing the characteristics of a mineral, you set it apart from others. In this way, you can identify it.

LUSTER. The luster of a mineral is the way it shines when in the light. There are two main kinds of luster, *metallic* and *nonmetallic*. A metallic luster is one that looks like the surface of a metal. The mineral

called pyrite, or fool's gold, has a metallic luster.

There are several kinds of nonmetallic lusters: *Adamantine* is the shine such as diamonds have. *Vitreous* luster is like a broken edge of glass. *Resinous* luster is like resin (the sap from a tree). *Pearly* luster is the shine such as pearls have. *Silky* luster is like silk. *Dull* describes a surface that has no shine at all.

HARDNESS. Some minerals are harder than others. A harder mineral can scratch a softer one. A scientist, Friedrich Mohs, set up a list of ten minerals. The lowest mineral (number 1) is softest and each higher one is harder. All other minerals and any other substances can be given a number of this scale according to hardness.

Rocks from Hardest to Softest	Scratch Test for Hardness
10. diamond	scratches all other rocks
9. corundum	scratches topaz
8. topaz	scratches quartz
7. quartz 6. orthoclase }	scratch glass
5. apatite 4. fluorite }	scratch with knife
3. calcite	scratch with penny
2. gypsum 1. talc }	scratch with fingernail

COLOR. Minerals are found in all colors. The color may be due to light passing through the mineral. Such a mineral is *transparent* if you can see objects through it, as through glass. It is *translucent* if you can see only light, but not objects, through it. Many transparent and translucent minerals are gems. Diamond, ruby, sapphire, emerald, and topaz are some transparent gem minerals. Rose quartz, moonstone, and serpentine are translucent gem minerals. Some minerals are translucent when they are in thick pieces and transparent in thin sheets. Mica is such a mineral. Minerals through which light cannot pass are *opaque*. Their color is due to the way light is reflected from their surface. Gold, copper, and turquoise are opaque minerals.

SPECIFIC GRAVITY. The weight of a mineral is an important characteristic. Its weight is usually called specific gravity. Specific gravity is found by comparing the weight of an amount of mineral and the weight of the same volume of pure water.

INDEX OF REFRACTION. When light passes through any substance, the direction in which the light travels is changed. The amount of change is called the index of refraction of the substance. This is an important characteristic of minerals, because different minerals have different indexes of refraction.

CRYSTAL STRUCTURE. There are several different kinds of crystals, each having a different shape. The shape of the crystals that make up each mineral is different, and is a good way to identify the mineral.

STREAK. The streak of a mineral is the color it has when ground up into a powder. The streak may be quite different from the color seen in a lump of the mineral. For example, lumps of iron ore *(hematite)* may be brown, green, or black, but all have a red-brown streak.

Useful Minerals

There are many useful minerals. Besides those that are valuable gemstones, the most useful minerals are metal ores. Iron is made from hematite, magnetite, and siderite ores. Aluminum comes from bauxite ore. Lead comes from galena ore. Tin is made from cassiterite ore. Nickel comes from pentlandite ore.

A very useful and interesting kind of mineral is *asbestos.* It is not a single mineral, but a soft, silky, flexible form of the minerals chrysolite, actinolite, tremolite, amosite, and crocidolite. Asbestos is useful because it will not burn in a fire. Asbestos is also used to insulate against heat and sound. Asbestos is light in weight and can be woven into fab-

rics that will not burn, decay, or be destroyed by strong chemicals.

For further information on:

Characteristics of Minerals, *see* ATOM, CHEMISTRY, CRYSTAL, ELEMENT, GAS, LIGHT, LIQUID, ROCK, SOLID, WEIGHT.

Formation of Minerals, *see* EARTH HISTORY, GEOLOGY, MATTER, SOLAR SYSTEM.

Kinds of Minerals, *see* DIAMOND, GEM, GOLD, IRON AND STEEL, METAL, PETROLEUM, SILVER, WATER.

Uses of Minerals, *see* COAL, CONSTRUCTION, FIRE, FUEL, JEWELRY, MANUFACTURING, MINES AND MINING.

MINES AND MINING

Ever since ancient times, man has been taking out of the Earth minerals and other valuable materials, such as gold, silver, diamonds, rubies, copper, iron, sulfur, and coal. When any one of these things is found in an amount large enough to make it worthwhile to be taken out of the Earth, it is called *ore.* Digging and washing ore out of the Earth is called *mining.* The holes that are dug to get at ores are *mines.*

A *deposit* is an accumulation of ore. Some kinds of deposits have special names. A long, branching deposit, surrounded by rock, is called a *vein* of ore. Gold and silver may be found in veins. A wide, flat deposit is often called a *bed.* Coal is found in beds. Oil and natural gas deposits are called *wells.*

Prospecting

Searching for ore is called *prospecting.* For thousands of years, prospecting was done by men (prospectors) who simply wandered around looking for signs of ore. In places where streams, rainwater, or landslides removed some of the earth above an ore deposit, the ore was exposed to the prospector's view—if one came along.

About 150 years ago, *geologists*—scientists who study the Earth—learned how to make maps of the

▲*Cinnabar is a mineral which contains mercury, a metallic element. Cinnabar is the world's only commercial source of mercury.*

Many mining techniques and some words used in mining (*skip, winze, sump,* for example) come from the old tin mining traditions in Cornwall, England. Cornish miners, who are called "Cousin Jacks" in U.S. iron mining, have taken their skills to mines all over the world.

▼*Crude chunks of cinnabar ore being carried along a conveyor belt. Mercury is extracted from this mineral by a roasting process.*

rocks in an area. Miners had noticed that certain kinds of ores usually were in or near certain kinds of rock. With maps to guide them to the proper kinds of rock, prospectors knew where they should dig for ore. As geology became a more accurate science, mining geologists became better able to locate ore deposits.

By the end of World War II, almost all the easy-to-find ore deposits had been found. Mining geologists then turned to prospecting with scientific instruments. One of these is the *seismograph,* which records the speed of shock waves traveling through the Earth. The prospector explodes dynamite in holes drilled in the ground. Shock waves from the explosion are recorded by the seismograph. If ore is in the area of the explosion, the speed of waves passing through the deposit will be different from their speed in the surrounding earth.

Prospectors fly instruments over an area in which they think there may be ore. One of these instruments is a *magnetometer.* It measures changes in the earth's magnetism, which is slightly different around a deposit of iron, nickel, or cobalt ore. A similar instrument is a *gravity meter,* which records changes in the strength of the earth's gravity. Such changes can tell of the presence of ore deposits. A *scintillation meter* can locate radioactive ores such as uranium.

▲*A mechanical loader scoops bauxite ore from an underground mine face. Bauxite is the main ore of aluminum.*

▼*A large machine called a gold dredge may be used to mine gold from sand lying beneath the surface of a stream.*

Ore

After finding a deposit, a mining engineer must decide whether it is ore—a deposit that it will pay to dig up. The deposit may be very deep, or it may be in rock that makes mining very difficult. If the engineer decides that it will cost more to get the ore out of the earth than the ore can be sold for, he will not try to mine it.

Sometimes, the way in which an ore deposit is mined will decide whether it is worth mining. Suppose only ten cents worth of gold is in every ton of gravel in a river bed. A lone miner, who can dig and search through only three or four tons of gravel a day, cannot get more than 40 cents for his day's work. So, a ten-cent-a-ton deposit of gold-bearing gravel would not be worth working for him. But a large dredge that can work though 18,000 tons of gravel a day will make it worthwhile to mine the same gravel. As more and cleverer mining methods and improvements are invented, miners find it worthwhile to mine ore deposits that they would have passed by a few years before.

Mining Methods

The three main ways of mining ore are: *placer, open pit,* and *underground.*

In placer mining, the miner is trying to get metals that exist in gravel as lumps or grains of pure metal. He uses strong jets of water to wash the gravel into a narrow box, or chute, called a *sluice box.* The sluice box has a rough bottom. Water running through the sluice washes away the lighter gravel, leaving the heavier metal on the bottom of the box. Gold is the chief metal mined in this way.

Panning is a kind of placer mining used mainly by prospectors during the gold rush in the 1800s. They scooped up water and sediment from streams into a flat pan. Swirling the water around in the pan

would reveal any pieces of gold in the sediment.

If ore deposits are near the surface, open pit mining is used. In this kind of mining, the soil and other kinds of earth—called the *overburden*—are dug, or *stripped*, away from the top of the ore deposit. Then, large amounts of ore are dug up cheaply by large power shovels. This method is used to mine iron, copper, and aluminum ore and coal. Mining coal from shallow pits is called *strip mining*.

When ore deposits are far underground or when the overburden is hard rock that is too costly to remove, miners dig deep holes to the ore. In underground mining, a wide hole, called a *shaft*, is dug straight down alongside the ore deposit. Then a horizontal tunnel, often called a *crosscut*, is dug from the shaft to the ore. Miners work in

a cleared area in the ore called a *stope*. The ore is sent in small cars to the shaft, where it is dumped into a container called a *skip hoist*. The skip, which is like an elevator car, is hoisted to the surface of the earth and dumped. The miners keep digging a stope, making it longer, as they follow the deposit of ore. When the stope has passed through the ore, or when the stope becomes too long to work in conveniently, a new one is begun.

Conserving Minerals

In the first few thousand years of mining, little of the world's supply of minerals was taken from the Earth. In the last 100 years, much more ore has been mined than in all the time before. Ore cannot be renewed, as crops can. Once ore is mined, it cannot be replaced. Some countries are using up their mineral resources so fast that they will have very little ore left by the year 2000. The United States is one of these countries which has already used up most of its best ore. For example, all the richest iron ore is gone. Because of new ways of prospecting and better methods of mining the poorer kinds of ore, the United States still has a fairly large reserve of many minerals. As the population grows, the amount of the reserve used up each year will increase. This amount can be lessened by reusing—or recycling—metals. You can help by collecting used cans and other kinds of junk metal and selling them to junk dealers. The junk will be melted and used to make new metal products. This

▲*Bingham copper mine in Bingham, Utah, is one of the largest open pit mines in North America* (left). *Explosives are often used in mining to blast chunks of ore from a layer of rock* (above). *These miners are placing sticks of dynamite in the wall of a tunnel.*

▼*An old drawing shows the shafts and tunnels of an underground mine in the days before air conditioning.*

▼ *Wagons that run on tracks or rails like trains are commonly used to move ore from the mine.*

▲ *An Irish miniature of an Evangelist painted sometime during the 700s.*

▲ *A Persian miniature painted sometime during the 1600s. The original is not much bigger than this.*

▶ November, *a miniature painted by the Limbourg brothers in France during the early 1400s.*

will make it unnecessary to take more ore from the Earth to get the metal.

ALSO READ: COAL, ELEMENT, GOLD, GOLD RUSH, METAL, MINERAL, NATURAL GAS, PETROLEUM.

MINIATURE   Miniatures are paintings done in a very small size. The artist must use very thin, pointed brushes to make his figures clear. The paintings are about the size of those shown here.

Miniature painting was a highly developed art in the Middle East. Before the 1500s, Muslim artists of Persia, Turkey, and India were creating beautiful miniatures. Miniature painting became popular in Europe during the 1500s to 1800s. The painting shown here of an Evangelist is a very early European miniature. Compare the heavy lines and stiff posture of the figure to the graceful lines and pose of the Persian miniature. They are both pictures of a man, but see how different they are in style.

The miniature titled *November* comes from a medieval calendar. Each month had a miniature picture showing an important activity of that month. The *November* miniature shows a swineherd with his dog taking care of the pigs. Two other men are trying to fetch pigs that have wandered into the woods. The trees are changing color, and in the background you can see a castle.

Imagine the fine brushwork it would take to paint such a tiny picture with so much detail!

You can create a miniature of your own using watercolors or colored pencils. Cut out a piece of white cardboard two or three inches square. Draw in your picture with black pencil and then color it in. If you paint with watercolors, be sure to use a brush that has very few hairs and a fine point. Mix very little water with the paints so that the colors do not run together in your painting. If you use colored pencils, be sure to keep the points very sharp for delicate work.

ALSO READ: ART, ART HISTORY, PAINTING.

MINISTRY see CLERGYMEN.

MINNESOTA   Minnesota is called "The Land of Ten Thousand Lakes." That may sound like a lot of lakes, but the correct number is even larger. If you count all the lakes of 25 acres or more, you will find more than 11,000 of them. The smaller lakes are far too numerous to count.

The Land and Climate
Minnesota is in the north central part of the United States. Canada lies along its northern border. To the west are North and South Dakota. The state of Iowa lies to the south. Wisconsin and Lake Superior are on the eastern border.

Besides being a land of lakes, Minnesota also has many rivers and streams. The state is named after the Minnesota River. The word *Minnesota* means "sky-blue water" and comes from the Sioux Indian language. Minnesota is also called the "North Star State."

Minnesota has two main parts. They are both very different. Long ranges of hills run across the northeastern part of the state. This region was once heavily forested in white pine and Norwegian pine, but people have cut down many of the trees. Some people needed clear land for farming. Others cut the trees for lumber. Large areas of woodland remain, and along with the lakes, Minnesota's forest areas have become popular vacation lands. Southern Minnesota and the valley of the Red River in the northwest were once prairie grasslands. Few trees grew in these areas, except along the banks of rivers. The old prairie is still very fertile and is now covered with rich farmlands.

Minnesota has cold winters and hot summers. The northern part of the state is extremely cold in winter. Rain and snow are much heavier in the east than in the west.

History

Sioux Indians once lived in the Minnesota forests. The men hunted deer and moose. The women gathered wild rice and swamp roots to cook. The Sioux also raised a few crops. By the 1600s, the Ojibwa (Chippewa) Indians had moved into northern Minnesota. The Ojibwa were members of a large eastern tribe. Europeans were taking over the Ojibwas' hunting grounds in the east, so the Ojibwa were forced to move westward. They fought the Sioux for new hunting grounds in the Minnesota area.

Europeans first came to Minnesota at about the same time. A French explorer named Daniel Greysolon arrived in 1679. His title was Sieur du Luth. The city of Duluth, Minnesota, is named in his honor. Du Luth made friends with the Sioux, and claimed the whole region of Minnesota for the king of France.

In 1680, Father Louis Hennepin, a French priest, discovered and named the Falls of St. Anthony. The city of Minneapolis now stands at the spot on the Mississippi River where St. Anthony Falls are located. No boats from the south could sail past the falls, which provided waterpower for the first settlements there.

French traders bought furs from the Indians, paying them with goods that the Indians wanted. The British first and the Americans later took over the fur trade. One of the most famous traders of the American period was a Negro named George Bonza. He was an especially good trader because he could talk to the Indians in their own language.

The U.S. Government had gained control of Minnesota by the early 1800s. In 1819, U.S. soldiers built Fort St. Anthony near the falls discovered by Father Hennepin. The soldiers had to make their own flour, so they built a flour mill to grind wheat. They also built a saw-

MINNESOTA

State flower
Pink-and-white lady's slipper

State bird
Common loon

State tree
Red pine

Capital
St. Paul
(309,980 people)

Area
84,068 square miles
(ranks 12th)

Population
3,805,069 people
(ranks 18th)

Statehood
May 11, 1858
(32nd state admitted)

Principal rivers
Mississippi River
Minnesota River

Highest point
Eagle Mts. (2,301 feet)

Largest city
Minneapolis (434,400 people)

◀Minnesota has great areas of unspoiled wilderness and thousands of beautiful lakes. These hikers are portaging—carrying their canoe from one lake to another to continue their canoe trip.

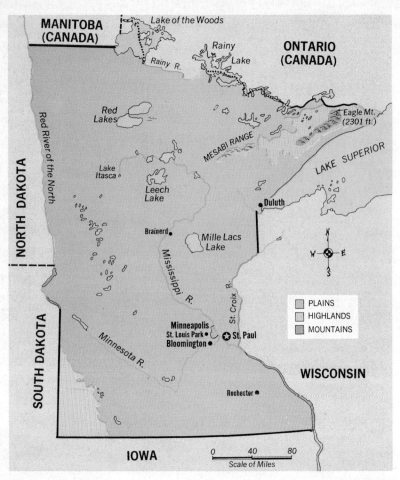

MANITOBA
(CANADA)

Lake of the Woods

Rainy
Lake

ONTARIO
(CANADA)

Rainy R.

Red River of the North

Red
Lakes

Eagle Mt.
(2301 ft.)

MESABI RANGE

LAKE SUPERIOR

NORTH DAKOTA

Lake
Itasca

Leech
Lake

Duluth

Brainerd

Mille Lacs
Lake

Mississippi R.

St. Croix R.

SOUTH DAKOTA

Minneapolis
St. Louis Park
Bloomington

St. Paul

Minnesota R.

PLAINS
HIGHLANDS
MOUNTAINS

WISCONSIN

Rochester

IOWA

0   40   80
Scale of Miles

▼ *A statue of Paul Bunyan, his musket, and his Blue Ox, Babe, on the shore of Lake Bemidji at Bemidji.*

mill to produce lumber. Both mills were run by waterpower from the falls. These were the first manufacturing plants in Minnesota.

The settlement that grew up around the falls became the city of Minneapolis. A neighboring town, St. Paul, began as an Indian village. By 1840, most of the people living there were French hunters and traders. They built a log church and named it for St. Paul. Soon people began calling the entire town by that name. Minneapolis and St. Paul grew until their boundaries touched. Now the two cities are side by side and look like one large city. They are called the "Twin Cities."

In the 1850s, the governor of the Minnesota region persuaded the Sioux and Ojibwa Indians to give up large areas of land. Settlers flocked in, coming mostly from the northeastern states. Many were Irishmen, Germans, Englishmen, and Canadians. Minnesota became a

state in 1858. When the Civil War started, the new state provided a regiment of soldiers for the Union Army. The Sioux saw the war as a chance to show how they had been cheated when they gave their land to the white man. Now that war was on, they thought they might be able to drive the settlers from the Indian hunting grounds. In 1862, Sioux warriors attacked the white settlements, but the Indians were eventually defeated.

The state developed rapidly after the Civil War. Lumbering became the leading industry for a while. Wheat growing also became an important business. The wheat was taken to Minneapolis, where mills ground it into flour. Iron mining in northeastern Minnesota began in 1884. The iron ore was hauled to Duluth, on the coast of Lake Superior. It was then loaded aboard steamboats and carried eastward across the Great Lakes. In 1892, the first ore was discovered in the famous Mesabi Range. The ore was very near the surface of the ground, and huge quantities were mined by the open pit method. The range's best ore is now gone, but the lower-grade ore, called *taconite*, still is being mined. Minnesota remains the nation's leading iron-mining state.

Minnesotans at Work

Manufacturing is now the principal source of income in Minnesota. More than half of all Minnesota's factory workers are employed in or near the Twin Cities. Office equipment, farm equipment, and mining machinery are three of the main products, but food processing is the state's major industry. Flour and butter are leading food products. Lumbering is still one of Minnesota's basic industries, although in the 1800s it was the state's main industry. The well-known tall tales about the giant lumberjack, Paul Bunyan, and his Blue Ox, Babe, were told in the lumber camps of Minnesota.

▲*A young fisherman waits patiently for a catch after cutting a hole through the ice on one of Minnesota's many lakes.*

Agriculture is the second most important industry in Minnesota. Cattle, hogs, and poultry are raised. Minnesota is known for its dairy products. Corn is the leading crop, but much of it is fed to livestock. Other crops, in their order of importance, include soybeans, hay, oats, and wheat.

Minnesota's hundreds of lakes and rivers have been popular with tourists for the past 100 years. Even before the Civil War, southern planters often traveled up the Mississippi River to St. Paul for summer vacations. Today, recreation and tourism are a big business in Minnesota. Fishermen and hunters come from all over the country to try their luck in the state's deep forests and plentiful lakes. During the summer, the lakes are full of boats, canoes, water-skiers, swimmers, and skindivers. In winter, ice skating, iceboating, snowmobiling, and ice fishing are popular sports.

ALSO READ: BUNYAN, PAUL; FLOUR MAKING; FUR TRADER; GREAT LAKES; IRON AND STEEL; OJIBWA INDIANS; PRAIRIE; SIOUX INDIANS; WESTWARD MOVEMENT.

MIRAGE On a hot summer day, while driving along the highway, you may have noticed puddles of water on the highway in front of the car. But when the car got closer, the puddles of water disappeared. What you saw was a mirage.

Where do mirages come from? On a hot day, the heat soaks into the highway. The hot pavement then throws some of the heat back into the air, like a radiator inside a house. This hot air floats about a foot above the highway. The top of the layer of hot air acts like a mirror. The hot air reflects the light coming from the sky, just as a mirror does. The "water" that you see is the blue sky reflected on hot air floating on top of the highway. Because the highway has a lighter color than the sky, the "puddles of water" in the mirage look dark.

Mirages can happen wherever there is a hot sun beating down on a flat surface. Some of the best mirages are seen at sea and in deserts. In the desert, the sun beats down on the sand. The sand becomes very hot. The layer of hot air above the sand then reflects the sky, and a traveler in the desert happily thinks he is looking at a cool oasis in the distance.

Sometimes a traveler in the desert thinks he sees palm trees, houses, and other objects floating in the air. This second kind of mirage happens when the ground is colder than the air. The air close to the ground is colder than the air higher up. High in the air, where the cold air and the hot air meet, the hot air acts like a mirror in the sky. Palm trees far away look as if they were floating in the sky.

ALSO READ: LIGHT, MIRROR.

MIRROR A mirror is any smooth surface that reflects light. Most mirrors in houses are made of glass. The glass is polished until it is very smooth. Then a film of silver or aluminum is laid on the back of the

▼*All kinds of mirages can be seen in the hot sun-drenched desert. The camels in the distance seem to be reflected in water. What appear to be clouds hover over the horizon.*

One of the largest mirrors in the world is the 200-inch Hale reflecting telescope at the Palomar Observatory in southern California. Eleven years were spent in grinding and polishing the concave front surface. The mirror weighs about 15 tons.

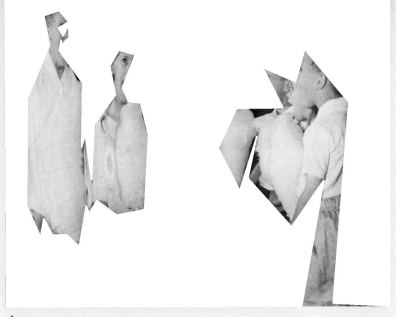

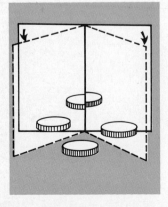

▲*These children are having fun viewing their distorted images in the funny mirrors at an amusement park.*

▼*Some countries use pairs of mirrors at dangerous traffic intersections. A car making the dangerous turn can see if any other vehicle is approaching.*

glass. The silver or aluminum backing reflects the light that falls on the glass. When you stand in front of a mirror, you see yourself because the light is reflected from you to the mirror and back from the mirror into your eyes.

The ancient Egyptians had highly polished bronze mirrors. In 1835, a German scientist, Justus von Liebig, discovered how to put a film of silver on the back of a piece of glass.

Mirrors do not have to be straight. Curved mirrors are used to direct light rays. If you look inside an automobile headlight, for example, you can see how the back of the headlight is made of polished metal. The metal is curved. The polished metal acts like a mirror. The metal reflects the light in such a way that all the light shines straight in front of the car. The driver can then see where he is going when he drives at night. If you take off the front a flashlight, you can see how the inside of the flashlight is curved the same way. The curved mirror makes the light shine in a powerful beam, instead of spreading out everywhere. Some telescopes are made of a large curved mirror. The mirror collects light rays that come from distant stars. The mirror directs all the rays to one place so the astronomer sees the light clearly.

A mirror gives a reflection. It is also possible to see a reflection of a reflection. Try this simple experiment. Lay a penny on a table. Take two mirrors and hold them upright and next to each other on the table with the edges touching. Be sure the penny is in front of the place where the mirrors meet. Now move the outer edges of the mirrors slowly forward, while keeping the inner edges touching. How many pennies can you see? You are seeing reflections of reflections.

ALSO READ: LENS, LIGHT, MIRAGE, TELESCOPE.

MISSILE   Any object thrown, fired or projected in some way at a target can be called a missile. Bullets and spitballs are missiles. But the word is most frequently used to refer to a military weapon that has an automatic control system and is usually powered by a rocket engine. A missile carries a *warhead*, consisting of explosives, used to destroy the missile's target.

A *guided missile* stays within Earth's atmosphere and is guided all the way to its target either by radio or radar command from the Earth or by a device within the missile. A *ballistic missile* follows a path that is partly outside the Earth's atmosphere. It is guided while it goes up, but after its rocket engine burns out, it returns to Earth in an unguided path called a ballistic trajectory. The path can be calculated.

Missiles are classified according to their launching point and target. Air-to-air missiles (AAM) are launched from airplanes and are aimed at other planes or at guided missiles. Air-to-surface missiles (ASM) are launched from airplanes and are aimed at targets on the Earth. Surface-to-air missiles (SAM) are launched from the Earth at targets in the air, such as planes or other missiles. Surface-to-surface missiles (SSM) are fired from launches on the Earth at targets on the ground. Underwater-to-surface missiles (USM) are fired from submarines at targets on the surface.

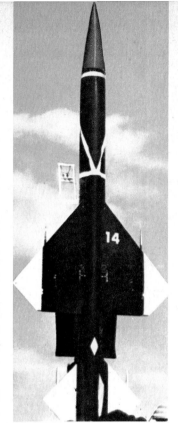

▲ *A Polaris missile seconds after being fired from a submarine. Polaris is a missile that can be fired from under water to any destination.*

A guidance system is the method used to steer a missile toward its target. A missile's guidance system gives instructions to sensitive and complicated machinery (the *control system*) that keeps the missile on course. Missiles controlled by a *command* guidance system receive radio instructions from stations on the ground or from another aircraft. For *preset* guidance systems, all instructions and adjustments for direction, speed, and altitude are put into an automatic pilot in the missile before the launch. Missiles operat-

ing on the *beam rider* system follow, or ride, a radar beam that is aimed at the target. In *homing* guidance systems, the missile contains sensitive machines that pick up and home (follow automatically) toward the target's radar beams, heat, or noise. *Inertial* guidance is a complex system used in missiles with long ranges (traveling distances). Inertial guidance involves a system of gyroscopes and other equipment that constantly pick up information during the flight about the missile's course, speed, and condition. This information is fed into the missile's computers, which provide directions and adjustments.

Ballistic missiles are designed primarily for nuclear attacks. They are classified according to their range. Intercontinental ballistic missiles (ICBMs) usually travel from 3,500 to 18,000 miles. Intermediate-range ballistic missiles (IRBMs) travel from 1,000 to 1,800 miles. Medium-range ballistic missiles (MRBMs) can travel only from 200 to 1,000 miles. A guided missile may carry nuclear or non-nuclear explosives. Missiles used as decoys to confuse the enemy carry no explosives.

The *propulsion* system of a missile may be a rocket engine, which carries its own oxygen, or an air-breathing engine, which depends on oxygen in the atmosphere. Since ballistic missiles go outside the Earth's atmosphere, they are propelled by rocket engines. Rocket engines are capable of greater speeds than air-breathing engines. Some rocket

▲ *The Bomarc is a surface-to-air missile used for long-range interception of enemy aircraft. It is guided by an "active homing device," an automatic means of guiding a missile to its target.*

▲ *The smallest surface-to-air missile used by the United States is the four-foot-long Redeye. A soldier can fire it from his shoulder at low-flying aircraft.*

◄ *The Zuni is a short-range air-to-air missile fired from an airplane at another airplane.*

▲ *The Hawk is a surface-to-air missile used as an antiaircraft weapon.*

engines use liquid fuel, which requires a complicated storage system. But modern rocket engines use solid fuel, which is easier to store and to protect from explosions.

ALSO READ: GYROSCOPE, MOTION, NUCLEAR ENERGY, ORBIT, ROCKET, SPACE, SPACE RESEARCH, SUBMARINE, WEAPONS.

MISSIONARY A missionary is a person who is dedicated to teaching and spreading his religious faith. He is convinced of his religious beliefs and tries to persuade other people to believe in them, too. In this way he helps his religion to grow. Missionaries have been important in the Christian religion more than in any of the other great religions. The first Christian missionaries were the 12 Apostles chosen by Jesus Christ. The preaching of Christian missionaries has been so effective that Christianity has become the largest religion in the world.

The Roman Catholic Church was

the first Christian body to organize its missionaries into groups called *missions*. Dominican and Benedictine monks led the earliest missions. The Jesuits and Franciscans later became large missionary groups. They started hundreds of colleges and established missions all over the world. Missionary work in the Protestant Church began around the 1700s. Protestant missionaries traveled to India, the South Seas, and the Orient. In the United States today, there are many missionary organizations.

Missionaries sometimes lead dangerous lives as they try to take their beliefs to others. Many have been killed by the people they were trying to help. Besides preaching religion, many missionaries also teach people how to farm, read and write, and live healthier lives. The German doctor Albert Schweitzer was a greatly admired "medical missionary" in Africa. Another famous missionary, John Eliot, came to America in the 1600s. He preached to the American Indians in Massachusetts and translated the Bible into their language. California's greatest missionary was a Spanish Franciscan priest named Father Junipero Serra. He founded the first of his 21 California missions (churches run by missionaries) in 1769. He is buried in the beautiful mission of San Carlos Borromeo, in Carmel, California.

ALSO READ: CHRISTIANITY; SALVATION ARMY; SCHWEITZER, ALBERT.

MISSISSIPPI Can you guess what Mississippi's newest industry is? A magazine put out by the state government says it is catfish farming. The homely catfish is not the finest of all food fishes, but many people like it. It is nourishing and it has a mild flavor. In several parts of the southern United States, people have taken up catfish farming. Mississippi leads all other states in the raising of catfish. A catfish farmer needs a

▶ *John Eliot, an early missionary to the American Indians.*

▲ *A beautiful flower garden, one of many in Mississippi. The warm, moist climate of Mississippi aids the growth of such luxuriant gardens.*

good pond. He stocks the pond with baby fish. When the fish grow large, he catches them and sells them. Most of Mississippi's catfish farms are in the region called the "Delta."

The Land and Climate
Mississippi belongs to a region of the United States often known as "the Deep South." The state stretches northward from the Gulf of Mexico to the state of Tennessee. The great Mississippi River forms the western boundary, separating Mississippi from the states of Arkansas and

Louisiana. The state of Alabama lies to the east.

The Delta lies in northeastern Mississippi. It is between the Mississippi River on the west and the Yazoo and Tallahatchie rivers on the east. This region is flat and very fertile. For centuries, the Mississippi River spread over the land during spring floods. When the water drained off, silt (topsoil) that the river had been carrying was left on the land. Deep, rich soil was built up in this way. Levees, or embankments, were built in the 1800s to control the floods. The Delta then became the leading cotton region.

Traveling eastward from the Delta, you come to hill country. The main ridge of hills, called the Bluff Hills, was once a rich and fertile area. But much of the soil has been worn out by the planting of cotton year after year. Plants cannot grow in this poor soil. This means that there are no plant roots to hold the soil together and rain washes it away. After every rain, the gullies are a little deeper and wider.

As you near the eastern border of the state, you come to the Black Prairie—a region of rich soil and grassland. Many of the settlers made their farms here, for there were no forests to clear away. Prairie farmers now raise dairy cattle and chickens, as well as crops.

MISSISSIPPI

State flower
Magnolia

State bird
Mockingbird

State tree
Magnolia

Capital and largest city
Jackson (153,968 people)

Area
47,716 square miles
(ranks 32nd)

Population
2,216,912
(ranks 29th)

Statehood
December 10, 1817
(20th state admitted)

Principal rivers
Tallahatchie River
Pearl River

Highest point
Woodall Mountain (806 feet) in the northeastern corner of the state

◀ *Fishing boats gather for the annual Blessing of the Fleet at Biloxi, Mississippi.*

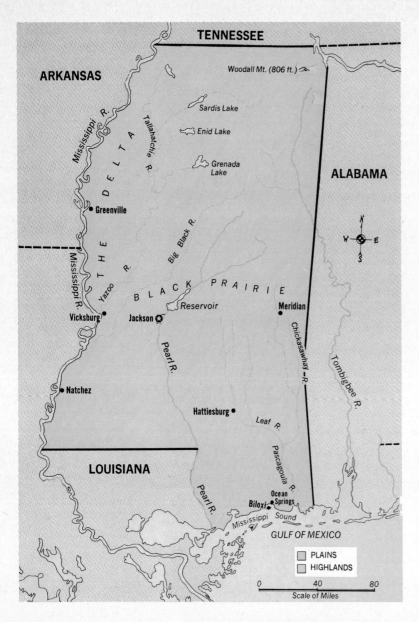

In the northeast corner of Mississippi are the Tennessee Hills. Slopes are steep here. They are difficult to plow and plant, and most farms are very small. Some farmers live in log houses like those of their grandfathers and great-grandfathers. Crops not found in other parts of Mississippi are raised in the Tennessee Hills. Among these are apples, grapes, and tobacco.

Now take a look at the southernmost part of the state. It has two sections. One section covers most of the southeast. It is known as the Piney Woods. Much of the soil here is poor. The hardy pine trees are the only plants that grow well. In the past, a large amount of timber was wastefully cut. The soil was left bare, except for stumps. But many areas have now been replanted. The northwestern part of the Piney Woods has the best soil. It is too thin for cotton, but tomatoes and other vegetables grow well here.

South of the Piney Woods lies Mississippi's coast. It is a small part of the long Gulf Coastal Plain. Its sandy soil is not good for crops, and some of the land is marshy. But mild winters and the blue Gulf of Mexico bring many tourists to the coast. The town of Biloxi is a busy fishing port. The Biloxi fishing fleet brings in Gulf shrimp, oysters, and fish called menhaden. Much of the seafood is processed at canneries in the town. Other factories make fertilizer from the menhaden.

Winters in Mississippi are short, and there are few really cold spells. The hot, drowsy summers are typical of most of the Deep South. The best season is fall. Nights are cool then, and the days are sunny and pleasantly warm.

History

Three Indian tribes lived in the Mississippi region before the European settlers arrived. They were the Choctaw, the Chickasaw, and the Natchez. The Indians lived mainly by farming. Spaniards visited the region in the 1500s. But the first European settlements were founded by the French. The colonist Pierre le Moyne, whose title was *Sieur d'Iberville*, brought settlers to Mississippi in 1699. His party built a fort and village on the Gulf coast. This settlement became the town of Ocean Springs.

Most of Mississippi was in the area that France gave to Great Britain in 1763, at the end of the French and Indian War. After the American Revolution, Mississippi came under the control of the United States. Americans from the East flocked to Mississippi. Raising crop after crop of cotton had ruined many of the

Eastern plantations. Planters bought land in the Delta and hill country of Mississippi. They marched gangs of Negro slaves westward to the big new plantations. Mississippi became a state of the Union in 1817.

In 1861, Mississippi broke away from the Union and helped to form the Confederate States of America. Jefferson Davis, who became president of the Confederacy, was living in Mississippi at the time. The abolition of slavery at the end of the Civil War almost destroyed the state's only big business, cotton-raising. The cotton plantations had depended entirely on their slave labor. The old way of life in the South began to break up. These troubled times are vividly described in the novels of the great American writer William Faulkner. Faulkner was born in New Albany, Mississippi. The cotton business began to improve again after *sharecropping* was adopted. Under this system, the landowners rented land to people, mostly Negroes, who worked the land and paid their rent with a share of the crop. The sharecroppers made a very poor living.

Poverty is still Mississippi's worst problem. But the state is encouraging new industries, and many people now have a chance to earn more than their fathers did. Another old problem troubles Mississippi. Here, as in other states, Negroes have been treated as second-class citizens. Civil rights leaders, such as Medgar Wiley Evers, have worked to alter these conditions. More Negroes are now voting. In a few towns, black men have been elected to public offices. Medgar Evers was assassinated, but his brother, Charles Evers, was elected mayor of Fayette, Mississippi, in 1969.

Mississippians at Work

Mississippi still looks like the home of country people. The land is mostly green fields and shady forests. There are no big cities and few

▲ *Jackson, Mississippi, became the state capital in 1822.*

large towns, but factories bring the most wealth to the state. Clothing leads all other manufactures. Wood products and food products follow. Jackson, the capital city, is one of the leading industrial centers of Mississippi. Oil and natural gas have been found in southern Mississippi. The state has several petroleum refineries.

Agriculture is still a major business. Cotton is no longer so important as it was in days gone by. But it is still the leading crop. Soybeans are another valuable crop. The raising of livestock—mostly cows and chickens—brings in more money than all the crops put together.

Another important industry in Mississippi is tourism. Visitors come to the colorful state festivals, such as the Shrimp Festival at Biloxi. In March and April, they take part in the annual Natchez Pilgrimage. Some of the most elegant plantation houses were built around the town of Natchez before the Civil War. People can visit these historic buildings, surrounded by the magnolia trees that have given Mississippi its nickname—the Magnolia State.

ALSO READ: CHOCTAW INDIANS; CIVIL RIGHTS MOVEMENT; CIVIL WAR; CONFEDERATE STATES OF AMERICA; COTTON; DAVIS, JEFFERSON; FRENCH AND INDIAN WAR; GULF OF MEXICO; MISSISSIPPI RIVER; SLAVERY.

▲*The Greater New Orleans Bridge spans the Mississippi River at New Orleans, Louisiana.*

MISSISSIPPI RIVER If you have read *The Adventures of Huckleberry Finn*, by Mark Twain, you will know about the excitement of taking a raft down the Mississippi River. Early settlers traveled down the long, wide, and lazy Mississippi on rafts.

The Mississippi is the longest river in the United States. It flows southward from the region of the Great Lakes to the Gulf of Mexico. From its source in the state of Minnesota to its mouth in the state of Mississippi, the river flows about 2,350 miles. Another long waterway, the Missouri River, flows into the Mississippi. The two rivers together stretch about 3,860 miles. Only the Amazon River system in South America and the Nile River system in North Africa are longer. The Mississippi system has 15,000 miles of waterways that can be used by ships and barges. Boats can travel up the Mississippi itself and several of its tributaries, or branch rivers. The major rivers flowing into the Mississippi are the Minnesota, Des Moines, Illinois, Missouri, Ohio,

Arkansas, and Ouachita. (See the map with the article on NORTH AMERICA.)

The Ojibwa (Chippewa) Indians named the river "Messipi," meaning "big river." The European settlers mispronounced the Indian word until it became the name we know today. The first European to see the river was probably Hernando de Soto, a Spanish explorer. De Soto explored the lower river valley in 1541.

French explorers came to the region more than 100 years later. Men such as Jacques Marquette, Louis Joliet, and Sieur de La Salle explored more of the river. France held the territory of the Mississippi until 1763. Then Spain and Great Britain owned the region. The United States bought most of the region under the Louisiana Purchase of 1803. The rest became part of the United States after the American Revolution. American settlers soon moved westward to farm these new lands. They shipped the goods they produced downstream to the port of New Orleans, on the Gulf

▶*A view of the Mississippi River flowing through a forest wilderness near McGregor, Mississippi. In some places the wide river contains numerous islands.*

of Mexico. Grain, meat, and coal came from the northern regions. Cotton, sugar, and tobacco were grown in the south. Barge men hauled upstream the manufactured goods and provisions that the settlers needed. Fishing became an important industry on the river and remained so for many years.

The early 1800s was the time of the famous stern-wheel riverboats on the Mississippi. With a shower of sparks, one riverboat would race another for the title of "fastest boat on the river." The writer Mark Twain worked for a while as a riverboat pilot. He wrote about his adventures in the book *Life on the Mississippi*. The Civil War and the railroad brought an end to the riverboats.

The Mississippi in most places is between one-half mile and a mile wide. Its depth is often between 50 and 100 feet. The river discharges a tremendous amount of water into the Gulf of Mexico. The force of the current also carries downstream tons of topsoil, sand, and gravel. Some of this dirt, or silt, is deposited on the river banks along the way. The rest has built up the big delta at the mouth of the river.

Spring rains and melting snow pour their waters into the drainage system of the Mississippi. The level of the river at times has risen as much as 50 to 55 feet above its low point. For many years, the river flooded its banks in the spring. The flood waters spread the rich silt over the land and built up the farmlands of the river valley. But the floods were dangerous. The worst floods occurred in 1927 and 1937. Homes and barns were swept away. Many people and animals were drowned. Crops were ruined. Government engineers have now built high banks, or levees, to stop the river from overflowing.

Today, river tugs push long strings of barges on the Mississippi. The Chicago Sanitary and Ship Canal now connects the Mississippi river system with the Great Lakes.

▲*Steamboats once cruised up and down the Mississippi River. In 1870, a race took place between the* Robert E. Lee *and the* Natchez. *The* Robert E. Lee *won.*

MISSOURI

State flower
Hawthorn

State bird
Bluebird

State tree
Dogwood

Capital
Jefferson City (32,407 people)

Area
69,676 square miles (ranks 19th)

Population
4,677,399 people (ranks 13th)

Statehood
August 10, 1821 (24th state admitted)

Principal river
Missouri River

Highest point
Taum Sauk Mountain (1,722 feet) in eastern Ozark Plateau

Largest city
St. Louis, 622,236 people (18th largest city in U.S.)

Barges can carry cargo more cheaply than railroad freight cars can carry it. The amount of goods shipped on the river is increasing. "Old Man River" is again becoming a major transportation route through the United States.

ALSO READ: DE SOTO, HERNANDO; OJIBWA INDIANS; RIVER; SHIPS AND SHIPPING; TWAIN, MARK.

MISSOURI The state of Missouri has a nickname straight out of American history. It is "Gateway to the West." The nickname is used, also, for the state's largest city, St. Louis.

At St. Louis, an unusual monument is a reminder of the "Gateway." It is a great arch rising from a green park. The arch is taller than the Washington Monument in the nation's capital. It is built of stainless steel and shines in the sunlight.

The Land and Climate

Missouri is in the Midwest of the United States. It is bounded by Arkansas on the south, Oklahoma, Kansas, and Nebraska on the west, and Iowa on the north. The mighty Mississippi River forms the eastern boundary, separating Missouri from the states of Illinois, Kentucky, and Tennessee.

Rivers offer Missouri water transportation in all directions. The Missouri River forms part of the state's western boundary and then flows across the center of the state to join the Mississippi. The river port of St. Louis grew up near the point where they join. A little to the north, the Illinois River flows into the Mississippi. The Ohio River joins the Mississippi to the south.

Northern Missouri is a region of flat grainlands. This region is part of the wide plain that curves west and south around the Great Lakes. In the western part of central Missouri is an area of rolling prairie land called the Osage Plains. South of the Missouri River, the Ozark Plateau covers most of southern Missouri. The plateau is a region of forested hills, sparkling lakes, and fish-filled rivers. In the extreme southeast corner of the state is a narrow section called the "Boot Heel." The land here is low and flat. It is part of the flood plain of the Mississippi River.

Missouri is generally cold in winter, and snowfall is fairly heavy in the northern regions. Summers are hot and humid. But some days of cool, dry weather bring relief from the heat. The growing season lasts half the year. Rain is plentiful, especially in the southeast.

▶*The bears attract a large crowd at Forest Park Zoo in St. Louis.*

History

In 1971, a new eight-cent postage stamp was issued to honor Missouri. The state was 150 years old. The picture on the stamp was part of a large wall painting. Thomas Hart Benton had done the painting for the Harry S. Truman Library at Independence. The stamp showed an American Indian meeting a frontiersman and a group of settlers. In the background were covered wagons pulled by oxen.

The Indians who once lived in Missouri belonged to several tribes. Those who most impressed the settlers were the Osage. They were taller than most Europeans and very athletic. Most of the Indians grew crops on the fertile plains and hunted the wild buffalo.

The earliest Europeans to arrive in the Missouri region were fur traders from New France (French Canada). Frenchmen found that lead could be mined in southeastern Missouri. About 1735, they built a port on the Mississippi as a base for shipping out the lead. They named the port Ste. Genevieve. This town is the oldest in Missouri. The river port of St. Louis was founded in 1764. It was named for a favorite saint of France. The port was built as a fur center. Furs were brought down the long Missouri River to St. Louis. They were packed there for shipment to Canada.

The United States, under President Thomas Jefferson, bought the huge Louisiana Territory from France in 1803. Missouri was a part of the territory. Thousands of American pioneers were already living in Missouri. Indians seldom attacked American settlers in Missouri. But some of the tribes sided with the British in the War of 1812. After this war, settlers came in ever-increasing numbers. Most were from southern states. Some settlers brought Negro slaves with them. Missouri Territory applied for permission to join the Union in 1818.

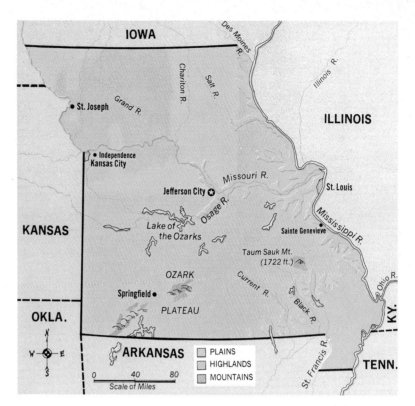

Many people in other parts of the nation disagreed with the idea of slavery. They claimed that if Missouri joined the Union, slavery should not be allowed in the new state. In 1821, the United States Congress agreed on the so-called Missouri Compromise. The compromise allowed Missouri to join the Union as a slave state, but ruled that slavery should not be permitted in other areas of the region that had been the Louisiana Territory.

Paddlewheel steamboats were now traveling up and down Missouri's rivers. They brought thousands of people from the East. Many of these people did not stay in Missouri. From St. Louis they went up the Missouri River to Independence. There, or at Westport (now a part of Kansas City). They then set out on the long and dangerous journey along the Oregon Trail to the West Coast.

After 1850, northerners began settling in Missouri. With them came immigrants from Europe—mostly Irish and Germans. The ideas of the new settlers often differed from those of the earlier set-

▶*The Mark Twain House and Museum is located in Hannibal, Missouri, where the great American author lived as a boy. The children in the picture are dressed as Tom Sawyer and his friend, Becky Thatcher.*

As a memorial to Winston Churchill, former Prime Minister of England, a church in London was taken down and built again in 1965 at Westminster College, Fulton, Missouri. Churchill had made a speech about the "Iron Curtain" of Communism there.

▼*The Gateway Arch in St. Louis, Missouri, is a symbol of the city as the "gateway to the west." The arch was completed in 1966.*

tlers from the South. When the Civil War broke out, Missourians fought Missourians. Some declared that the state was one of the Confederate States. Others declared that Missouri was loyal to the United States. This second group had strong Union forces on its side.

By the time the war ended, the old Missouri was no more. Covered-wagon days were over. The slaves had been freed. Negroes now raised cotton on rented lands. They were called *sharecroppers* because their rent was a share of the crop. Steamboats had lost business to the new railroads. St. Louis had become one of the nation's leading rail centers. Agriculture, mining, and manufacturing were making swift progress in the state.

A great fair was held in St. Louis in 1904. It celebrated the Louisiana Purchase of 1803. In 1927, a group of St. Louis businessmen gave a young American aviator called Charles Lindbergh money to build an airplane. Lindbergh named his airplane *The Spirit of St. Louis.* He amazed the world by flying it to France on the first nonstop solo flight across the Atlantic Ocean.

Missourians at Work

St. Louis is the principal center of Missouri's major industry, manufacturing. The leading product of both state and city is transportation equipment. It consists largely of automobiles. Airplanes are also built in the St. Louis area. Food products and chemicals are other important manufactures of the state.

Agriculture is Missouri's second largest industry. Livestock products, rather than crops, bring the most wealth to the state. These products include cattle, hogs, milk, chickens, and eggs. The main crops are soybeans and corn.

Missouri also has a busy tourist trade. Many visitors are interested in the famous people who have lived in the state. The writer Samuel Langhorne Clemens, known as Mark Twain, spent much of his childhood in the town of Hannibal. His book *The Adventures of Tom Sawyer* tells of a boy's experiences in a town like Hannibal. George Washington Carver, Negro teacher and scientist who worked to help Southern farmers, was another famous Missourian. John Joseph Pershing, the general who commanded American troops in France during World War I, and Harry S. Truman, President of the United States, were both born in Missouri. Every year, thousands of people visit the places connected with the lives of these Missourians.

ALSO READ: CARVER, GEORGE WASHINGTON; CIVIL WAR; CONFEDERATE STATES OF AMERICA; FUR TRADER; LOUISIANA PURCHASE; OREGON TRAIL; PONY EXPRESS; PRAIRIE; TRUMAN, HARRY S.; TWAIN, MARK; WAR OF 1812; WESTWARD MOVEMENT.